Lecture Notes in Computer Science   8448

Commenced Publication in 1973
Founding and Former Series Editors:
Gerhard Goos, Juris Hartmanis, and Jan van Leeuwen

T0253954

Jorge Cuellar (Ed.)

Smart Grid Security

Second International Workshop,
SmartGridSec 2014
Munich, Germany, February 26, 2014
Revised Selected Papers

 Springer

Editor
Jorge Cuellar
Siemens AG
Munich
Germany

ISBN 978-3-319-10328-0   ISBN 978-3-319-10329-7 (eBook)
DOI 10.1007/978-3-319-10329-7

Library of Congress Control Number: 2014946607

Springer Cham Heidelberg New York Dordrecht London

Printed on acid-free paper

Springer is part of Springer Science+Business Media (www.springer.com)

Preface

This volume brings together a selection of papers presented at SmartGridSec 2014 the Second Open NESSoS - EIT ICT Labs Workshop on Smart Grid Security, held at the Technical University of Munich, on February 26th, 2014. The papers were carefully peer-reviewed and the versions published here are corrected and extended for the purposes of these post-proceedings.

NESSoS – the Network of Excellence on Engineering Secure Future Internet Software Services and Systems – organized the workshop in collaboration with the action line smart energy systems of the EIT ICT Labs. NESSoS aims to establish Europe as the scientific leader in engineering secure software by addressing the current fragmentation of activities across Europe through the establishment of a joint virtual research lab on Engineering Secure Software Services, integrating the research, dissemination, and technology transfer activities of the researchers and practitioners in the area. NESSoS believes that in order to build secure systems, it is necessary to use, from the beginning, sound security engineering processes. Although the project already finished at the end of March, 2014, the community will be creating the IFIP Working Group 11.14 on Secure Engineering, where the activities will continue. The EIT ICT Labs is one of the Knowledge and Innovation Communities (KICs) set up by the European Institute of Innovation and Technology (EIT), as an initiative of the European Union. EIT ICT Labs brings together researchers and practitioners to work across the 'Knowledge Triangle' of education-research-innovation. EIT ICT Labs' partners are top ranked universities, leading research centres, and global companies in the field of ICT.

The engineering, deployment, and operation of the future Smart Grid will be an enormous project that will require the active participation of many stakeholders with different interests and views regarding the security and privacy goals, technologies, and solutions. There is an increasing need for workshops that bring together researchers from different communities, from academia and industry, to discuss open research topics in the area of future Smart Grid security.

The following set of papers illustrate the wide topic range related to the future Smart Grid:

A. Paverd, A. Martin, and I. Brown take a closer look at a particular strategy for demand response: demand bidding. Analyzing the realistic adversary models, they conclude that the current proposals cannot achieve the privacy goals that should be expected. They propose a new solution for this problem based on a trusted remote entity based on TPM technology.

D. Bytschkow, J. Quilbeuf, G. Igna, and H. Ruess propose a model-based design methodology for embedded systems, relying in particular on a separation kernel, as the one developed by MILS.

K. Beckers, M. Heisel, L. Krautsevich, F. Martinelli, and A. Yautsiukhin provide a structured method to analyze, in the context of Smart Grid, the attacker motivation as a hierarchy of goals, and relate to specific vulnerability attack graphs.

A. Armando, R. Carbone, E.G. Chekole, C. Petrazzuolo, A. Ranalli, and S. Ranise propose a framework to harmonize and enforce the requirements of different stakeholders in different domains, as they often appear in Smart Grid, based on the attribute based access control for a selective release of smart metering data in multi-domain smart grids.

J. King-Lacroix and A. Martin propose a multi-stakeholder network architecture for the smart home and, correspondingly, a set of modifications to ZigBee. The goal is to solve the trust issues between end-users and providers or operators.

Pöhls and Karwe tackle a question of resolving a conflict between privacy and integrity: Privacy can often be protected by passing data in a lower resolution, but in that case, how can end-to-end integrity be guaranteed?

K. Beckers, S. Faßbender, M. Heisel, and S. Suppan present a structured method for identifying possible security threats in the smart home scenario and analyzing their severity and relevance.

C. Rottondi, S. Fontana, and G. Verticale the interaction between Electric Vehicles (EVs) and the Smart Grid and their privacy-preserving interaction.

T. Hartmann, F. Fouquet, J. Klein, G. Nain, and Y. Le Traon suggest that unforeseen attacks and failures cannot be effectively countered proactively, but that a reactive and corrective approach based on simulation and reasoning techniques will be necessary to intelligently monitor and continuously adapt the smart grid to new conditions.

M. Karwe and J. Strüker discuss privacy energy issues and potential solutions in Demand Response systems, which are the cornerstone of the first step in a future smart grid, and how the Smart Metering Gateway concept of the German BSI can accommodate the different types of Demand Response.

F. Moyano, C. Fernández-Gago, K. Beckers, and M. Heisel claim that, complimentary to classical authentication and authorization mechanisms, the concepts of trust and reputation should play an explicit role when deciding how to interact with external agents in an open system like the Smart Grid. They propose a general framework to integrate such concepts in a Smart Grid environment.

T. Holczer, M. Félegyházi, Dl Buza, F. Juhász, and G. Miru present a proposal for honeypot systems to detect targeted attacks against industrial control systems and in particular smart energy systems.

This workshop has been partially funded by the European Commission through the FP7 project NESSoS (FP7 256890). We are also glad to acknowledge the excellent support from EasyChair both during the review process as well as for preparing the post-proceedings.

May 2014   Jorge Cuellar
                                                                Santiago Suppan

Organization

Program Committee

Alessandro Armando — Fondazione Bruno Kessler, Italy
Gabriele Costa — University of Genoa, Italy
Alberto Crespo-Garcia — Atos, France
Jorge Cuellar — Siemens AG, CT RTC ITS, Germany
Lieven Desmet — Katholieke Universiteit Leuven, Belgium
Keqin Li — SAP, France
Javier Lopez — University of Malaga, Spain
Fabio Massacci — University of Trento, Italy
Marius Minea — Universitatea Politehnica Timişoara, Romania
Martin Ochoa — Technical University of Munich, Germany
George Oikonomou — University of Bristol, UK
Santiago Suppan — University of Regensburg, Germany
Elias Tragos — Foundation for Research and Technology (FORTH), Greece
Luca Viganò — Kings College, UK

Contents

Security and Privacy in Smart Grid Demand Response Systems

Andrew Paverd[1]([⊠]), Andrew Martin[1], and Ian Brown[2]

[1] Department of Computer Science, University of Oxford, Oxford, UK
{andrew.paverd,andrew.martin}@cs.ox.ac.uk
[2] Oxford Internet Institute, University of Oxford, Oxford, UK
ian.brown@oii.ox.ac.uk

Abstract. Various research efforts have focussed on the security and privacy concerns arising from the introduction of smart energy meters. However, in addition to smart metering, the ultimate vision of the smart grid includes bi-directional communication between consumers and suppliers to facilitate certain types of Demand Response (DR) strategies such as demand bidding (DR-DB). In this work we explore the security and privacy implications arising from this bi-directional communication. This paper builds on the preliminary work in this field to define a set of security and privacy goals for DR systems and to identify appropriate and realistic adversary models. We use these adversary models to analyse a DR-DB system, based on the Open Automated Demand Response (OpenADR) specifications, in terms of the security and privacy goals. Our analysis shows that whilst the system can achieve the defined security goals, the current system architecture cannot achieve the privacy goals in the presence of honest-but-curious adversaries. To address this issue, we present a preliminary proposal for an enhanced architecture which includes a trusted third party based on approaches and technologies from the field of Trusted Computing.

1 Introduction

It is widely acknowledged that the upgrade to a smart energy grid presents multiple new challenges in terms of security and privacy. There has been extensive research on the security and privacy issues that arise from the Advanced Metering Infrastructure (AMI) in which smart meters record fine-grained energy consumption measurements and send these to the energy supplier or other external entities. In particular, privacy-preserving smart metering has been the subject of numerous research efforts and various privacy-preserving protocols have been proposed [1–4].

However, whilst the AMI is a critical part of the smart grid infrastructure, it is not the only aspect from which security and privacy concerns arise. In addition to the AMI protocols for measuring energy consumption, the future architecture of the smart grid includes Demand Response (DR) protocols for managing energy consumption. Specific types of DR, such as demand bidding (DR-DB) protocols,

© Springer International Publishing Switzerland 2014
J. Cuellar (Ed.): SmartGridSec 2014, LNCS 8448, pp. 1–15, 2014.
DOI: 10.1007/978-3-319-10329-7_1

involve bi-directional communication between the consumers and entities such as the energy supplier in order to co-ordinate the consumers' actions towards reducing their consumption during periods of high demand. As a result of this bi-directional communication, these protocols also present various security and privacy challenges that must be addressed.

The Open Automated Demand Response (OpenADR) specification is an example of a data model that can be used in DR communication. OpenADR 1.0 [5] was developed by the Demand Response Research Center operated by Lawrence Berkeley National Laboratory as a means for communicating DR information between energy suppliers, network operators and consumers. This formed the foundation of OpenADR 2.0 [6] which has now been developed by the OpenADR Alliance, an industry coalition that promotes the development and adoption of OpenADR-compliant systems. The alliance claims that over 60 vendors are currently producing OpenADR-compliant systems [7]. Section 2 of this paper provides background information about DR and presents an overview of OpenADR.

Building on preliminary research in the area of security and privacy for DR systems, this paper describes the threats to security and privacy that arise from bi-directional DR communication. Although we use the OpenADR specification as a case study, our analyses can be applied to similar DR systems. Section 3 defines the security and privacy goals that we have identified for a generic DR system. Section 4 presents the possible adversary models and describes their capabilities. Using these adversary models, Sect. 5 presents an analysis of a DR-DB system, based on the OpenADR specification, in terms of the security and privacy goals. In order to address the identified privacy challenges, this paper presents a preliminary proposal for a technical architecture that enhances consumers' privacy in DR protocols. Using approaches and technologies from the field of Trusted Computing (TC), this architecture is designed to mitigate against the major security and privacy threats that have been identified. An overview of this proposed architecture is presented in Sect. 6 but the full design and analysis will be carried out as future work. The three main contributions of this paper are therefore: the development of a threat model for DR protocols through the combination of appropriate adversary models and security and privacy goals; the application of this model to a concrete protocol based on the OpenADR specification; and the proposed architecture for mitigating against these threats.

2 Background

This section contextualizes the work by providing background information about demand response (DR) systems in general as well as an overview of OpenADR.

2.1 Demand Response Systems

In the absence of grid-scale storage capacity, electrical energy must be used as it is generated. Electrical energy consumption can be divided into a *base-load* that remains relatively constant and a *peak-load* that varies with time. As demand for energy increases relative to supply, it is necessary to either increase generation or reduce demand. Although additional peak-load generation capacity might be available, it is often expensive and might not be sufficient to satisfy the full demand. The same objective can be achieved by reducing peak demand through the use of demand response (DR) techniques.

The United States Department of Energy (DoE) defines DR as:

"Changes in electric usage by end-use customers from their normal consumption patterns in response to changes in the price of electricity over time, or to incentive payments designed to induce lower electricity use at times of high wholesale market prices or when system reliability is jeopardized." [8]

DR refers to a set of actions with the aim of dynamically reducing energy demand at specific times and in specific locations in response to a relative shortage in supply. These so called *DR events* could be caused either by an increase in demand or a decrease in generation capacity at a particular time. It is well known that peak-load demand increases at specific times during the day (known as *peak times*) due to human behaviour and energy generation capacity is dimensioned to accommodate these known variations. However, in addition to this variability in demand, we are also faced with increasing variability in supply as we integrate renewable energy sources such as wind and solar power into the grid.

The simplest and most extreme form of DR is forced curtailment or *load-shedding* in which specific consumers are forcibly disconnected in order to reduce demand. However, load-shedding can result in significant productivity and economic losses for the affected areas. There has been significant interest in improving this situation through more participative forms of DR that involve the consumers in the DR activities. As indicated in the US DoE definition [8] and explained in the categorization by Albadi and El-Saadany [9], there are two major categories of participative DR, namely *price-based* and *incentive-based* DR:

Price-Based Demand Response. In a price-based system, the DR manager uses time-based pricing in an effort to reduce demand at certain times. If possible, consumers will reduce demand when the price is high in order to minimize their energy bills. This could be implemented in various ways:

- **Time-of-use (ToU) pricing:** The energy price varies predictably according to the time at which it is used.
- **Critical peak pricing:** The energy price is specifically increased for periods of peak demand.
- **Dynamic pricing:** The energy price varies dynamically in time or geographic location depending on the ratio between supply and demand.

All of these approaches require a reliable mechanism for communicating the current price information to the consumers (e.g. in-home displays) as well as the implementation of appropriate billing (e.g. ToU billing using smart meters).

Incentive-Based Demand Response. As an alternative to price-based DR, incentive-based schemes provide certain incentives (usually financial in nature) to consumers who participate in DR events.

One type of incentive-based DR is a *demand bidding* (DR-DB) system. A DR-DB system requires a bidding protocol in which the DR manager (e.g. the energy supplier) initiates a DR event and consumers send *bids* indicating the amount by which they are willing to reduce demand at the specified time. These bids might include each consumer's desired incentive price if this is not specified by the DR manager. The DR manager accepts these bids until the DR objective has been met. Although it is not required, it may be desirable to check that consumers with accepted bids actually do reduce or shift their consumption accordingly. An overview of the communication in this type of protocol is shown in Fig. 1.

The bi-directional communication in the bidding protocol provides a feedback loop for the DR manager. Without this feedback, the DR manager would be required to predict the effects of specific DR actions on consumers' behaviour. Depending on the dynamics of the system, incorrect predictions could lead to instability in the system characterized by large swings in demand. Instead, the inclusion of the bidding protocol makes this a closed-loop feedback system which can be controlled effectively.

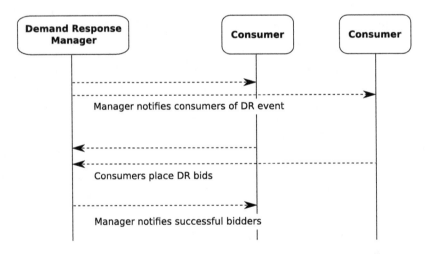

Fig. 1. Bidding process in a generic demand bidding (DR-DB) system.

2.2   OpenADR

The OpenADR specifications describe an open standards-based communications data model to facilitate DR communication between service providers and consumers [5,6]. The specification defines various XML-based messages that can be exchanged over any IP-based network using protocols such as Hypertext Transfer

Protocol (HTTP), Simple Object Access Protocol (SOAP) or XML Messaging and Presence Protocol (XMPP) [5,6]. The OpenADR 1.0 specification [5] introduces the concept of the Demand Response Automation Server (DRAS). The role of this component is to automate the communication between various entities in the system. The DRAS augments the generic bidding procedure by serving as an intermediary between the DR manager (usually the energy supplier) and the consumers. The DR manager informs the DRAS of a DR event and the DRAS in turn publishes this information to the consumers. Consumers have the option to set up standing bids with the DRAS so that when a new DR event is announced, they can either place new bids, maintain their standing bids or cancel their standing bids by opting-out of the event. The DRAS forwards the new bids or standing bids to the DR manager who accepts bids until the DR objective is met. These interactions are shown in Fig. 2 [5].

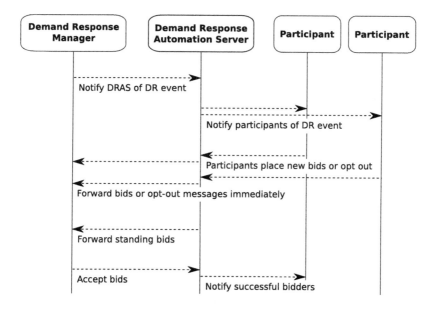

Fig. 2. Bidding process in an OpenADR system [5,10].

The OpenADR 2.0 specification [6], developed by the OpenADR alliance, differs significantly from the OpenADR 1.0 specification. In OpenADR 2.0, there are two types of nodes in the system: nodes that publish or transmit information about events are called *Virtual Top Nodes* (VTNs) and nodes that receive and respond to information are called *Virtual End Nodes* (VENs). The specification intentionally does not define the behaviour on the nodes once a message has been received. Although it is not defined in the specification, the functional role of the DRAS can therefore be recreated using a specifically-designed VTN. There is no peer-to-peer communication between VENs but a hierarchical structure can be used in which a node receives information as a VEN and retransmits it downwards to subordinate nodes as a VTN. Since the behaviour of the nodes is not specified, it is possible that this hierarchical structure can also be used in the reverse (upwards) direction since a VTN can retransmit information from its subordinate VENs to nodes further up the hierarchy. This also makes it possible for a node to aggregate information from multiple subordinate nodes. In this paper, all references to the DRAS are therefore based on the OpenADR 1.0 specification since this provides a concrete definition of this component's behaviour. In general, our analysis is also applicable to OpenADR 2.0 systems which may or may not include intermediary nodes.

3   Security and Privacy Goals

This section defines a set of security and privacy goals for a DR system. These represent the overall goals for the system rather than the individual security and privacy requirements for specific scenarios or the mechanisms through which these are achieved. These goals are used as a frame of reference for the analysis in Sect. 5. Although the security and privacy goals are presented separately, it will be shown that there is a strong relationship between them.

3.1   Security Goals

Given the critical nature of the electricity supply infrastructure, the primary security objective is to ensure that only legitimate entities can participate in the DR protocol. This can be defined through the following two goals:

S-1: Consumers must be able to verify the authenticity and integrity of all DR events and bid notifications.
S-2: The DR manager must be able to verify the authenticity and integrity of all DR bids.

Goal **S-1** refers to any DR event in either a price-based or incentive-based approach and also includes the acceptances of bids in an incentive-based approach. This goal means that actions such as setting a higher ToU energy price or requesting bids for energy reduction can only be performed by a legitimate entity since the authenticity of the message must be verifiable. It also means that these messages cannot be modified by an adversary since the integrity must be verifiable. Goal **S-2** is only applicable in the incentive-based approach and enforces the same restrictions as **S-1** on messages sent by the consumers containing bids for energy reduction.

Similar versions of these security goals are present in the OpenADR 2.0 specification which also describes mechanisms for achieving these goals. The specification defines two security levels: standard and high security [6]. All OpenADR-compliant systems must implement at least standard level security in which Transport Layer Security (TLS) with mutual authentication is used to protect the confidentiality and integrity of the communication and authenticate the communicating entities [6]. Some OpenADR systems implement the high security level in which XML signatures are used in addition to TLS to ensure the integrity and authenticity of the messages [6]. In the OpenADR specification, the confidentiality of the messages is an important concern but in this paper we classify this as a privacy goal as described in the next subsection.

In addition to the above goals, the specific hardware elements used in the smart grid might introduce requirements on the security mechanisms, for example, that any cryptographic operations used in the protocol must be achievable on a smart meter with limited computational capabilities. However, the requirements of the security mechanisms as well as the mechanisms themselves are beyond the scope of this section. It should be noted that the security goals presented in this section are broadly similar to those used in most other protocols for secure communication. From a communication perspective, DR systems do not introduce any new security goals beyond those already in place elsewhere. However, it is precisely because of these security goals that certain conflicts with the privacy goals arise as explained in our analysis. Therefore, it is critical to recognize the existence and impact of these seemingly general security goals.

3.2   Privacy Goals

The privacy goals for the system aim to protect the privacy of individual consumers. Initially, the participants in DR programmes have been large consumers such as industrial sites or building complexes. However, it is anticipated that DR programmes will be extended to all consumers including residential homes. For residential consumers, the protection of personal or private information is an important requirement in the smart grid. This is illustrated by the significant privacy concerns raised in response to the introduction of smart meters [11–13] as well as the various research efforts to develop privacy-preserving smart metering protocols [1–4]. However, despite their importance, these privacy goals are not addressed in the OpenADR specifications. The specifications only call for confidentiality of the communicated messages with respect to an external adversary. Building on the research about privacy-preserving smart metering as well as the preliminary research on privacy in DR systems by Karwe and Strüker [10], we define the following privacy goals:

P-1: Untrusted entities must not be able to link DR bids to individual consumers.

P-2: Untrusted entities must not be able to infer private information about individual consumers from the DR system.

These goals should be interpreted from the perspective of the individual consumer as he or she is the owner of the private information. Goal **P-1** requires that entities that are not trusted by the consumer must not be able to link DR bids to specific consumers since this could reveal private information about the consumer. If bids were visible to an untrusted entity and could be linked to individual consumers, the untrusted entity would learn information such as the consumers chosen energy supplier and tariff plan. Furthermore, the energy reduction specified in the bid reveals some information about the consumer's total energy consumption. In the same way that frequent energy measurements from smart meters can be used to make inferences about the occupants of resident premises, DR bids could also be used to infer private information. For example, a bid to decrease a large load, equal to that of a plug-in electric vehicle, indicates that the consumer probably owns such a vehicle and would otherwise be recharging it. The ability to link the bids to individual consumers also allows the untrusted entity to build up a profile of the consumer's behaviour. Any deviations from this profile could lead to further inferences about the user's behaviour. Continuing the previous example: if a particular consumer regularly bids to stop recharging an electric vehicle at peak times, any deviation from this pattern could indicate that the electric vehicle and its owner are away from home at that time. Even if an untrusted entity cannot view the individual bids or link them to specific consumers, goal **P-2** aims to ensure that untrusted entities either outside or within the system cannot make inferences such as those described above from the DR system.

4   Adversary Models

This section defines the adversary models used in our analyses in terms of the adversary's capabilities. The main adversary models used in this work are the Dolev-Yao (D-Y) model and the Honest-But-Curious (HBC) model.

4.1   Dolev-Yao Adversary

In the model proposed by Dolev and Yao [14], the adversary has full control of the communication network. The adversary can eavesdrop, intercept, block or modify messages as well as replay old messages or synthesize falsified messages. The adversary is only limited by the constraints of the cryptographic systems. It is assumed that the adversary cannot break cryptographic primitives. This means the adversary can neither read encrypted messages without the correct decryption key, nor forge cryptographic signatures, nor reverse cryptographic hash functions. Although the D-Y model is already considered to be the strongest type of adversary, it is sometimes also assumed that the DY adversary might be able to guess passwords with some defined success probability or recover encryption keys after a defined period of time.

4.2   Honest-But-Curious Adversary

In contrast to the D-Y model, the HBC adversary is more limited in terms of its capabilities. The HBC adversary does not deviate from the defined protocol in terms of sending and receiving messages. This adversary is also limited by the constraints of cryptographic systems and cannot break cryptographic primitives. However, this adversary aims to learn as much as possible from any messages it can receive. This usually also involves linking messages together or making inferences based on message contents. This model is sometimes referred to as the semi-honest model [15]. The HBC model differs from a passive D-Y adversary. The passive D-Y adversary attempts to avoid detection by not performing any active actions (i.e. by neither modifying messages nor sending falsified messages) but will still attempt to eavesdrop on all messages in the system. In contrast, the HBC adversary does not attempt to eavesdrop on messages for which it is not the intended recipient. Therefore, the HBC model is deliberately more limited than even a passive D-Y adversary so that it can be used to accurately model the behaviour of real entities in our system.

5   Analysis of a Demand Bidding System

This section presents an analysis of a DR-DB system, based on the OpenADR specification, in terms of the security and privacy goals defined in Sect. 3 and the adversary models described in Sect. 4. The aim is to provide a realistic representation of the potential adversaries within the system using an appropriate model for each adversary. This representation can then be analysed with respect to the defined security and privacy goals. Figure 3 shows the communication architecture of the system and indicates the potential adversaries we consider in this analysis.

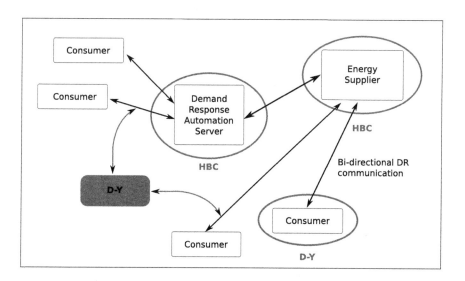

Fig. 3. Adversary model for a demand response system.

5.1   External D-Y Adversary

The most widely used adversary representation is that of an external D-Y adversary who controls the communication network. This adversary is neither authorized to initiate events nor respond to events and so must be prevented from doing so in order to satisfy **S-1** and **S-2**. In the OpenADR specifications, this is achieved through the use of mutually authenticated TLS connections between all nodes and optional XML signatures on messages [6]. The privacy goals **P-1** and **P-2** are also achieved with respect to this adversary because of the confidentiality provided by TLS. The adversary could perform traffic analysis on the encrypted messages but could be prevented from learning any private information by introducing dummy traffic from the consumer at regular intervals. Although it is assumed that the adversary cannot break the underlying cryptographic primitives, the security and privacy of the system are still fully dependent on all secret keys being protected from the adversary. If any of the nodes exhibits end-point vulnerabilities, it might be possible for the adversary to obtain these keys. Therefore, the protection of these keys is of critical importance. Techniques such as that described in [16] aim to address this challenge taking into account the unique constraints of the smart grid.

5.2   Consumer as a D-Y Adversary

The second possible type of adversary in the system is a dishonest or malicious consumer. This adversary is modelled as a D-Y adversary because he or she might deviate from the defined protocol. In the worst case it can be assumed that this adversary exhibits the same level of control over the network as the external D-Y adversary. This is a realistic assumption because the dishonest consumer might collaborate with the external adversary or the external adversary might also be a consumer in the system. This adversary is stronger than the external D-Y adversary because he or she is also a legitimate agent in the communication protocol and thus has access to a set of cryptographic keys required to respond to DR events. For example, this adversary could represent a dishonest consumer who attempts to claim larger incentives by submitting high bids but does not reduce demand by the bid amount. Assuming that the bids are attributable to the dishonest consumer because of TLS mutual authentication (**S-2**), it should be possible for the supplier to identify and take action against this adversary. A more malicious consumer might try to masquerade as multiple different consumers in order to evade detection. Unless the system has a robust mechanism for distinguishing between different consumers, this attack will succeed. If the false bids are not detected, this type of attack could be used to destabilize the electricity grid through the submission of multiple false bids from a large number of consumers. The privacy goals would still be maintained under the same conditions as for the external D-Y adversary. Since OpenADR does not permit peer-to-peer communication between VENs, the adversary gains no personal information about other consumers by becoming a consumer in the protocol.

5.3   DRAS as an HBC Adversary

The third type of possible adversary is the DRAS as an HBC adversary as described by Karwe and Strüker [10]. In this section we use the term *DRAS* to refer to the functionality of the DRAS node as defined in the OpenADR 1.0 specification [5] or to the equivalent functionality provided by an OpenADR 2.0 VTN. Since this entity is an important part of the infrastructure, it must be assumed to be weaker than a D-Y adversary due to external forces such as regulation, auditing and legal intervention. If this entity had the capabilities of a D-Y adversary, it would have the capability to cause a catastrophic system failure by sending falsified data to the energy supplier. Real-world implementations are therefore designed to minimize the probability of this occurrence and so the most realistic way to model these implementations is to use an HBC rather than a D-Y adversary model. It is therefore assumed that the DRAS will follow the defined protocol and will not violate the security goals (**S-1** and **S-2**). However, since the DRAS acts as an intermediary node in the communication architecture, it already has legitimate access to all the messages passing between consumers and the supplier. Even if it executes the protocol correctly, it could still violate the privacy goals (**P-1** and **P-2**) if it is not trusted by consumers. Using only information it has legitimately obtained, the DRAS could link bids to individual consumers and therefore make inferences about these consumers and their behaviour. Karwe and Strüker [10] propose a solution to this problem by introducing end-to-end encryption between the consumers and the DR manager so that messages cannot be read by the DRAS.

5.4 Supplier as an HBC Adversary

The final type of adversary is the energy supplier as an HBC adversary. As in the previous section, it is assumed that external forces such as regulation limit the capabilities of the supplier. Giving this entity the capabilities of a full D-Y adversary would again result in catastrophic system failure since this entity is the only legitimate initiator of DR events. Therefore, an HBC adversary model must be used to achieve a realistic representation of the system. As above, the security goals are satisfied because the supplier is always assumed to follow the protocol correctly. However, the supplier can violate the privacy goals by linking bids to individual consumers and making inferences based on these bids. This challenge cannot be overcome by anonymizing bids as this would allow the external D-Y adversary or the consumer D-Y adversary to violate the security goals by submitting multiple falsified bids which could not be attributed to specific consumers. Furthermore, one of the functional requirements is that the supplier must be able to link bids to individual consumers in order to allocate the relevant incentives. This means that with the current architecture, neither of the privacy goals can be achieved unless the supplier is trusted. However, in reality energy suppliers are not always trusted by consumers as illustrated by the Dutch case in 2008 [13, 17]. This challenge could be addressed through regulation of the energy supplier or through modification of the system architecture as we propose in the next section.

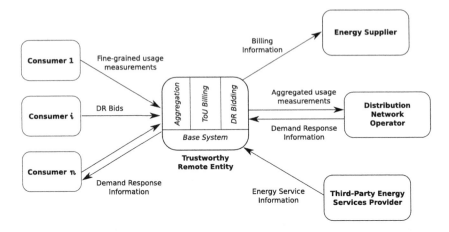

Fig. 4. Enhanced system architecture using a Trustworthy Remote Entity [18].

6   Proposed Architecture

In order to address the privacy challenges identified above, we propose an enhanced system architecture to facilitate communication between consumers and other entities such as energy suppliers or distribution network operators (DNOs). This architecture has been developed as part of our ongoing research into privacy-enhancing technologies for the smart grid [18]. Figure 4 shows our proposed system architecture. The significant innovation of this architecture is the inclusion of a trusted third party called a Trusted Remote Entity (TRE). The TRE is an information processing node situated as an intermediary between the consumers and all external entities. The TRE makes extensive use of Trusted Computing (TC) technologies and approaches. As specified by the Trusted Computing Group (TCG), TC can be used to obtain various security guarantees about computational systems. The TCG-specified Trusted Platform Module (TPM) is a secure cryptographic co-processor that can be used as a root of trust in the system [19]. The *secure boot* procedure ensures that the system will boot into a secure state and the process of *remote attestation* uses the TPM to generate unforgeable proofs of this state which are sent to the relying parties in order to establish trust. The TRE uses these approaches to prove its secure state to all the relying parties. Unlike TC in the PC domain, the TRE avoids the problem of scalability in attestation by running a very small Trusted Computing Base (TCB). A full description of the TRE will be presented in future work.

The fundamental aspect of the TRE is that it is mutually trusted by parties that do not necessarily trust each other. As explained in Sect. 5, there is evidence that consumers do not necessarily trust the energy supplier to store and perform computations on their private information. Similarly, the energy supplier does not necessarily trust the consumers to calculate their own energy bills honestly. However, in our architecture, both consumers and the energy supplier trust the TRE to perform these operations on their behalf. Critically, these parties have good grounds for trusting the TRE because of its use of TC approaches and technologies. Whilst the use of TC does not remove all risks from this architecture, it significantly reduces the likelihood of a large class of software-based threats. TC secure boot and remote attestation virtually eliminate the possibility of a remote adversary compromising the software of the TRE without being detected immediately. TC does not mitigate against all hardware-based threats such as eavesdropping on the physical memory bus within the system, however, attacks of this type are significantly more complicated and expensive than software-based attacks and so present a significantly lower risk. In practice, these risks would be mitigated through certification or auditing processes. Just as the hardware of a TPM is trusted based on a certificate from its manufacturer, a similar certificate from the TRE manufacturer could be used to establish trust in the TRE hardware which would in turn support trust in the TRE software.

6.1   Distributed TREs

There will be multiple TREs throughout the network, each serving a group of consumers. The maximum number of consumers per TRE will depend on the computational and network capacities of the TRE but it is expected to be in the order of thousands of consumers per TRE. One of the primary weaknesses of any architecture that includes a trusted third party is that this node could become both a single point of failure as well as the most attractive target for attack. This would also be true of the TRE if it were a single node in the architecture. However, the use of multiple distinct TREs (i.e. with differing cryptographic keys etc.) throughout the network mitigates against this risk. There is still a non-zero probability that a single attack could affect all TREs in the network but this is very similar to an attack affecting all smart meters in the grid. The smart meter attack is arguably more likely since the meters generally do not include the hardware-based security capabilities used in the TRE.

6.2   Smart Grid TRE Functionality

In the smart grid, the TRE provides three main types of functionality: Firstly it aggregates the high-frequency measurements from smart meters before sending them to the DNO for use in network optimization. Secondly, it performs ToU billing calculations on behalf of the energy supplier. Thirdly, it provides the functionality of a DRAS in an OpenADR 1.0 system or an aggregator in an OpenADR 2.0 architecture. In this role, the TRE does not forward the bids to the energy supplier but instead aggregates the bids so that they cannot be linked to individual consumers. Since the TRE also performs the billing calculations, it can apply the respective incentives to successful bidders without revealing their identities to the supplier. This architecture therefore mitigates against both types of HBC adversaries identified in the previous section. Consumers can use TC remote attestation to verify that a particular TRE is trustworthy. Even if the energy supplier or DNO are untrusted HBC adversaries, the aggregation of energy measurements and DR bids performed by the TRE prevents these adversaries from learning any private information about consumers.

In OpenADR 2.0, the TRE appears as a VTN for the consumers and as a VEN for the energy supplier. This means that the TRE can be deployed as a plug-in enhancement to the smart grid without requiring any modification of the primary information flows. The only additional communication that would be required are the remote attestation protocols for establishing trust in the TRE. Furthermore, a heterogeneous smart grid architecture could be used in which some users communicate directly with the supplier whilst others communicate via a TRE. In a real-world deployment scenario, the TREs could therefore be deployed gradually without causing major disruptions to the smart grid. The specific TRE deployment scenarios are the subject of future research.

7 Conclusion

Security and privacy concerns arising from the introduction of smart meters have been the subject of various research efforts. However, less attention has been given to the security and privacy of demand response protocols, such as demand bidding (DR-DB), which will be an important part of the future smart grid. This paper builds on preliminary work in this area to define a set of high level security and privacy goals for demand bidding systems highlighting the fact that the bi-directional communication used in these systems poses a risk to consumers' privacy. We identify the appropriate types of adversary models and use these to present an analysis of a DR-DB system based on the OpenADR specifications, in terms of the security and privacy goals. Although this system achieves the security goals, it cannot achieve the defined privacy goals if external entities such as the energy supplier are not trusted by the consumers. In order to address this issue, we have proposed a system architecture to enhance consumers' privacy in the smart grid. The key innovation of this architecture is the inclusion of a Trustworthy Remote Entity (TRE) which uses Trusted Computing (TC) approaches and technologies to establish trust relationships with both the consumers and the external entities. The TRE is mutually trusted by parties that do not necessarily trust each other and the use of TC provides good grounds for this trust. Through the functionality provided by the TRE, the defined security and privacy goals can be achieved whilst maintaining the overall functionality of the demand response system.

Acknowledgements. The research described in this paper was conducted as part of the *Future Home Networks and Services* project at the University of Oxford, funded by BT.

References

1. Efthymiou, C., Kalogridis, G.: Smart grid privacy via anonymization of smart metering data. In: Proceedings of IEEE International Conference on Smart Grid Communications (SmartGridComm), pp. 238–243 (2010)
2. Danezis, G., Kohlweiss, M., Rial, A.: Differentially private billing with rebates. In: Filler, T., Pevný, T., Craver, S., Ker, A. (eds.) IH 2011. LNCS, vol. 6958, pp. 148–162. Springer, Heidelberg (2011)
3. Ács, G., Castelluccia, C.: I have a DREAM! (DiffeRentially privatE smArt Metering). In: Filler, T., Pevný, T., Craver, S., Ker, A. (eds.) IH 2011. LNCS, vol. 6958, pp. 118–132. Springer, Heidelberg (2011)
4. Borges, F., Martucci, L.A., Muhlhauser, M.: Analysis of privacy-enhancing protocols based on anonymity networks. In: Proceedings of IEEE Third International Conference on Smart Grid Communications (SmartGridComm), pp. 378–383, November 2012
5. Piette, M.A., Ghatikar, G., Kiliccote, S., Koch, E., Hennage, D., Palensky, P., McParland, C.: Open automated demand response communications specification (version 1.0). Technical report, California Energy Commission, PIER Program, April 2009
6. OpenADR Alliance: OpenADR 2.0b profile specification. Technical report (2013)
7. OpenADR Alliance: The openADR primer. Technical report (2012)
8. United States Department of Energy: Benefits of demand response in electricity markets and recommendations for achieving them. Technical report, February 2006
9. Albadi, M., El-Saadany, E.: A summary of demand response in electricity markets. Electr. Power Syst. Res. 78(11), 1989–1996 (2008)
10. Karwe, M., Strüker, J.: Maintaining privacy in data rich demand response applications. In: Cuellar, J. (ed.) SmartGridSec 2012. LNCS, vol. 7823, pp. 85–95. Springer, Heidelberg (2013)
11. Quinn, E.L.: Privacy and the New Energy Infrastructure. SSRN eLibrary (2009)
12. Brown, I.: Britain's smart meter programme: a case study in privacy by design. Int. Rev. Law Comput. Technol. 28, 172–184 (2013)
13. Cuijpers, C., Koops, B.J.: Smart metering and privacy in Europe: lessons from the Dutch case. In: Gutwirth, S., Leenes, R., de Hert, P., Poullet, Y. (eds.) European Data Protection: Coming of Age, pp. 269–293. Springer, Dordrecht (2013)
14. Dolev, D., Yao, A.: On the security of public key protocols. IEEE Trans. Inf. Theory 29(2), 198–208 (1983)
15. Goldreich, O.: Foundations of Cryptography: Basic Applications, vol. 2. Cambridge University Press, Cambridge (2009)
16. Paverd, A.J., Martin, A.P.: Hardware security for device authentication in the smart grid. In: Cuellar, J. (ed.) SmartGridSec 2012. LNCS, vol. 7823, pp. 72–84. Springer, Heidelberg (2013)
17. Cuijpers, C., Koops, B.J.: Het wetsvoorstel slimme meters: een privacytoets op basis van art. 8 EVRM Onderzoek in opdracht van de Consumentenbond. Technical report, Universiteit van Tilburg (2008)
18. Paverd, A.J.: Student research abstract: trustworthy remote entities in the smart grid. In: ACM Symposium on Applied Computing (SAC) (2013)
19. Trusted Computing Group: TPM main specifications, version 1.2, revision 116, part 1: design principles. Technical report (2011)

Distributed MILS Architectural Approach for Secure Smart Grids

Denis Bytschkow$^{(\boxtimes)}$, Jean Quilbeuf, Georgeta Igna, and Harald Ruess

fortiss GmbH, An-Institut Technische Universität München,
Guerickestr. 25, 80805 München, Germany
{bytschkow,quilbeuf,igna,ruess}@fortiss.org
http://www.fortiss.org

Abstract. Successful decentralized and prosumer-based smart grids need to be at least as dependable and secure as the prevailing one-way, generation-transmission-distribution-consumer power grids. With this motivation in mind, we propose a two-phase model-based design methodology for secure architectural design and secure deployment of such a security architecture on a distributed separation kernel. In particular, we are modeling essential parts of a smart micro grid with several interacting prosumers, and demonstrate exemplary security/privacy requirements of this smart grid. The security policy architecture of this smart grid is deployed on a secure distributed platform, relying on a combination of separation kernels and deterministic network, as developed in the Distributed MILS project.

Keywords: Smart grid security · Distributed MILS · Separation kernel · Formal verification · Security policy architecture · Configuration compiler

1 Introduction

The electricity industry is in the middle of a paradigmatic shift towards smart power grids in order to meet the emerging needs of a highly reliable, efficient and sustainable society. In particular, the management of renewable, decentralized energy sources, higher volatility of power production, the consumer's active behavior coupled with sustainability objectives, and efforts towards new market designs drive the on-going transformation of the traditional power grid.

The control of smart grids requires significant change towards decentralized energy management systems (EMS) with a tight coupling of energy control with

This work has been carried out as part of the D-MILS project (www.d-mils.org) which is funded by the European Commission under the 7th Framework Programme for Information and Communications Technology. The smart grid case study has been supported by Siemens, the EIT ICT Labs, and the Bavarian Ministry of Economics.

J. Cuellar (Ed.): SmartGridSec 2014, LNCS 8448, pp. 16–29, 2014.
DOI: 10.1007/978-3-319-10329-7_2

new monitoring, processing, optimizing, and controlling devices based on real-time information and communication technology (ICT). Moreover, electricity consumers are evolving into economically motivated *prosumers* that not only consume, but can also produce and store electricity. Prosumers can become smart energy ecosystems if they are equipped with market access and suitable ICT that allow them to achieve their own objectives.

Prosumer-based smart grid systems, however, are subject to a multitude of new types of attacks and threats [5]. Smart meter data may be manipulated to consume electricity without or with reduced payment. Manipulation of actuator components may damage the physical prosumer system, or even allow a burglar to break in. Finally, attacks to the communication infrastructure may lead to leaks of private and financial data.

A number of security guidelines and requirement specifications for smart grid infrastructure have recently been developed, including the ENISA Smart Grid Security report [13], the ENISA guidelines for security measures [12], and the NIST report NIST-IR-7628 [17]. The ISO/IEC TR 27019 report provides security guidelines based on ISO/IEC 27002 for process control systems specific to the energy industry. It has been pointed out, however, that engineering dependable and secure energy systems based on these guidelines is rather costly and time-consuming due to the need for extensive reviewing and testing of critical smart grid protocols, their low-level implementations, and the inherent dynamics of the environment of smart grid components [22].

In this paper we are proposing a novel approach for engineering secure smart grids based on model-based design methodology for embedded systems. In particular, we are proposing the model-based MILS approach for designing and implementing dependable and secure smart grids. MILS [1, 21] was originally an acronym for Multiple Independent Levels of Security and is popularly characterized as the use of a separation kernels and information flow mechanisms to support both untrusted and trusted applications from diverse security domains on one computational system. Key concepts of the MILS architectural approach include separation, component integration, policy architecture, and physical resource sharing [3]. Separation concepts are consistent with approaches like intransitive noninterference [19] and partitioning in integrated-modular avionics [20]. Nowadays MILS is a standard platform in the US for deploying ultra-dependable mixed-criticality systems, but it is still virtually unknown in Europe. The Distributed MILS (D-MILS) project [9] extends the classical work of MILS to distributed embedded systems by realizing a distributed separation kernel by means of deterministic and predictable network communication (e.g. via time-triggered Ethernet). In this way D-MILS provides the capability to use one policy architecture that seamlessly spans across multiple MILS nodes—as required for smart grids. Moreover time and space separation of the D-MILS platform might be used to minimize the effect of faults or attacks to certain regions only, thereby avoiding rolling blackouts. Given a high-level model of the system, security properties in D-MILS are established in two phases

1. The policy architecture defined by the high-level model is established and enforced by the configured D-MILS platform.
2. Security properties are checked on a high-level model assuming that the policy architecture is enforced.

The policy architecture indicates how information is allowed to flow amongst the different components of the system. Consequently the construction of security assurance cases is separated into (1) establishing security of the high-level model and (2) enforcing the policy architecture defined by the high-level model through configuration of the distributed platform. The D-MILS platform[1] is specified to have provable domain isolation and information flow controls, thereby increasing assurance of the absence of hidden channels and unwanted information flow. We are using the D-MILS architectural approach for demonstrating various privacy requirements for a prosumer-based smart grid.

In this paper we are applying and demonstrating key concepts of the D-MILS methodology for establishing representative security properties of a smart micro grid. This case study is based on the smart grid demonstrator at fortiss [15], which has been built-up in the context of the European network of smart grid living labs of the EIT ICT Labs. This micro grid is mainly used for experimenting with distributed controls for (self-) stabilization of prosumer-based smart grids.

This paper is organised as follows. In Sect. 2, we introduce the smart grid example that we will use to illustrate the D-MILS approach. In Sect. 3, we present the D-MILS platform. In Sect. 4 we show how our case study is formalized using AF3. Finally, in Sect. 5 we show how (1) the policy architecture is enforced by configuring the platform and (2) how a simple security property is verified assuming that the underlying policy architecture is enforced by the platform.

2   Case Study

The smart micro grid entails a large variety of security requirements. Figure 1 shows an overview of the system. The system consists of a finite number of prosumers communicating with a Micro Grid EMS. Communication channels are represented by arrows in the figure.

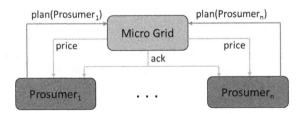

Fig. 1. High-level description of the smart micro grid system

---

[1] The D-MILS platform consists of a LynxSecure hypervisor provided by LynuxWorks and a TTEthernet solution provided by TTTech.

Each prosumer communicates with the Micro Grid through well-defined interfaces. Initially, the Micro Grid sends the energy price (through channel `price`) for the next day. As a response, each prosumer sends its planned consumption and production (through channel `plan`) for the next day to the Micro Grid. The Micro Grid validates the plans received by checking that the overall energy flow through the grid implied by these plans does not exceed the power line capacity. The Micro Grid sends back an acknowledgment message `ack` that contains the value 0 if the plans are within the power line capacity, otherwise it contains the amount of energy that exceeds the line capacity. Based on this acknowledgment message `ack`, each prosumer is responsible to update its own plan and send it back to the Micro Grid. The negotiation terminates when `ack=0`, meaning that the energy flow on the grid does not exceed the line capacity.

The security requirements that the Micro Grid system should fulfill are described in detail in [10]. In this paper, however, we focus on one of the most relevant requirements, which is related to privacy

RQ: No prosumer knows the consumption of another prosumer.

Using the D-MILS approach, the requirement RQ is ensured by two simpler requirements:

RQ1: No prosumer is able to bypass the defined communication channels to find out the consumption plan of any other prosumer.

RQ2: No prosumer is able to deduce the consumption plan of any other prosumer with the received information.

The first requirement refers to the low-level implementation of the system. This requirement is enforced through separation capabilities of the platform and its configuration by a configuration compiler (Sect. 5.1). The configuration files are built from a formal model of the system. A configured D-MILS platform guarantees the absence of unintended communication channels that are not in the formal model. The second requirement is ensured by checking that the formal model satisfies a security hyperproperty as described in Sect. 5.2.

3   D-MILS Platform

The D-MILS platform consists of a set of MILS nodes that communicate over a deterministic network. A MILS node implements a minimum separation kernel, which is a low-level hypervisor that controls the information exchange between the applications and virtualizes hardware resources. Its minimalistic design allows the separation kernel to be exhaustively tested and evaluated to meet low-level properties, such as being not by-passable and tamper-proof. The networking system, e.g. time-triggered Ethernet, guarantees message delivery and separation.

The separation kernel of each node as well as each switch of the network is statically configured. The configuration guarantees the absence of unintended information exchange in the system deployed on the distributed MILS platform. An example of a possible D-MILS platform configuration is shown in Fig. 2.

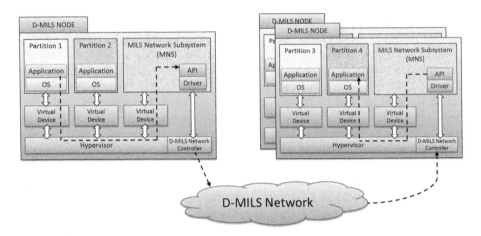

Fig. 2. D-MILS platform and possible information flows between different partitions

The platform consists of several MILS nodes and a Time-Triggered Ethernet as the networking system. The D-MILS configuration allocates a partition for each component of the system. Communications inside a node are handled by the local hypervisor, which also provides the resources as virtual devices for the local partitions. In each node, a dedicated partition called MILS Network Subsystem (MNS) handles the communications over the network. The D-MILS network ensures separation of (virtual) communication channels between the nodes through time partitioning. A virtual channel is depicted in Fig. 2 as a dashed line.

4   Formalization of the Information Flow

The system representation of Fig. 1 illustrates the intended communication channels. We formalize the system as a component-based model. We use AUTOFOCUS 3 (AF3), which is a modeling tool[2] based on the semantics of the FOCUS theory [4]. Each component has a well-defined interface explicitly represented as a set of ports. AF3 provides strong data encapsulation, i.e. each data variable resides within an atomic component and each atomic component has exclusive access to its variables. Therefore, data-sharing is only possible through explicit communication channels.

Components can be hierarchically decomposed into subcomponents in order to model complex systems in a comprehensible manner. Components are synchronously executed based on a discrete global time. The semantics of a component can be specified with state-automata, tables with input/output specification, or a stateless code specification. This semantics defines a *stream* [4] for each port, representing the successive values taken by that port at each time step.

---

[2] AF3 is an open source tool available at http://af3.fortiss.org.

Figure 3 shows our model. The model contains three prosumers, a micro grid and communication channels to the environment. Black dots represent output ports, whereas the white dots represent input ports. Arrows encode the communication channels. The communication between the components of the model define the policy architecture.

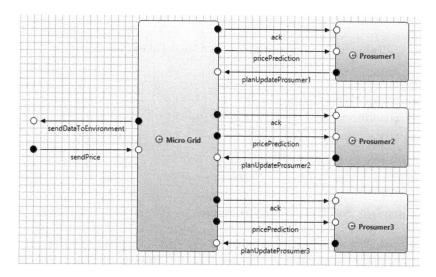

Fig. 3. The connections between the components define the policy architecture for the smart micro grid system.

The Micro Grid receives the energy price for the next day and transmits it to prosumers through the channels `pricePrediction`. The prosumers react to the price by generating their plan for the next day. Each prosumer `Prosumer` i sends its plan through the channel `planUpdateProsumer` i. A plan consists of a nonnegative production plan P_i, a non-positive consumption plan C_i and battery usage plan B_i indicating whether the battery will store energy (negative value) or provide energy (positive value). We summarize this information in a tuple (P_i, C_i, B_i). We furthermore assume that for each prosumer i, $P_i \in \{0, 1, 2\}$, $C_i \in \{-3, -2, -1, 0\}$ and $B_i \in \{-1, 0, 1\}$. By adding the three values, we get the global contribution of the prosumers to the grid. For the plans to be accepted, the balance of energy produced/consumed must be admissible for the system, which is specified by line capacity bounds L and H. More precisely, the set of plans is accepted if $L \leq \sum_{i=1}^{n}(P_i + C_i + B_i) \leq H$. In this case, the Micro Grid sends zero on the `ack` port. In the sequel, we define that $L = -7$ and $H = 4$. If the sum is below L or above H, the difference is sent back on the `ack` port to the prosumers. In this case, each prosumer updates its plan accordingly and sends it back to the Micro Grid. This negotiation process terminates when the plans are accepted.

The trace of an execution consists of successive values written on the ports at each step. The first steps of a trace (for ports planUpdateProsumer{1, 2, 3} and ack) are depicted in Table 1. The ack port is represented once since it is the same for each prosumer. This trace represents a negotiation, where the plans initially consume too much energy (an excess of four energy units in the first round, and one unit in the second). Accordingly, Prosumers 1 and 2 reduce their consumption by discharging the battery instead of charging it.

Table 1. The beginning of a trace for the smart micro grid

Execution step	1	2	3	4	5	6	...
planUpdateProsumer1	$(0, -3, -1)$		$(0, -3, 0)$		$(0, -3, 1)$		...
planUpdateProsumer2	$(0, -3, -1)$		$(0, -3, 0)$		$(0, -3, 1)$		...
planUpdateProsumer3	$(0, -3, 0)$		$(0, -2, 0)$		$(0, -2, 0)$		...
ack		-4		-1		0	...

5   Ensuring Security Properties

As said in Sect. 2, the D-MILS approach separates our main requirement RQ into two simpler requirements. The requirement RQ1 is obtained by enforcing the policy architecture defined by the connections in the high-level model. A platform configuration automatically derived from the high-level model by a configuration compiler is used for this purpose, as described in Subsect. 5.1.

At the software component level, security policies are expressed through hyperproperties [8]. The assumption that communications match the policy architecture is supported by the platform configuration. Hyperproperties allow us to formalize security requirements such as RQ2, as shown in Subsect. 5.2.

5.1   Ensuring Security of the Platform

A D-MILS platform establishes and enforces an intransitive security policy, provided that it is configured properly. Such a security policy defines communication channels between components. A configured D-MILS platform ensures that the only possible communications are the ones defined in the security policy. In particular, it guarantees that there are no hidden channels.

A D-MILS platform consists of a set of nodes, connected through a network. Each node is a physical machine equipped with a separation kernel. The latter defines *partitions* that are completely isolated and host components. Two components running on two distinct partitions of the same node are able to communicate only if the configuration allows it. The communication between components deployed on distinct nodes relies on a network able to enforce separation of channels. In the D-MILS project, a time-triggered network is used for

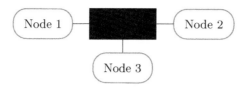

Fig. 4. A simple D-MILS platform

this purpose and separation is enforced through time partitioning. In the sequel, we assume a D-MILS platform as depicted in Fig. 4.

The configuration compiler is a tool that produces a configuration for each node and each switch of the platform. To this purpose, the configuration compiler is fed with the policy architecture, such as in Fig. 3, a model of the platform, such as in Fig. 4 and deployment information. For instance, one could assume that Prosumer 1 and Micro Grid components from Fig. 3 are deployed on nodes 1 and 2 from Fig. 4 respectively, and that Node 3 hosts both Prosumer 2 and Prosumer 3. Therefore, the configuration compiler generates configuration files such that Node 3 runs two separate partitions and that the communication channels between partitions are restricted to the channels of Fig. 3. The deployed system is depicted in Fig. 5. Each node contains a dedicated partition for hosting a Mils Network Subsystem (MNS) in charge of the communications over the time-triggered network.

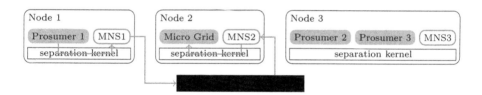

Fig. 5. A communication channel in a deployed D-MILS smart micro grid.

In order to state some correctness conditions for the MNS components, we derive an intermediate model between the high-level model and the corresponding deployed software. The intermediate model includes the components of the high-level model and the MNS components. Two different types of channels are defined:

– Channels between components deployed on the same node. These channels model communications handled by the separation kernel.
– Channels between MNS components. Each of these channels model a virtual link defined over the time-triggered network.

The channels between components hosted on different nodes are modified to be routed through the MNS components. Figure 6 shows how a channel *ab* between components deployed on distinct nodes is transformed. For each inter node-channel, a new virtual link is defined. In the figure, vl_{ab} is the virtual link defined to support the channel ab from the high-level model. For each channel of the high-level model either incoming to the node or outgoing from the node, the MNS component includes two corresponding ports. One port is connected to the component of the node involved in the channel, the other port to the virtual link associated to the channel. Each MNS transfers outgoing messages on the virtual link corresponding to the input port that received the message. Similarly, it transfers incoming messages on the output port corresponding to the virtual link that conveyed the message.

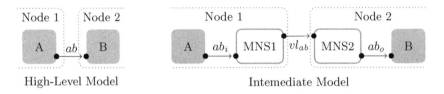

Fig. 6. Transformation of a channel between components deployed on distinct nodes.

Using this model, we say that the set of MNS components is correct if it implements the information flow described in the high-level model as in Fig. 1 for our example. On Fig. 6, the MNS are correct if in every execution, the sequence of values observed on the channel ab_i and the sequence of values observed on the channel ab_o are identical. A sufficient condition for correctness is stated through filter functions [6]. A filter function refines an existing information flow by specifying whether a given message is allowed according to the history of received and sent messages. In our case, a separate filter function is attached to each output port of the MNS component. The filter function allows an outgoing message only in the sequence of messages seen on the output port is a prefix of the sequence of message seen on the corresponding input port. The combination of these filters function correspond to our correctness criteria. Consider again the Fig. 6, the filter function on ab_o requires that it transmits the same sequence of messages as vl_{ab}. Similarly, the filter function on vl_{ab} requires that it transmits the same sequence of messages as ab_i. According to [18], checking that the filter functions are respected can be done locally for each MNS and does not depend on the implementation of other components.

Essentially, the platform guarantees that the information exchanged bet ween components follows the channels defined in the high-level model. Each component is only aware of the values sent to its input ports. For instance, each prosumer can only see the information sent by the Micro Grid component, and cannot directly communicate with another prosumer. However, a prosumer obtain get some information about other prosumers through the Micro Grid component.

5.2   Checking Security of the High-Level Model

In this section, we focus on requirement RQ2 which demands that no prosumer can deduce the consumption plan of any other prosumer. In order to formalize this requirement, we use the theory of knowledge [14]. In this theory, an agent observes only a part of the system and knows the set of all possible traces allowed by the system. If a particular property holds in all traces that are (1) possible and (2) consistent with the current observation, then the agent knows that this property holds in the current execution. In our case, the agent is a prosumer and its observation is restricted to its input and output ports. We want to ensure that the property "the consumption plan of prosumer i is X" cannot be deduced by any other prosumer.

For our analysis, we focus on the knowledge gained during one exchange of plans and acknowledgements. In our case, the set of traces is determined by the bounds imposed on the prosumer plans and the line capacity. Recall that each prosumer i may send any plan (P_i, C_i, B_i) such that $P_i \in \{0, 1, 2\}$, $C_i \in \{-3, -2, -1, 0\}$ and $B_i \in \{-1, 0, 1\}$. Then, the Micro Grid returns the value 0 on the port ack if $-7 \leq \sum_{i=1}^{n}(P_i + C_i + B_i) \leq 4$, otherwise, it returns the difference between the sum of the plans and the bound exceeded. We assume that each prosumer knows the set of possible traces, or, equivalently, the bounds for the prosumer plans and the line capacity. Such an assumption is supported by the fact that these bounds may be publicly available (line capacity), estimated (production from solar energy), or learned by observing multiple executions of the system.

Figure 7 presents a set of possible traces and the corresponding observations made by Prosumer 3. The bounds imply that only one trace is consistent with Observation 1, as it corresponds to the case where both Prosumer 1 and Prosumer 2 requested 4 units of energy ($P_1 = P_2 = 0$, $C_1 = C_2 = -3$ and $B_1 = B_2 = -1$), which is an extreme value. In this case, there is only one trace consistent with Observation 1, where $C_2 = -3$. Thus Prosumer 3 can deduce from Observation 1 that the consumption plan of Prosumer 2 is -3. However, several traces are consistent with Observation 2. In some traces $C_2 = -3$ whereas in some others $C_2 = -2$. Therefore, Prosumer 3 cannot deduce the exact consumption plan of Prosumer 2 from Observation 2. We conclude that this implementation is insecure because it allows one case (i.e. Observation 1) where a prosumer can infer the consumption of another prosumer.

The implementation is secure if there is no observation that allows a given prosumer to deduce the consumption of another one. This intuitive definition is formalized as follows. We denote by τ a trace (in our case a set of plans and the corresponding acknowledgement), and by T the set of all possible traces. Given a set of ports V, we denote by $\tau|_V$ the values taken by the ports in V when executing τ. In particular, prosumer i can observe the ports planUpdateProsumer i (abbreviated pUP$_i$) and ack. Hence, $\tau|_{\{\text{pUP}_i, \text{ack}\}}$ denotes the observation of prosumer i during the execution of τ. For ease of notation, we denote by $\tau|_{C_i}$ the value of the consumption in the plan sent by Prosumer i. We formalize the property "Prosumer i is not able to deduce the consumption plan of prosumer j" by

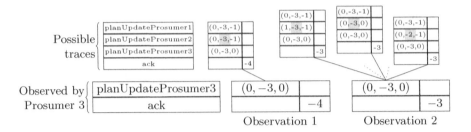

Fig. 7. Some possible traces and corresponding local observations. There is a single trace consistent with Observation 1, and several for Observation 2. The list of possible traces is not exhaustive.

$$\forall \tau \in T \; \exists \tau' \in T \quad \tau|_{\{\text{pUP}_i,\text{ack}\}} = \tau'|_{\{\text{pUP}_i,\text{ack}\}} \wedge \tau|_{C_j} \neq \tau'|_{C_j} \tag{1}$$

The formula states that for any trace τ of the system, there exists at least another trace τ' where Prosumer i observes the same values as in τ, but such that the consumption of j differs between τ and τ'.

For this kind of properties, it is not sufficient to check that each trace individually complies with the property. Rather, the property depends on the exact set of traces T allowed by the system. Such properties are called hyperproperties and were introduced by Clarkson and Schneider [8]. Several formalisms exist to specify such security properties. Van der Meyden proposed several semantics for intransitive non-interference [16]. Intransitive non-interference is possibly reinforced through filter functions [6], that are used in [18] to specify a weaker security property for the same Micro Grid as discussed here. Balliu uses epistemic logic [2] in a more general case than ours, Clarkson et al. defines a temporal logics for hyperproperties [7].

In order to check the security property, we wrote a SMT-lib script. The script encodes the constraints for a trace where a prosumer i can deduce the consumption of another prosumer j. Formally, we search for a trace τ such that

$$\tau \in T \wedge \forall \tau' \in T \; \tau|_{\{\text{pUP}_i,\text{ack}\}} = \tau'|_{\{\text{pUP}_i,\text{ack}\}} \implies \tau|_{C_j} = \tau'|_{C_j} \tag{2}$$

If these constraints are unsatisfiable for each pair i, j such that $i \neq j$, no prosumer can deduce the consumption of another prosumer. Z3 [11] found a trace satisfying the constraint (2), which corresponds to Observation 1 from Fig. 7. Thus, the system is insecure.

In order to make the system secure, we add further constraints on prosumers plans. We ask that the global contribution of the prosumer remains within the bounds corresponding to the maximal consumption or production. Formally, for a plan (P_i, C_i, B_i), we require that $-3 \leq P_i + C_i + B_i \leq 2$. In this case, the extreme values for each plan can be reached in several ways, as in Observation 2 of Fig. 7, which hides the real value of the consumption. By adding these constraints on the prosumers plans, we modify the set of traces T allowed by the system. Consequently, Z3 outputs that the constraint (2) is unsatisfiable, meaning that the security property (1) is met.

6   Conclusion

We have outlined an application of the two-phase D-MILS architectural methodology for demonstrating security properties of the distributed implementation of a prosumer-based smart grid.

The low-level platform view of D-MILS is provided by a secure technology layer, which guarantees the sharing of resources using components, such as separation kernels and partitioning communications systems that deliver the required guarantee of separation. A correct configuration of those components provides the assurance that no unintended channels exist, and data leakage is prevented on the resource sharing level.

The high-level architectural view is represented by a formal model, which constitutes the system design and defines available channels for data exchange. The assurance argument that the high-level model indeed satisfies the given security goals is independent of low-level considerations of the platform implementation. This high-level architectural model is used as input for the configuration compiler, which produces configurations of the D-MILS components, which enforce the intended high-level information flow on the low-level technical platform; in particular, a correct configuration compiler does not introduce any hidden channels on the resource-sharing platform.

The separation into an architectural and a platform-dependent part structures and considerably simplifies the construction of assurance cases for security properties of the micro grid case study.

We have demonstrated that representative privacy properties of the micro grid case study can be encoded in terms of hyperproperties. We proposed a preliminary encoding of facts deduced from the execution traces which are visible at the input ports. These encodings allowed us to detect a case where privacy is broken and propose an alternative model that is more secure. The analysis can be extended by taking into account the history of actions (instead of one step of execution as currently). Ultimately, the privacy property should be stated in term of the quality of approximation that a prosumer can obtain from a given observation.

Altogether, our smart grid case study demonstrates that the D-MILS approach is suitable to reason about security requirements. Together with a secure low-level technical platform, which can be configured to allow desired information flow channels, and more importantly prevent undesired information flow channels, the D-MILS approach provides an environment for design, analysis, verification, and implementation of scalable, interoperable and affordable trustworthy smart grid architectures. However, significant progress along several lines is needed for reaching our ultimate goal of a complete and cost-effective solution for securing smart grids. In particular, the D-MILS methodology as outlined needs to be supported by (1) a high-level architectural language (e.g. AADL) for specifying the security policy architecture and a wide variety of security properties, (2) a suitable automated and suitable *verification framework*, (3) *assurance and verification methods* for compositional assurance, and (4) a *runtime monitoring plane* for testing, diagnosis, assessment, auditing and management of

D-MILS systems. Moreover, the current versions of D-MILS are static and do not support the evolution of smart grids in time, as configurations are determined a priori and cannot be dynamically changed during runtime. Both the D-MILS architectural design methodology and platform need to be extended to support dynamically changing information flow policies and platform configurations.

References

1. Alves-Foss, J., Harrison, W.S., Oman, P., Taylor, C.: The MILS architecture for high-assurance embedded systems. Int. J. Embed. Syst. **2**(3/4), 239–247 (2006)
2. Balliu, M.: A logic for information flow analysis of distributed programs. In: Riis Nielson, H., Gollmann, D. (eds.) NordSec 2013. LNCS, vol. 8208, pp. 84–99. Springer, Heidelberg (2013)
3. Boettcher, C., DeLong, R., Rushby, J., Sifre, W.: The MILS component integration approach to secure information sharing. In: IEEE/AIAA 27th Digital Avionics Systems Conference, 2008, DASC 2008, pp. 1.C.2-1–1.C.2-14. IEEE (2008)
4. Broy, M., Stølen, K.: Specification and Development of Interactive Systems: Focus on Streams, Interfaces, and Refinement. Springer, Secaucus (2001)
5. Camek, A., Holzl, F., Bytschkow, D.: Providing security to a smart grid prosumer system based on a service oriented architecture in an office environment. In: Proceedings of Innovative Smart Grid Technologies (ISGT), 2013 IEEE PES (2013)
6. Chong, S., van der Meyden, R.: Using architecture to reason about information security. In: Layered Assurance Workshop (2012)
7. Clarkson, M.R., Finkbeiner, B., Koleini, M., Micinski, K.K., Rabe, M.N., Sánchez, C.: Temporal logics for hyperproperties. In: Abadi, M., Kremer, S. (eds.) POST 2014 (ETAPS 2014). LNCS, vol. 8414, pp. 265–284. Springer, Heidelberg (2014)
8. Clarkson, M.R., Schneider, F.B.: Hyperproperties. J. Comput. Secur. **18**(6), 1157–1210 (2010)
9. D-MILS: Distributed MILS for dependable information and communication infrastructures. STREP, FP7. http://www.d-mils.org
10. D-MILS: Safety and security requirements for the fortiss Smart Micro Grid demonstrator (2013), d-MILS project deliverable
11. de Moura, L., Bjørner, N.S.: Z3: an efficient SMT solver. In: Ramakrishnan, C.R., Rehof, J. (eds.) TACAS 2008. LNCS, vol. 4963, pp. 337–340. Springer, Heidelberg (2008)
12. ENISA: Appropriate security measures for smart grids - guidelines to assess the sophistication of security measures implementation. Study of the European Network and Information Security Agency (ENISA) (2012)
13. ENISA: Smart grid security - recommendations for Europe and member states. Study of the European Network and Information Security Agency (ENISA) (2012)
14. Fagin, R., Halpern, J.Y., Moses, Y., Vardi, M.Y.: Reasoning About Knowledge. MIT Press, Cambridge (1995)
15. Koss, D., Sellmayr, F., Bauereiß, S., Bytschkow, D., Gupta, P.K., Schätz, B.: Establishing a smart grid node architecture and demonstrator in an office environment using the SOA approach. In: SE4SG, ICSE, pp. 8–14. IEEE (2012)
16. van der Meyden, R.: What, indeed, is intransitive noninterference? In: Biskup, J., López, J. (eds.) ESORICS 2007. LNCS, vol. 4734, pp. 235–250. Springer, Heidelberg (2007)

17. NIST: NIST IR 7628: guidelines for smart grid cyber security (2011). http://csrc.nist.gov/publications/PubsNISTIRs.html
18. Quilbeuf, J., Igna, G., Bytschkow, D., Ruess, H.: Security policies for distributed systems. CoRR abs/1310.3723 (2013)
19. Rushby, J.: Noninterference, transitivity, and channel-control security policies. SRI International, Computer Science Laboratory (1992)
20. Rushby, J.: Partitioning in avionics architectures: requirements, mechanisms, and assurance. Technical report, DTIC Document (2000)
21. Vanfleet, W.M., et al.: MILS: architecture for high assurance embedded computing. Cross Talk **18**, 12–16 (2005)
22. Yardley, T., Berthier, R., Nicol, D., Sanders, W.: Smart grid protocol testing through cyber-physical testbeds. In: ISGT, 2013 IEEE PES, pp. 1–6 (2013)

Determining the Probability of Smart Grid Attacks by Combining Attack Tree and Attack Graph Analysis

Kristian Beckers[1], Maritta Heisel[1], Leanid Krautsevich[2]([⊠]), Fabio Martinelli[2], Rene Meis[1], and Artsiom Yautsiukhin[2]

[1] paluno – The Ruhr Institute for Software Technology – University of Duisburg-Essen, Essen, Germany
{kristian.beckers,maritta.heisel,rene.meis}@paluno.uni-due.de
[2] Istituto di Informatica E Telematica – Consiglio Nazionale Delle Ricerche, Via G. Moruzzi 1, 56124 Pisa, Italy
{leanid.krautsevich,fabio.martinelli,artsiom.yautsiukhin}@iit.cnr.it

Abstract. Smart grid is an intelligent energy distribution system consisting of multiple information and communication technologies (ICT). One of the challenges for such complex and heterogeneous system as smart grid is to unite security analysis on a high level of abstraction and concrete behavioral attack patterns that exploit low-level vulnerabilities. We provide a structured method that combines the Si* language, which can express attacker motivations as a goal hierarchy, and vulnerability specific attack graphs, which shows every step available for an attacker. We derive system specific information from the low-level representation of the system for a high-level probabilistic analysis.

Keywords: Smart grid · Threat analysis · Attack graphs · Attack trees · Si* model

1 Introduction

The smart grid is an electricity grid (or network) that intelligently manages the behavior and actions of its participants. The benefit of this network is envisioned to be a more economic, sustainable, and secure supply of energy. The part of the smart grid called smart metering system meters the consumption or production of energy and forward the data to external entities. This data is further used for billing and steering the energy production. In this paper, we focus on the analysis of security issues in the smart grid to help developers and administrators to protect their systems against possible attackers.

This research was partially supported by the EU FP7 Network of Excellence on Engineering Secure Future Internet Software Services and Systems (NESSoS, no 256980) and SESAMO, no 295354 projects.

© Springer International Publishing Switzerland 2014
J. Cuellar (Ed.): SmartGridSec 2014, LNCS 8448, pp. 30–47, 2014.
DOI: 10.1007/978-3-319-10329-7_3

Running Example. In our running example, we focus on attacks on an energy supplier called *Huntsville Consortium*. The Huntsville Consortium requires information about the prosumers energy consumption for billing purposes. The Huntsville Consortium acquires this information via an ICT system in the smart grid (see Sect. 4 for details). The energy supplier is interested in a protection against a certain group of attackers, e.g., network attackers, which are considered the most relevant for the system.

There are high-level and low-level views on attacks execution. The analysis of attacks often starts with determination of high-level attack scenarios [4,7], e.g., determination of goals of attackers. There is the Si* framework for high-level describing and analyzing the system from the viewpoint of actors. The Si* framework provides the ability to model the actors, their relations and goals, as well as the technology needed to fulfill the goals. We use the Si* framework [11] for modeling and decomposing attackers goals. The result of decomposing goals is a usual attack tree [12,18].

In addition to attack tree modeling notation, the Si* framework provides the means to model a high-level abstraction of a system, which is related to goals in the attack tree. Moreover, the Si* framework has been created to analyze secure socio-technical systems by making their capabilities explicit. In particular, the framework allows to express delegation and transfer of capabilities and the expected behavior of actors (in our example the energy supplier delegates tasks and capabilities to subcontractors). Thus, Si* provides the means to describe the context of the attacker goals in addition to usual description and decomposition of goals. There are several examples of application of Si* to the analysis of security in general [1,10,13] and smart grid in particular [2].

At the low level, an attacker realizes his/her attack plan by exploiting vulnerabilities existing in a system. High-level attack trees usually do not considered these vulnerabilities. Attack graphs are a low-level description of a system that organizes vulnerabilities in such a way that denotes the propagation of gained privileges during an attack [6,14].

Attack graphs are constructed by security personnel, while a real attacker does not have this complete picture of the existing vulnerabilities. In contrast, the attacker has only a rough plan (attack tree) and focuses only on the relevant parts of the system for her plan. Therefore, our contribution proposes to limit the analysis of the attack graph to the plan of the attacker represented in the attack tree. To achieve this, we propose to map Si* attack trees to attack graphs and explicitly considers how the attacker may satisfy his/her high-level goals by exploiting low-level vulnerabilities.

To sum up, we aim at an approach that connects two views on attacks execution in the smart grid. We provide a mapping between a high-level view on attacks expressed in the Si* language as an attack tree composed of sub-goals and a low-level view expressed as an attack graph consisting of vulnerabilities. This mapping helps us to aggregate the information available at a low-level and to analyze attacker plans. We use this aggregated information for a quantitative analysis, which allows the evaluation of probabilities of attackers goals to be achieved analyzing vulnerabilities that should be exploited while pursuing the goal. We suppose that such analysis allows more efficient investment distribution to achieve a more secure smart grid system.

The paper is organized as follows. Section 2 reviews the related work. Section 3 describes our structured method and Sect. 4 exemplifies the application of our method to our running example. Section 5 presents conclusions and the future work.

2   Related Work

Several methods were proposed for modeling an attacker during system engineering in the past. The aim of such methods was to understand the socio-technical view of the system and find the ways how an attacker may affect the work of the system.

Liu et al. [10] presented an i*-based framework for agent-oriented software engineering and requirements analysis. The framework is mainly focused on insider attackers rather than on hackers threatening a system from the outside. Mouratidis et al. [13] proposed a similar approach using scenarios to analyse a reaction of information systems on potential security attacks during the development process. The authors consider a simple single attacker and model the attacker as an i* actor who is trying to achieve her goal by completing sub-goals. Lamsweerde [19] considered attack scenarios during the development of services on the application layer. He considered obstacles as anti-goals for the system and, thus, as goals for the attacker. Asnar and Massacci [1] added risks related to the goals of a system to the Si* framework. The work has no explicit focus on the source of the risk (e.g., on attackers).

In this work we focus on goals of the attacker and their decomposition. In fact, this goal decomposition is similar to the attack tree technique, introduced by B. Schneier [18]. Since then, the attack trees have been acknowledged as a useful technique for analysis of attacker behaviour [4,12]. The usage of Si* from the attacker's point of view is similar to the attack tree technique, but allows modelling additional aspects of possible attacks (e.g., attacker motivation).

An attack graph is a technique for security modelling and analysis of a system which specifies states, related to the privileges the attacker may have, and transitions between them. There are two types of attack graphs in the literature. The first type denotes every state as a set of all privileges the attacker possesses at a certain stage of an attack [6]. The graph in this case is acyclic if we assume that an attacker cannot loose her privileges. The advantage of this model is that such type of analysis as Markov Decision Process (MDP) may be applied to it [8,9,17]. The main drawback of this model is the state-explosion problem. The second type was proposed by Noel and Jajodia [14] who represented nodes as disjoint sets of privileges. An attacker possesses several privileges at some stage of an attack, "owns" several nodes, i.e., the privileges she has is a union of the privileges assigned to these nodes. A transition requires "owning" certain nodes and leads to a new privilege. This model is free from the state explosion problem, but requires handling cycles and cannot be used for analysis with MDP.

Several authors considered transformation of attack trees into models which allows analysis of attacker steps as a sequence. Qin and Lee [16] proposed a conversion of attack trees into causal networks representing an order of execution of steps contained in the tree. Dalton et al. [5] and Piètre-Cambacédès and Boisou [15] proposed a transformation of attack trees into Petri Nets. The purpose of the transformation to Petri Nets is to use simulation to determine the likelihood of particular sequences of steps of the attacker, meaning paths in the attack tree. In contrast, we are proposing a mapping between an existing attack tree (expressed as a Si* model) and an existing attack graph. We rely on the precise information and existing probabilities in the attack graph and map these to the attack tree rather than determining probabilities via simulation.

3 A Method for Combining Attack Trees and Attack Graphs

Our approach is attacker centric, which means that we analyse a system against a certain type of an attacker (e.g., a network attacker). The attacker achieves high-level goals executing low-level actions. For example, the attacker exploits vulnerabilities in an operating system and database software installed on a server in order to get an access to billing data. High-level goals of the attacker are usually described as an attack tree while low-level actions as an attack graph. We aim at finding sequences of low-level actions that an attacker needs to execute in order to achieve her high-level goals. We formalize attack trees and attack graphs and then present a formal approach for mapping goals to sequences of actions. This sequence is exploited latter for a probabilistic analysis of the attacker's plan. The analysis could be further exploited in the development of a defensive strategy against the attacker of the selected type.

Figure 1 shows our security analysis method that is explained further in this section. In the following we describe the steps of our approach in details.

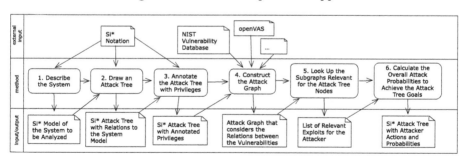

Fig. 1. An overview of our method for combining attack trees and attack graphs

Step 1. Describe the System. Describe the system in a high level of abstraction using the Si* notation. All stakeholders and electronic systems in the scope of the analysis shall be in this system description. Ensure that all relations between elements of the system are a part of the Si* diagram.

Step 2. Draw an Attack Tree. Select a type of attacker for the analysis from the types: network attacker, software attacker, social engineering attacker, or physical attacker (c.f., [2,3]). Elicit the main motivations of the attacker using Si* soft goals and a corresponding main goal of the attacker. Divide the main goal into subgoals until all leaf goals of the tree concern a part of the system described in Step 1. Draw a relation from each leaf goal to a part of the system. The attack tree is the overall plan of the attacker.

The Si* language provides three types of operators for goal decomposition: (i) AND, (ii) OR, and (iii) MEANS-END. The AND operator means that all subgoals must be satisfied to fulfill the target node. The OR operator means, that at least one sub-goal must be satisfied. We do not consider the MEANS-END operator that simply points out that the subgoals are required but they are not enough to satisfy the target goal. A goal tree of an attacker formed with only AND and OR operators is a well-known attack tree [18].

In our paper we use a formalization of attack trees described in [12]. The goal tree of an attacker is $T = (N, \mapsto, n_0)$ where N is a set of goals, $n_0 \in N$ is a top goal, and $\mapsto$ is a finite acyclic relation: $\mapsto \subseteq N \times \mathbb{M}(N)$, where $\mathbb{M}(N)$ is a multiset[1] of goals N. Note, that if $n \mapsto \mathbb{M}(N')$, then $n \notin N'$, because T is a tree.

Step 3. Annotate the Attack Tree with Privileges. Firstly, annotate each leaf goal of the tree with the initial (start) privileges that are required to start achieving the goals. Secondly, determine the resulting (end) privileges that the attacker gains after achieving each leaf goal.

In this work by a "privilege" we mean access rights, possessed resources, information, etc., required for or gained after an execution of an attack. Let P be a set of all possible privileges in a system and $\mathbb{P}(P)$ be a powerset of this set. We assume there are two functions for getting such sets:

$$tprivsbgn : N \to \mathbb{P}(P) \qquad (1)$$

$$tprivsend : N \to \mathbb{P}(P) \qquad (2)$$

The function *tprivsbgn* returns the set of privileges that the attacker needs to begin achieving a certain goal $n \in N$. The function *tprivsend* returns the resulting set of privileges that the attacker possesses after achieving the goal n.

Step 4. Construct the Attack Graph. Conduct vulnerability scanning and derive available actions *Act* of the attacker using different scanning tools (e.g., openVAS[2]). This is a usual procedure before construction of attack graphs although the procedure may be tedious and time consuming [6,14]. Afterwards, construct an attack graph based on the available actions.

In this work, we follow the model of attack graphs as it is presented in [6]. In order to build an attack graph, we use a set of attacker's actions *Act*.

---

[1] In fact, Si* does not allow using the same subgoals in different parts of the tree, but we still keep multiset of nodes (instead of a powerset) for compliance with [12].

[2] http://www.openvas.org/

Every action of an attacker $a \in Act$ is a single exploit of a vulnerability obtained as a result of vulnerability scanning. Let also $Act \subseteq \mathbb{P}(P) \times \mathbb{P}(P)$ be a relation such that:

$$(P^b, P^e) \in Act \; . \; P^b, P^e \in \mathbb{P}(P), P^b \subset P^e \tag{3}$$

Where P^b is a minimal set of privileges required to perform the action and P^e is the resulting set of privileges. In a system, the execution of an action may require some initial privileges. For example, an attacker needs to get root privileges on a server in order to run an exploit against a database installed on the server. Please note that we make the usual for attack graphs assumption that privileges once gained remain until the end of an attack [6].

In the sequel, we use superscript b to indicate the initial privileges when e specifies the ending privileges. We also use two special functions: fst and snd, which return the first and the second element of a Cartesian product, i.e., $fst\ a = P^b$ and $snd\ a = P^e$ for $a = (P^b, P^e)$. Finally, for the sake of brevity we define the privileges gained during step $a_i = (P_i^b, P_i^e) \in Act$ as: $\Delta_i = P_i^e \backslash P_i^b = snd\ a_i \backslash fst\ a_i$.

Let $seq\ Act$ be a set of all possible sequences of elements from Act and $s \in seq\ Act$ be a sequence of actions of an attacker:

$$s = a_1 \ldots a_n \; . \; \forall i \in \{1, \ldots, n\}, \; a_i \in Act, \tag{4}$$

$$\forall j \in \{2, \ldots, n\}, fst\ a_j \subseteq \bigcup_{k=1}^{j-1} snd\ a_k, snd\ a_j \nsubseteq \bigcup_{k=1}^{j-1} snd\ a_k$$

An i-th element of a sequence s is an action $a_i = s[i]$, $i \in \{1, ..., n\}$, and $n = \#s$ is the length of the sequence.

Definition 1. *Let P be a set of all possible privileges and Act be a set of all possible attacker actions found in the system. Then, the attack graph $\mathcal{G} \subseteq \mathbb{P}(\mathbb{P}(P) \times Act \times \mathbb{P}(P))$ associated to P and Act is defined as follows:*

$$G := \{(P^b, a, P^e) \in \mathbb{P}(P) \times Act \times \mathbb{P}(P) \mid \tag{5}$$
$$1)\ fst\ a \subseteq P^b,\ 2)\ P^e = P^b \cup snd\ a,\ 3)\ snd\ a \backslash fst\ a \nsubseteq P^b\}$$

In words, the attack graph is defined as a set of edges, which relate to actions and allow an attacker to move from one set of privileges to a wider set. A vertex in the attack graph is a set of privileges. The attack graph defined in Definition 1 is a direct acyclic graph (DAG).

A path π in an attack graph is a sequence of edges. We may say that the π is also an attack graph with ordered edges. We define sequential numbers for these edges $\pi[i]$ for all $i \in \{1, \ldots, n\}$ where $n = \#\pi$. We assume that there is a function $Paths(P^b, P^e)$ that returns all paths from P^b to P^e.

In our analysis we are interested in sequences of attacker's actions that are required to satisfy some goal of the attacker. We would like to derive these sequences from an attack graph as a subgraph. However, there is the following issue with the graph in Definition 1. One action in the real world can refer to multiple edges in the graph. Thus, the multiple distinct paths can refer to the same sequence of actions in the real world.

To address this issue, we, first, define a relation between a sequence of actions and a path.

Definition 2. *Let Act be a set of actions, $s \in seq\ Act$ be some sequence of these actions, G be an attack graph, $\Pi(G)$ be a set of paths π in G. Then, we define the relation $\rightrightarrows \subseteq seq\ Act \times \Pi(G)$:*

$$\rightrightarrows := \{(s, \pi) \mid s \in seq\ Act,\ \pi \in Act,\ \#s = \#\pi, \tag{6}$$
$$\forall i \in \{1, \dots, \#\pi\},\ \pi[i] = (P^b, s[i], P^e), P^b, P^e \in \mathbb{P}(P)\}$$

Second, we would like to show formally that it is enough to consider paths starting from a single vertex with required amount of initial privileges, because paths from other vertices containing the same amount of privileges will correspond to the same sequences.

Theorem 1. *Let s be some sequence of actions and G be an attack graph. Then:*

$$\forall \tilde{P}^b \in \mathbb{P}(P) \ . \ \forall i \in \{1, \dots, \#s\}, \tag{7}$$
$$1)\ fst\ a_i \backslash \bigcup_{j=1}^{i-1} \Delta_j \subseteq \tilde{P}^b,\ 2)\ \Delta_i \backslash \bigcup_{j=1}^{i-1} \Delta_j \not\subseteq \tilde{P}^b \Rightarrow$$
$$\exists \hat{\pi} \in Paths(\tilde{P}^b, \tilde{P}^e) \ . \ s \rightrightarrows \hat{\pi}$$

Where $\tilde{P}^e = \tilde{P}^b \cup \bigcup_{i=1}^{\#s} \Delta_i$.

Thus, an attacker can execute the sequence where for each next step she either has the privileges at the beginning or she gains the privileges during earlier steps of the sequence (condition 1). Moreover, in any step of the sequence the attacker must gain something she did not have at the beginning and did not gain during earlier steps (condition 2).

Proof. We prove by induction that there is a path from some $\tilde{P}^b \in \mathbb{P}(P)$ which satisfies the conditions of Theorem 1. To do that, we need to show, that for every action a_k, $k \in \{1, \dots, n\}$, $n = \#s$ there is always an edge related to this action. This edge starts with $\tilde{P}_k^b$ to which there is a path from $\tilde{P}^b$ related to the sequence of actions from s predeceasing a_k. We use Definition 1 to prove the existence of such edge.

First, we always can reach $\tilde{P}_0 = \tilde{P}^b$ with an empty s.

Second, lets assume, that there is a path $\hat{\pi}_{k-1}$ from $\tilde{P}^b$ to $\tilde{P}_k^b$, which relates to a sequence s_{k-1} formed with $k-1$ first actions of s (i.e., $s_{k-1} \rightrightarrows \hat{\pi}_{k-1}$). Using Eq. 5 we prove that there is always an edge $(\tilde{P}_k^b, a_k, \tilde{P}_{k+1}^b) \in G$.

The amount of privileges an attacker gains after executing some action a_i is Δ_i. Therefore, the set of privileges $\tilde{P}^b_k$ is equal to the privileges $\tilde{P}^b$ plus all privileges gained after executing $k-1$ steps, i.e., $\tilde{P}^b_k = \tilde{P}^b \cup \bigcup_{i=1}^{k-1} \Delta_i$. Now according to the first condition in the theorem, we have:

$$\tilde{P}^b_k = \tilde{P}^b \cup \bigcup_{i=1}^{k-1} \Delta_i \supseteq (\bigcup_{i=1}^{\#s} \textit{fst } a_i \setminus \bigcup_{j=1}^{i-1} \Delta_j) \cup \bigcup_{i=1}^{k-1} \Delta_i \supseteq \tag{8}$$

$$(\textit{fst } a_k \setminus \bigcup_{j=1}^{k-1} \Delta_j) \cup \bigcup_{i=1}^{k-1} \Delta_i = \textit{fst } a_k$$

Thus, $\textit{fst } a_k \subseteq \tilde{P}^b_k$, which is the first conditions in Eq. 5.

The second condition of Eq. 5 is satisfied because both $\tilde{P}^b_k$, $\textit{snd } a_k \in \mathbb{P}(P)$, therefore there is always a set of privileges $\tilde{P}^b_k \cup \textit{snd } a_k \in \mathbb{P}(P)$.

According to the second condition of the theorem we see that $\tilde{P}^b_k = \tilde{P}^b \cup \bigcup_{i=1}^{k-1} \Delta_i \not\supseteq \Delta_k$, thus, $\textit{snd } a_i \setminus \textit{fst } a_i \not\subseteq P^b_k$. Therefore, the third condition of Eq. 5 is satisfied and the edge $(\tilde{P}^b_k, a_k, \tilde{P}^b_{k+1})$ exists in the graph G.

To conclude the step we define an auxiliary function $front(P')$ which gives a minimal set of vertices where a set of privileges P' is achieved:

Definition 3. *Let $P' \subseteq P$ be some set of privileges and G be an attack graph. Then, the function $front : \mathbb{P}(P) \to \mathbb{P}(\mathbb{P}(P))$ is defined as follows:*

$$front(P') := \{P^f \in \mathbb{P}(P) \mid \exists (P^b, a, P^f) \in G, \ P' \not\subseteq P^b, \ P' \subseteq P^f\} \tag{9}$$

According to Theorem 1, the same sequences, that require initial privileges P', start from every vertex in $front(P')$.

Step 5. Look Up the Subgraphs Relevant for the Attack Tree Nodes. Query the graph from the set of the initial privileges of a leaf goal to the resulting privileges. Derive the further subgraphs for each node to refine the high level attacker goals to concrete attack actions.

Before we start mapping goals from a goal tree with parts of an attack graph we must make some assumptions. First, we assume that an attack graph and a goal tree were created separately but for the same system. Therefore, they must correspond to each other. We assume that the attacker behaves only according to the plan and use only the privileges specified in the goal tree. Another important aspect of goal tree is that its leaves should be independent from each other, i.e., the way of execution of one goal should not affect another one apart of the sequence of actions. Usually, quantitative analysis of attack trees makes the same assumption (see for example [18]).

In particular, these assumptions mean the following.

- We ignore the paths which require more privileges than specified by the starting privileges assigned to a goal (assumption of correspondence).

- The actions which do not lead the attacker to his goal are possible but they should not affect our analysis (assumption of "useless" actions).
- The attacker heads towards the states where *only* the target privileges are satisfied (plus some irrelevant privileges). In other words, no privileges to be obtained on the later steps should be gained at early ones (assumption of independence).

The later assumption, which follows from the independence of goals, shows that we have to consider every goal in the context of the whole tree.

Let us have a complete attack graph G for a system and a goal tree T of an attacker. And let us aim at finding a subgraph corresponding to a leaf goal n from the tree. In fact, we are interested only in a part of the complete attack graph. The complete graph created in Definition 1 is usually huge and most parts are not considered in the plan of the attacker (the tree) and, thus, are not relevant for us. Therefore, we purge the graph as most attack graph techniques do (e.g., [6]). We consider only the part of the graph which can be potentially exploited by the attacker. Thus, we consider an attacker with initial set of privileges P^i and the target set of privileges P^t. Therefore, we are interested only in the part of G which is built by all paths from $front(P^i)$ to all nodes from $front(P^t)$. This selection does not affect the following discussion, but reduces the computational power required to implement our method.

In order to find the subgraph G_n which realizes the leaf goal n from the tree we need to know the initial privileges P^b of an attacker and final privileges P^e corresponding to the goal. According to Eqs. 1 and 2:

$$P^b = tprivsbgn(n) \tag{10}$$

$$P^e = tprivsend(n) \tag{11}$$

Next we look for the set of vertices (sets of privileges) $\boldsymbol{P}^{fb}$ in the graph from which the attacker may start achieving the goal n and vertices $\boldsymbol{P}^{fe}$ where this goal is achieved.

First, we select all possible sequences of actions which lead an attacker from starting privileges to end privileges and which require *only* P^b as starting set of privileges.

$$S^b := \{s \in seq\ Act \mid \exists \pi \in Paths(\tilde{P}^b, \tilde{P}^e),\ \tilde{P}^b \in front(P^b), \tag{12}$$

$$\tilde{P}^e \in front(P^e),\ s \rightrightarrows \pi,\ \forall i \in \{1, \ldots, \#s\},\ fst\ a_i \subseteq P^b \cup \bigcup_{j=1}^{i-1} \Delta_j\}$$

We need also a set of sequences of actions from end privileges to target privileges, since our tree must be independent from the perspective of future steps.

$$S^e := \{s : seq\ Act \mid \exists \pi \in Paths(\tilde{P}^e, \tilde{P}^t),\ \tilde{P}^e \in front(P^e), \tag{13}$$

$$\tilde{P}^t \in front(P^t),\ s \rightrightarrows \pi,\ \forall i \in \{1, \ldots, \#s\},\ fst\ a_i \subseteq P^e \cup \bigcup_{j=1}^{i-1} \Delta_j\}$$

Second, we are able to filter fronts for P^b and P^e to remove the sets of privileges, which already have the privileges scheduled to be obtained on the later steps (assumption of independence).

$$\boldsymbol{P}^{fb} := \{P^{fb} \in \mathbb{P}(P) \mid P^{fb} \in front(P^b),\ \forall s \in S^b, \tag{14}$$

$$\forall i \in \{1, \ldots, \#s\},\ \Delta_i \nsubseteq P^{fb}\}$$

$$\boldsymbol{P}^{fe} := \{P^{fe} \in \mathbb{P}(P) \mid P^{fe} \in front(P^e),\ \forall s \in S^e, \tag{15}$$

$$\forall i \in \{1, \ldots, \#s\},\ \Delta_i \nsubseteq P^{fe}\}$$

The subgraph G_n corresponding to the goal n consists of paths from vertices in $\boldsymbol{P}^{fb}$ to vertices in $\boldsymbol{P}^{fe}$. However we may consider only one arbitrary vertex $P^{fb} \in \boldsymbol{P}^{fb}$ and look for paths to all $P^{fe} \in \boldsymbol{P}^{fe}$ since all sequences of actions corresponding to paths from other vertices in $\boldsymbol{P}^{fb}$ are *the same due to* Theorem 1:

$$G_n = \bigcup_{\forall P^{fe} \in \boldsymbol{P}^{fe}} \{\pi \in \Pi(G) \mid \pi \in Paths(P^{fb}, P^{fe}), \tag{16}$$

$$\nexists (P', a, P'') \in \pi,\ P', P'' \in \boldsymbol{P}_f^b,\ P', P'' \in \boldsymbol{P}^{fe},$$

$$\exists s \in S^b,\ s \rightrightarrows \pi\}$$

Equation 16 gives us a subgraph formed with an aggregated set of paths from P_f^b to $\boldsymbol{P}_f^e$ (first line), which do not contain any other nodes from these sets, apart of P_f^b and P_f^e (second line), and which do not use additional privileges that are gained on the further steps (third line). The attacker will follow one of the paths specified in G_n in order to achieve the goal n.

We would like to make a small remark. Some goals in a goal tree state *what* the attacker should achieve (e.g., "get login and password") when other goals also define *how* to achieve the goal (e.g., "eavesdrop login and password" or "bribe an employee to get login and password"). The goals of the second type restrict the ways for getting to the desired state. In order to address this restriction someone can define a function which assigns a set of essential actions for every goal in a goal tree:

$$esseqs : N \to \mathbb{P}(seq\ Act) \tag{17}$$

This function should be further used to filter the set of sequences S^b in order to obtain only sequences relevant to the way of achieving the goal.

Step 6. Calculate the Overall Attack Probabilities to Achieve the Attack Tree Goals. Analyze obtained subgraphs and calculate the probabilities of achieving corresponding subgoals. Annotate the attack tree with the probabilities. Derive the overall probability for the attacker to achieve the main goal.

To find the probability of successful achievement of a goal n (denoted as $\mathbf{pr}[n]$) we need to find the probability to get from an initial vertex P_f^b of G_n to one of the target vertices from $\boldsymbol{P}_f^e$ (see Eq. 15). We assume that an attacker

```
   Input  : P^s − starting vulnerability
   Output: pr[n] − probability of successful exploitation
   Global : G − associated graph
            P^e − set of target privileges
   Data: pr[P] − probability to reach a certain vertex
   pr[a] − probability to perform action a successfully
   pr^{fail} − probability to fail at a certain step
   P^f − a fork, i.e., a vulnerability with several outgoing edges
   G^P − a shortest path
 1 function computeProbability(P^s)
 2     pr[n] = 1;
 3     Find G^P = shortestPath(P^s, P^e);
 4     for ∀(P', a, P'') ∈ G^P forward do
 5         pr[n] = pr[n] · pr[a];
 6         pr[P''] = pr[n];
 7         pr[a] = 1;
 8     for ∀(P', a, P'') ∈ G^P backward do
 9         Find nearest fork at P^f or exit;
10         Restore pr[a], where a ⇒ x̃;
11         pr^{fail} = pr[P'] · (1 − pr[a]);
12         pr[a] = 0;
13         pr[n] = pr[n] + pr^{fail}·computeProbability(P^f);
14         Restore pr[a];
15     return pr[n];
```

Algorithm 1. Computation of probabilities for a goal

may fail to exploit a vulnerability (e.g., when it is already patched or it is too hard) and, thus, for every action we have a probability of successful exploitation, denoted as $\mathbf{pr}[a]$.

We consider a greedy attacker who would like to execute the attack with the highest probability of success. Thus, the attacker tries the most probable path to achieve the goal. Since the attacker may fail to make an action and thus, to complete the most probable path, the attacker will try an alternative path, and so on until she reaches her goal (or fail all paths). We assume, that we have an adapted algorithm of Edsger Dijkstra for a search of the shortest path P_f^b to $\boldsymbol{P}_f^e$, called here as **shortestPath**.

Although, one action cannot be used in one attack several times, the same action may be used in different attacks. Thus, if an attacker successfully performs an action during execution of one attack but then switches to another attack, then there is no need to perform the same step again. We assign the probability of all edges referring to the successfully performed action to one. Once failed an action cannot be used in other attacks and we change its probability to zero. Algorithm 1 shows a recursive function **computeProbability** which consists of two parts. The first part contains a search for a shortest path (line 2), computation of the probability of successful exploitation of the path (line 4), computation of the probability to reach a certain amount of privileges (line 5), and changing of the probability associated with an action to 1 (as successfully performed).

The second part follows the path backwards assuming that an action failed to succeed. In this case the attacker should find an alternative path. Thus, she is going back to the last set of privileges, where alternatives are possible, called a *fork* (step 8). Note, that only the nearest fork should be considered, since it contains all privileges of the vertexes down in the path, and thus all possible alternatives for the considered failure are rooted in this vertex. Since the attacker considers alternatives only in case of a failure of the shortest path, then we compute the probability of such failure (line 10). Then we put to 0 the probability of the action which is considered as failed. After that, we add the probability to re-consider the course of action to the overall probability (line 12). Finally, we restore the initial value of the probability of the considered action (since in the next round of the cycle we will assume another action to fail).

When the probabilities for leaf goals are computed and assigned, we can find the set of leaf goals, which lead an attacker to target goal with highest probability of success. The countermeasures should be applied against the vulnerabilities from the subgraphs corresponding to these leaf goals.

4   Application of Our Method to a Smart Grid Scenario

We illustrate the application of our method to a smart grid example in the following.

Step 1. Describe the System. Figure reffig:networkspsattacker (upper part) presents the part of an Si* diagram of our smart grid scenario, which we would like to use as an illustrative example. The actor *Huntsville Consortium* plays the role of the *Energy Supplier* (circles in the Fig. 2). The *Huntsville Consortium* has the main goal *Sell Energy* for which the subgoals *Collect Prosumer Data* and *Calculate Bill* need to be fulfilled (rounded rectangles in Fig. 2). Various resources (represented as rectangles) are required for achieving these goals, *Prosumer Information* is required for *Collect Prosumer Data* goal and *Aggregated Billing Data* is required for the goal *Calculate Bill*. Another goal of the consortium is to *Provide Grid Services*, which also can be broken down into the three subgoals: *Manage ESS*, *Manage EMS*, and *Manage Smart Meters*.

The energy supplier server (ESS) collects metering data from the smart meters, as well as stores and aggregates this data. The *Manage ESS* goal requires obviously an *ESS*. The ESS uses a specific *ESS Network Gateway* to communicate with the smart meters and authorized external entities, e.g., the *Billing Operator* uses the *Billing Operator's Laptop* to get billing data, which are stored in the *ESS Database (DB)*. The *Billing Operator* requires this data to fulfill the goal *Calculate Bill*, which is also delegate from the *Huntsville Consortium*.

The home energy management system (EMS) controls the smart appliances in the smart home. It is a computer system that visualizes the prosumers energy consumption and support the selection of offers for buying and selling energy. The EMS relies upon a *Network Gateway* to communicate with authorized external parties. The goal *Manage EMS* is delegated to the *Meter Point Operator*, who conducts the maintenance for the EMS. The *Meter Point Operator* has also been delegated the goal *Manage Smart Meters*, meaning he/she conducts the maintenance for Smart Meters. The maintenance can be conducted partially from a remote location, which makes this goal also reliant on the *Network Gateway*. We focus on attacks on the energy supplier, i.e., *Huntsville Consortium*.

Note that we include the entire scope (large oval with all the actor's goals inside) of the actor *Huntsville Consortium*. In particular, goals that are delegated to other actors, as well. For the sake of brevity, we show only the threats involving the goal *Manage ESS*.

Step 2. Draw an Attack Tree. We show exemplary our threat analysis for a network attacker (the discussion on other types of attackers and their intentions could be found in [2,3]). The network attacker is of interest for this scenario, because the smart home scenario relies on a secure ICT network. The grid is not usable anymore when data cannot be transmitted over it. Figure 2 (bottom part) describes the possible plan of a network attacker as an attack tree in Si*. The network attacker (see Fig. 2) is motivated by *Financial Gain, Self Interest*, and *Curiosity*. Driven by these motivations the attacker forms the goal to *Change Metering Data*. This goal represents a threat that can harm *Aggregated Billing Data, Prosumer Information* and others. There are different ways to achieve this goal. For example, the attacker may *Change Metering Data during Transmission* or *Get Local Access to ESS, Gain Access to Database Locally* and directly change data in the ESS database.

The attack tree is designed with the scope of the analysis in mind, meaning the scope of the Huntsville Consortium (Fig. 2 top part). This is reflected by the relations from each leaf goal to a resource in the scope. For example, the leaf goal *Gain Access to Database Locally* has a relation to the resource *ESS Database*. This resource is exploited by the attacker to satisfy the leaf goal. It represents an entry point of the attacker into the scope.

Hence, our Si* diagram contains: the scope of the analysis, the motivations of the attacker, the subsequent goals, and resulting entry points of the attacker from leaf goals to the scope. In the future, we will use all these information to check of our threat analysis for completeness with validation conditions. For example, we can check if all leaf goals exploit at least one resource in the scope. In addition, we could check if there are resources in the scope that do not represent entry points.

Remember that this diagram (Fig. 2) represents the high-level plan of the attacker. Later we enrich the information in the plan with low-level details existing in the system related attack graph (Fig. 3).

Step 3. Annotate the Attack Tree with Privileges. We show the privileges relevant for our running example in Table 1. The table lists the initial and resulting privileges for each leaf goal in the tree. The initial privileges are the ones required to start a sequence of actions to achieve the goal. The resulting privileges contain the gained privileges by the sequence of actions in addition to the initial privileges.

Step 4. Construct the Attack Graph. The Billing Operator has an infrastructure in order to achieve the goal *Manage ESS*. We assume that the infrastructure consists of a laptop and a workstation that are used by an administrator in order to manage the ESS. We assume that the laptop has Windows OS installed and

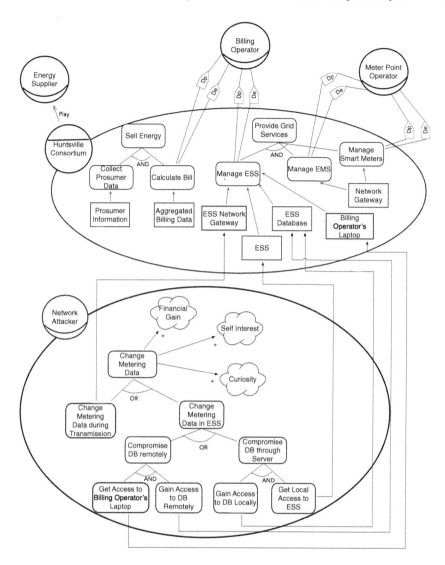

Fig. 2. Si* model for a network attacker in our smart grid example

the workstation has Linux OS installed. The laptop and the workstation are connected by VPN. There is the ESS itself with a database server installed. The server runs FreeBSD OS and the database server is Oracle MySQL. The server and the workstation are connected by LAN. Clients access the server via network that is based on the RuggedCom equipment with RuggedCom OS installed.

The vulnerabilities related to the infrastructure are listed in Table 2. The table contains CVE vulnerability codes, software that contains a vulnerability, and sets of initial and resulting privileges for each vulnerability. The privilege

Table 1. Available privileges considered in our running example

Goal name	Initial privileges	Resulting privileges
Change data during the transmission	∅	{ruggedcom}
Get access to billing operator's laptop	∅	{laptop}
Gain access to the DB remotely	{laptop}	{laptop,mysql}
Get local access to ESS	∅	{server}
Gain access to the DB locally	{server}	{server,mysql}

Table 2. Actions available for the attacker in our example

CVE code	Software	Initial privileges	Resulting privileges
CVE-2011-3108	Chrome browser	∅	$\{laptop\}$
CVE-2009-4781	TUKEVA Pass.Man.	$\{laptop\}$	$\{laptop, database\}$
CVE-2012-2369	Pidgin	∅	$\{workstation\}$
CVE-2011-4862	FreeBSD	$\{workstation\}$	$\{workstation, server\}$
CVE-2012-0173	Windows	$\{workstation\}$	$\{workstation, laptop\}$
CVE-2011-4913	Linux	$\{laptop\}$	$\{workstation, laptop\}$
CVE-2013-6926	Rugged OS	∅	$\{ruggedcom\}$
CVE-2012-0114	MySQL	$\{server\}$	$\{server, database\}$

values mean the root access to the specified network node. These vulnerabilities are obtained from the NIST Vulnerability Database[3].

An attack graph related to the infrastructure is presented in Fig. 3 and the list of privileges for each vertex is presented in Table 3. The edges of the graph are labeled by CVE vulnerability codes from Table 2. In this graph we show only one edge related to the action *CVE-2013-6926* for simplicity's sake. We use the names of vertices from Table 3 such as v_1 and v_3 instead of the full set of privileges, i.e. such that $\{workstation\}$ and $\{workstation, server, database\}$.

Step 5. Look Up the Subgraphs relevant for the Attack Tree Nodes. The main privilege to achieve is to have possibility to modify metering data, which could be seen as a subset of vertices where root access to RuggedCom or database (e.g., to reach v_3, v_5, v_8, v_9 or v_{10}). There are three alternative ways to achieve the main goal for the attacker (see corresponding subgoals on Fig. 2). The first one is to fulfill the subgoal *Change Metering Data during Transmission* (n_{tran}) compromising RuggedCom equipment. The goal in this case specifies the way, how the goal should be achieved, i.e., "during transmission", and $esseqs(n_{tran}) = \{\langle CVE\text{-}2013\text{-}6926 \rangle\}$. The mapping is straightforward: one goal to a subgraph $G_{n_{tran}} = \{(v_0, CVE\text{-}2013\text{-}6926, v_8)\}$.

Other ways require either getting root access to the server or to a workstation and then getting root access to the database. Consider *Get Local Access to ESS* goal

---

[3] NIST Vulnerability Database: http://nvd.nist.gov/.

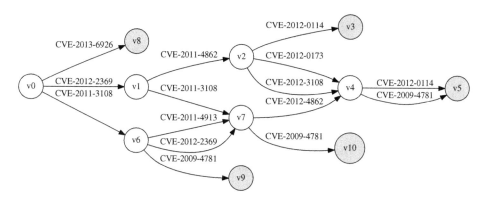

Fig. 3. A part of the attack graph for our smart grid example

(n_{ESS}). In our example, $tprivsbgn(n_{ESS}) = \emptyset$ and $tprivsend(n_{ESS}) = \{freebsd\}$ and:

$$esseqs(n_{ESS}) = \{\langle \text{CVE-2012-2369}, \text{CVE-2011-4862} \rangle, \qquad (18)$$
$$\langle \text{CVE-2012-2369}, \text{CVE-2011-3108}, \text{CVE-2011-4862} \rangle,$$
$$\langle \text{CVE-2011-3108}, \text{CVE-2011-4913}, \text{CVE-2012-4862} \rangle,$$
$$\langle \text{CVE-2011-3108}, \text{CVE-2011-2369}, \text{CVE-2012-4862} \rangle \}$$

Thus, the attacker should move from v_0 to v_2 or v_4 and, by Eq. 16, $G_{n_{ESS}}$ includes vertices $v_0, v_1, v_2, v_4, v_6, v_7$ and the edges between them, apart of CVE-2012-0173 and CVE-2012-3108 which are eliminated by the second line of Eq. 16. We see that the next subgoal *Gain Access to DB locally* (n_{DBl}) can be achieved by the same action CVE-2012-0114 from v_2 and v_4, when vulnerability CVE-2009-4781 is not considered in this case, since the attacker decided to get *Remote Access*

Table 3. Privileges corresponding to the nodes of the attack graph

Node	Set of privileges
v_0	$\emptyset$
v_1	$\{workstation\}$
v_2	$\{workstation, server\}$
v_3	$\{workstation, server, database\}$
v_4	$\{workstation, server, laptop\}$
v_5	$\{workstation, server, laptop, database\}$
v_6	$\{laptop\}$
v_7	$\{laptop, workstation\}$
v_8	$\{ruggedcom\}$
v_9	$\{laptop, database\}$
v_{10}	$\{laptop, workstation, database\}$

to ESS using the privileges from the earlier steps. I.e.:

$$G_{n_{DBl}} = \{(v_2, \text{CVE-2012-0114}, v_3), (v_4, \text{CVE-2012-0114}, v_5)\} \qquad (19)$$

which are equivalent from the point of view of applied actions. Thus, their probability is the same. Similar reasoning could be applied to the third alternative, which leads from v_0 to v_4, v_6 or v_7 and then CVE-2009-4781 is the last action for *Gain Access to DB remotely*.

Step 6. Calculate the Overall Attack Probabilities to Achieve the Attack Tree Goals. The shortest path in $G_{n_{ESS}}$ is $\langle$CVE-2012-2369,CVE-2011-4862$\rangle$. If the probabilities of the actions are $\mathbf{pr}_1 = 0.6$ and $\mathbf{pr}_2 = 0.9$, then the overall probability to execute only this path is 0.54. Note that, in case CVE-2011-4862 is patched, there is no way for the attacker to achieve his goal (since the same vulnerability must be used to follow from v_7 to v_4). In case of CVE-2012-2369 patched, there is a path to achieve the goal and the attacker should add its probability (let it be 0.36) to the overall computation. Thus, the attacker first tries CVE-2012-2369, fails, and then she follows the only available path. The probability to *Get Access to ESS* is $(1 - 0.6) * 0.36 + 0.54 = 0.684$.

5   Conclusions

We contributed a structured method for threat analysis that concerns the mapping of the plan of the attacker (represented as an attack tree) to concrete vulnerabilities of a system (documented in an attack graph). We showed that it is possible to extract a part of a complex graph, which relates to a specific goal in the attack tree. We found that the complexity of the analysis of attack graphs can be significantly reduced because for a specific attacker we can consider only a part of the whole attack graph. We proposed an algorithm that computes the overall probability of success of an attacker on the basis of the mapping. Finally, we illustrated our method on a smart grid example.

In the future, we will consider in detail how the method can be used to identify the most appropriate countermeasures. Furthermore, we plan to identify further attacker motivations and provide a more extensive application of our approach in collaboration with industrial partners. Finally, we are planing to refine our method for creating an ISO 27001 compliant Information Security Management System.

References

1. Asnar, Yudistira, Massacci, Fabio: A method for security governance, risk, and compliance(GRC): a goal-process approach. In: Aldini, Alessandro, Gorrieri, Roberto (eds.) FOSAD 2011. LNCS, vol. 6858, pp. 152–184. Springer, Heidelberg (2011)

2. Beckers, K.: Goal-based establishment of an information security management system compliant to ISO 27001. In: Geffert, V., Preneel, B., Rovan, B., Štuller, J., Tjoa, A.M. (eds.) SOFSEM 2014. LNCS, vol. 8327, pp. 102–113. Springer, Heidelberg (2014)
3. Beckers, K., Côté, I., Hatebur, D., Faßbender, S., Heisel, M.: Common Criteria CompliAnt Software Development (CC-CASD). In: Proceedings of 28th SAC, pp. 937–943. ACM (2013)
4. Bistarelli, S., Fioravanti, F., Peretti, P.: Defense trees for economic evaluation of security investments. In: Proceedings of the 1st ARES, pp. 416–423. IEEE (2006)
5. Dalton II, G.C., Colombi, J.M., Mills, R.F., Raines, R.A.: Analyzing attack trees using generalized stochastic petri nets. In: Proceedings of the IAS, pp. 116–123. IEEE (2006)
6. Jha, S., Sheyner, O., Wing, J.: Two formal analyses of attack graphs. In: Proceedings of the 2002 IEEE CSF, p. 49. IEEE (2002)
7. Jürjens, J.: Using UMLsec and goal trees for secure systems development. In: Proceedings of the 2002 SAC, pp. 1026–1030. ACM Press (2002)
8. Krautsevich, L., Martinelli, F., Yautsiukhin, A.: Towards modelling adaptive attacker's behaviour. In: Garcia-Alfaro, J., Cuppens, F., Cuppens-Boulahia, N., Miri, A., Tawbi, N. (eds.) FPS 2012. LNCS, vol. 7743, pp. 357–364. Springer, Heidelberg (2013)
9. LeMay, E., Ford, M.D., Keefe, K., Sanders, W.H., Muehrcke, C.: Model-based security metrics using adversary view security evaluation (advise). In: Proceedings of the 8th QEST, pp. 191–200. IEEE (2011)
10. Liu, L., Yu, E., Mylopoulos, J.: Security and privacy requirements analysis within a social setting. In: Proceedings of the 11th RE, pp. 151–161. IEEE (2003)
11. Massacci, Fabio, Mylopoulos, John, Zannone, Nicola: Security requirements engineering: the SI* modeling language and the secure tropos methodology. In: Ras, Zbigniew W., Tsay, Li-Shiang (eds.) Advances in Intelligent Information Systems. SCI, vol. 265, pp. 147–174. Springer, Heidelberg (2010)
12. Mauw, S., Oostdijk, M.: Foundations of attack trees. In: Won, D.H., Kim, S. (eds.) ICISC 2005. LNCS, vol. 3935, pp. 186–198. Springer, Heidelberg (2006)
13. Mouratidis, H., Giorgini, P., Manson, G.: Using security attack scenarios to analyse security during information systems design. In: Proceedings of ICEIS, pp. 10–17 (2004)
14. Noel, S., Jajodia, S.: Managing attack graph complexity through visual hierarchical aggregation. In: Proceedings of the VizSEC/DMSEC (2004)
15. Piètre-Cambacédès, L., Bouissou, M.: Beyond attack trees: Dynamic security modeling with boolean logic driven markov processes (bdmp). In: Proceedings of the EDCC, pp. 199–208. IEEE (2010)
16. Qin, X., Lee, W.: Attack plan recognition and prediction using causal networks. In: Proceedings of the 20th ACSAC, pp. 370–379. IEEE (2004)
17. Sarraute, C., Richarte, G., Obes, J.L.: An algorithm to find optimal attack paths in nondeterministic scenarios. In: Proceedings of the 4th AISec, pp. 71–80. ACM (2011)
18. Schneier, B.: Attack trees: Modelling security threats. Dr. Dobb's journal, December 1999
19. van Lamsweerde, A.: Elaborating security requirements by construction of intentional anti-models. In: Proceedings of the 26th ICSE, pp. 148–157. IEEE (2004)

Selective Release of Smart Metering Data in Multi-domain Smart Grids

Alessandro Armando[1,2], Roberto Carbone[1]([✉]), Eyasu Getahun Chekole[1],
Claudio Petrazzuolo[3], Andrea Ranalli[3], and Silvio Ranise[1]

[1] Security & Trust Unit, FBK-irst, Trento, Italy
{armando,carbone,chekole,ranise}@fbk.eu
[2] DIBRIS, Università degli Studi di Genova, Genova, Italy
alessandro.armando@unige.it
[3] Telecom Italia S.p.A. - Innovation Department, Rome, Italy
{claudio.petrazzuolo,andrea.ranalli}@telecomitalia.it

Abstract. In the context of energy efficiency, smart metering solutions are receiving growing attention as they support the automatic collection of (fine-grained) consumption data of appliances. While the capability of a stakeholder (such as a consumer, an utility, or a third-party service) to access smart metering data can give rise to innovative services for users, it makes the control of data release and usage significantly more complex. It is thus extremely important to put in place an adequate access control mechanism that takes into account the authorization requirements of the various stakeholders. To address this issue, we propose a framework based on the Attribute Based Access Control model for the selective release of smart metering data in cloud-based solutions for smart grids.

We applied our framework to a scenario proposed by Energy@Home, a non-profit association of companies with the mission of developing and promoting techniques for energy efficiency in smart homes. As a proof of concept, we implemented our approach on top of the open-source Spring Security framework.

1 Introduction

Energy grids are the backbones of our economy and society. There has been a push to make such grids "smart," i.e. to make them capable of re-distributing energy according to the time-varying consumer needs, in order to reduce energy consumption under the pressure of the economic crisis and the reduced availability of natural resources (e.g., fossil fuels). A key enabler to make a grid smart is the capability of collecting fine-grained energy consumption data by means of an advanced (smart) metering infrastructure permitting the collection of tens of data points per second. This is made possible by the adoption of Information and Communication Technologies (ICTs) that allow for collecting, transmitting, and storing huge amount of user energy consumption data, derived from a variety of devices such as generators, breakers, and home appliances.

© Springer International Publishing Switzerland 2014
J. Cuellar (Ed.): SmartGridSec 2014, LNCS 8448, pp. 48–62, 2014.
DOI: 10.1007/978-3-319-10329-7_4

Designing and implementing the ICT infrastructure for smart metering is well-known to be difficult and error prone in particular with respect to security issues, such as confidentiality, integrity, and privacy of consumer data; see, e.g., [1] for more on this and related problems. To reduce development time and cost, while guaranteeing a high level of security, cloud computing has been proposed as the appropriate solution to store smart metering data and make them available to consumers, utilities, and third-party services [2]. In fact, cloud computing holds the promise to significantly reduce infrastructure management by on-demand provisioning of computing and, at the same time, permitting the re-use of well-engineered security solutions. Additionally, it has been observed that cloud computing reduces the environmental impact of ICTs [3].

Despite these attractive features, cloud security is not satisfactory for such critical infrastructures as smart grids, exposed to cyber-attacks that can potentially disrupt the energy supply in large regions of a country with catastrophic economical and social consequences. At a much lesser scale but equally important for security, other serious problems may arise from the integration of Personally Identifiable Information (PII) of consumers from smart meters and other resources, such as social networks. In fact, integrated data may hinder privacy by giving insights into the activities and behaviors of users; e.g., when they are at home, if they are cooking or looking at a television show, and so on (see, e.g., [4]). It is thus obvious that data security and privacy are the main concerns for consumers, utilities, and third-party services [5].

Besides authentication, encryption, and monitoring, one of the most important mechanisms to put in place for securing cloud solutions is access control. This helps reducing the exposure to security issues related to confidentiality, integrity, and availability of utilities and third-party services using cloud services [5]. We consider the problem of selectively releasing smart metering data among three stakeholders—namely consumers, utilities, and third-party service providers—by using a suitable access control system with the goal of sharing data according to the intention of the stakeholders and restricting data usage for agreed purposes. For instance, only the age and the weekly energy consumption of a consumer can be used for statistical purposes by an utility whereas the name and the daily energy consumption should not be disclosed. The situation is further complicated by regulations and laws, that need to be enforced by the cloud platform, requiring not only the protection of the PII of consumers but also the transparency of the energy pricing strategy operated by utilities.

There are two main research questions to be solved for designing an access control system in a cloud-based smart metering scenario. First, how can a stakeholder be able to define and maintain its own access control policy while the cloud provider can limit the scope of applicability of each access control policy to the suitable set of users and resources managed by each stakeholder? A suitable answer to this question would permit policy designers to focus on authorization conditions that are crucial to grant/deny access and disregard the scope of applicability of the policies. Second, how can the cloud provider be able to enforce an access control policy composed by the policies of the various stakeholders together with applicable laws and regulations? An answer to this question would be a suitable mechanism to combine the various policies in a simple and flexible way while taking into account their scope of applicability.

In this paper, we provide answers to the two research questions above by building on top of the Attribute Based Access Control (ABAC) model (see, e.g., [6,7]) because of its flexibility in coping with a wide variety of authorization requirements. We first introduce the notion of "access control domain" for restricting the scope of applicability of the access control policy of a stakeholder to the appropriate sub-set of users and resources in the cloud. Then, we define a mechanism for combining access control policies—constrained by access control domains—so that security is preserved (i.e. authorizations denied by the policy of a stakeholder are also denied by their combination) and autonomy is guaranteed (i.e. authorizations granted by the policy of a stakeholder are also granted by their combination) provided this does not conflict with the policy of the cloud provider (i.e. in other words, autonomy is sacrificed when considering the authorization requirements concerning regulations and laws for which the cloud provider is ultimately responsible).

To evaluate the practical applicability of our solution, we consider the Energy@Home (E@H, for short)[1] cloud platform whose goal is to create and promote services and applications for efficient use of energy in residential buildings. In particular, we have implemented a prototype of the access control system (in the Spring Security framework[2]) to be integrated in the open source project JEMMA (Java-based Energy Management Application) of the E@H Association.

Plan of the paper. Section 2 briefly describes the E@H Association and gives an overview of the E@H scenario. Section 3 describes our proposal of a flexible access control mechanism for the selective release of data with several access control domains. Section 4 shows how our approach can be applied to the E@H scenario previously described. Section 5 briefly describes the enforcement of our access control system. Section 6 briefly discusses related work. Section 7 concludes the paper by sketching future work.

2   Energy@Home

Smart grids have been considered crucial for the future of Europe by the European Commission, that has promoted some activities for their development.[3] In particular, smart meters have been identified as the central components of smart grids, permitting adaptive load balancing, targeted pricing strategies, and the exploitation of a wide range of (non carbon-based) energy sources (e.g., photovoltaic). In this context, the Energy@Home (E@H) Association was founded by four major Italian companies (namely, Electrolux, Enel Distribution, Indesit

---

[1] http://www.energy-home.it
[2] http://projects.spring.io/spring-security
[3] http://ec.europa.eu/energy/gas_electricity/smartgrids/smartgrids_en.htm

Company and Telecom Italia), and now includes 19 members ranging from electrical system suppliers and the industry of household appliances, ICT suppliers, to public and private research institutes. The main goal of the E@H Association is to create and to promote systemic and collaborative techniques, tools and methodologies for efficient use of energy in residential buildings. In particular, the E@H Association focuses on gaining a deeper understanding of the sharing and usage of smart metering data among the various stakeholders, which in turn can stimulate the creation of new services based on innovative business models. For instance, consumers which are also capable of producing some amounts of energy can negotiate better prices from utilities depending on the load and balance of the network. Key to achieve this result is a careful analysis of the impact of the regulatory framework so as to determine which technological constraints it imposes on smart metering infrastructures.

2.1   The Energy@Home Scenario

The E@H Association envisions an eco-system of interoperating devices based upon a communication infrastructure that enables provisioning of third-party services in the Home Area Network (HAN). Figure 1 shows a high-level description of a scenario in which the E@H eco-system provides consumers with a variety of services ranging from energy consumption awareness to integrated energy management. The figure contains the main stakeholders, grouped in domains, of the E@H scenario: consumers in the HAN domain (whose energy consumption is recorded by sensors and appliances using the ZigBee technology), stakeholders in the Operations domain (providing services and applications for fault analysis, monitoring, load control and optimization of the energy infrastructure), and stakeholders in the Market domain (providing services for pricing, auditing, energy retailing and brokering). Figure 1 also depicts how the various stakeholders are interconnected. The Home Residential Gateway acts as the central coordinator for all devices in the HAN. The Home Gateway and the Virtual Private Network (VPN), both provided by Telecom Italia, constitute the Energy Services Interface (ESI) between the HAN and the Telecom Italia Cloud Data Center (CDC). In this way, the storage and management of smart metering data is moved to the CDC and in case a third-party service desires to obtain some energy consumption information shall contact the CDC, without having direct access to the Home Gateway. This implies the migration of security, privacy, and data integrity issues to the CDC.

In this paper, we focus on the design of a suitable access control mechanism to guarantee the confidentiality, integrity, and availability of smart metering data based on the cloud. In particular, we are interested to understand how to mediate access to the data that are produced, exchanged, stored, and used by customers (in the HAN domain), the cloud provider (CDC), and third-party services (in the Market or Operation domains). The idea is that smart metering data stored in the cloud (CDC) can be accessed by other stakeholders according to consumer policies. For instance, universities interested in real data to fine-tune and improve energy-optimization algorithms or companies looking for

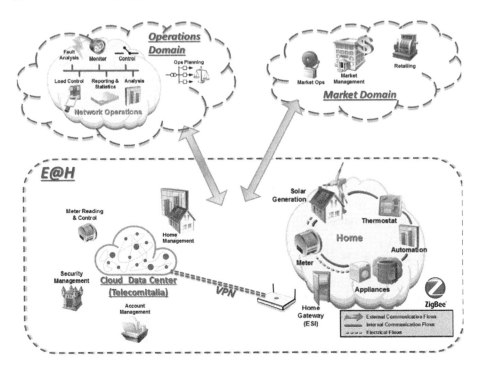

Fig. 1. Overview of the Energy@Home scenario

exploiting new trends in the energy market can access anonymized and aggregated smart metering data. More fine-grained but still anonymized data can be used by manufacturers to reduce the energy consumption of certain appliances (e.g., washing machines). Of particular interest in this respect are third-party services that elaborate individual smart metering data for energy awareness with the goal of increasing the consumer awareness of energy usage which may reduce environmental impact.[4] Prominent examples of services for energy awareness are the so called *energy social networks*, which exploit the connection, sharing, comparing, and real-time update capabilities of social media to foster a sense of belonging, achievement, competition, ease of use, and sustainability to motivate consumers and conserve energy.[5] For example, services and applications for accessing each individual's home energy consumption data allow consumers to compete with their friends, family, or neighbours about who can cut the most energy use. Another example is the use of services and applications that give consumers the option to receive tips and information on energy usage from utilities based on their energy consumption profiles derived from their smart metering data. Indeed, for all these services and applications to be successful, it is critical

---

[4] http://www.energyawareness.eu/beaware

[5] http://www.huffingtonpost.com/f-michael-valocchi/ibm-want-to-cut-energy-usage_b_1836486.html

a high level of security concerning the release and usage of consumer data. In cloud-based solutions, such as the E@H scenario, it is the cloud provider (CDC) that is ultimately responsible to combine and enforce the policies of the various stakeholders. Indeed, it should enforce the policies that were previously agreed with the customers or the third-party services, e.g., at the time of signing a contract. However, the contract may specify the possibility for consumers to perform modifications to their policies (by means of a simple interface as it will be discussed in Sect. 5). Another important aspect is that the cloud provider is also responsible to guarantee that existing laws and regulations are enforced by means of suitable policies on data release and usage. As a consequence, the cloud provider (Telecom Italia in the E@H scenario) becomes the security supervisor for the administration and enforcement of access control policies.

3   Selective Release of Data in a Multi-domain Environment

To accommodate the heterogeneity and complexity of authorization conditions for the release of smart metering data, we use authorization policies based on the Attribute Based Access Control (ABAC) model; see, e.g., [6,7]. In ABAC, access rights are granted or denied depending on the security-relevant characteristics—called attributes—of the entities involved in access control: a *subject* (e.g., a user or an application) asking to perform an *action* (e.g., read, write, update) on a *resource* (e.g., a file, a document, or a database record) in an *environment*, i.e. a collection of contextual information (e.g., location, time of day). By suitably defining attributes, it is possible not only to simulate and combine a wide range of classical access control models but also refine them so as to supplement rather than supplanting the classical models; see, e.g., [8] for a discussion on these and related issues.

Unfortunately, the ABAC model alone does not offer suitable mechanisms for the specification of ABAC policies regulating the release of smart metering data in the cloud. There are two main problems to address.

First, the cloud provider should be able to limit the scope of applicability of each access control policy—called the *access control domain*—of the various stakeholders, namely consumers, utilities, and third-party services. I.e. we need a mechanism to specify to which set of subjects, resources, and environments a certain policy is applicable. For this, we introduce ways to define a condition on the attributes of subjects, resources, and environments characterizing an access control domain. (Intuitively, an access control domain contains the authorization relevant aspects of the Home, Market, and Operations domains (see Fig. 1) discussed in Sect. 2.1.) The advantage of the notion of access control domain are two-fold. On the one hand, the cloud provider is in the position to confine the effect of a policy to the set of subjects, resources, and environments that has been negotiated with the stakeholder. On the other hand, policy designers may focus on the conditions of the attributes that are crucial to grant or deny access and disregard the conditions for membership of subjects, resources, and environments to the appropriate access control domain.

Second, the cloud provider should be able to *combine* its own policy—reflecting the business rules but also applicable laws and regulations—with those of the various stakeholders. While the scope of applicability of an access control policy of a stakeholder is limited to a certain access control domain, this is not the case for the policy of the cloud provider whose applicability extends to any subject, resource, and environment in the cloud. For this, we propose a combination mechanism yielding a global policy (to be enforced by the cloud provider) such that (a) the access control domain to which the subject, resource, and environment in the authorization query belong is identified, (b) the policy of the stakeholder associated to the access control domain is applied, (c) the policy of the cloud provider is also applied, and (d) if both authorization decisions are 'grant,' then the final decision is also 'grant;' otherwise (i.e. at least one decision is 'deny'), the final decision is 'deny.' For the mechanism to be well-defined, we assume that just one stakeholder is responsible to define a policy for a given access control domain (this is equivalent to say that the domains are pairwise disjoint). In this way, any tuple of subject, resource, and environment extracted from an authorization query belongs to exactly one access control domain. In the smart metering scenario such an assumption seems reasonable and, most importantly, easy to satisfy by adding to every subject, resource, and environment, an attribute whose values are the collections of identifiers for access control domains.

In the rest of this section, we develop a precise model for the two notions discussed above on top of a formalization of the ABAC model in the specification framework of [9].

3.1 Mathematical Model

We regard subjects, resources, actions, and environments (called entities) as records whose fields are the attributes. An entity is uniquely identified by the values associated to its attributes. The semantics of an *ABAC policy* $A(s, a, r, e)$—regardless of the language in which it is written—is given by a collection of structures, each one composed by a universe—a non-empty set of values for the attributes—and a Boolean function (predicate) over the values of the attributes expressing a relation among a subject s, a resource r, an action a, and an environment e. Given subject s, action a, resource r, and environment e, we say that s can execute action a on resource r in environment e according to the ABAC policy A iff the Boolean function A applied to the values given by the attribute assignments for s, r, a, and e (in symbols, $A(s, a, r, e)$) returns true.

We say that a structure in the semantics of an ABAC policy *satisfies* the policy. An ABAC policy is *consistent* iff the collection of structures satisfying the specification is non-empty. The semantics of the *composition* of a set of ABAC policies is given by the collection of the structures satisfying all component specifications. Following [9], we observe that structures in the semantics of an ABAC policy correspond to standard interpretations in first-order logic (FOL). This allows us to use the language of FOL for writing ABAC policies so that (i) the semantics of a policy can be seen as an assertion of FOL, (ii) the semantics of a composition is the conjunction of their assertions (this is the view of "conjunction as composition" in [9]), and (iii) the composition of some ABAC policies is consistent iff the conjunction of their assertions is satisfiable.

Similarly to an ABAC policy, an *access control domain* $D(s, r, e)$ is given by a collection of structures, each one composed by a universe and a predicate over the values of the attributes identifying a set of tuples formed by a subject s, a resource r, and an environment e. As for ABAC policies, we can give the semantics of an access control domain as an assertion of FOL. Let D be an access control domain, called *global*, we say that $D_1, ..., D_n$ is a partition of D when D_i and D_j are mutually inconsistent (i.e. the conjunction $D_i \wedge D_j$ is unsatisfiable) for each distinct i and j in $\{1, ..., n\}$ and the union of the predicates in $D_1, ..., D_n$ is equal to the predicate in D (i.e. the disjunction of $D_1, ..., D_n$ is logically equivalent to D).

We are now in the position to define how an access control domain D restricts the scope of applicability of a policy A. The semantics of the *constrained* ABAC policy $A|_D$ contains the structures of A not satisfying D or those satisfying A. When using assertions of FOL for both A and D, this amounts to saying that $A|_D$ is the implication $D \Rightarrow A$. Notice that this implies that a subject s can perform action a on resource r in environment e according to the constrained policy $A|_D$ when the subject s, resource r, and environment e do not belong to the access control domain D. As we will see, this is desirable when composing constrained ABAC policies.

Let A be an ABAC policy (of the cloud provider) and D be an access control domain (identifying all subjects, resources, and environments in the cloud)—both called *global*—and A_i be an ABAC policy (of stakeholder i) and D_i be an access control domain (identifying those subjects, resources, and environments in the cloud under the jurisdiction of stakeholder i)—called *local*—for $i = 1, ..., n$. Assume also that $D_1, ..., D_n$ is a partition of D (i.e. just one stakeholder is responsible to define a policy for a given access control domain). The *globally composed* ABAC policy $G := A|_D \wedge \bigwedge_{i=1}^{n} A_i|_{D_i}$ is the composition of $A|_D, A_1|_{D_1}, ..., A_n|_{D_n}$. Since $D_1, ..., D_n$ is a partition of D, there must be $i^* \in \{1, ..., n\}$ such that $D_{i^*}(s, r, e)$ is true for every subject s, resource r, and environment e in the global domain D while $D_i(s, r, e)$ is false for any $i \neq i^*$. This implies that there must exist $i^* \in \{1, ..., n\}$ such that $G(s, a, r, e)$ is equivalent to $A|_D(s, a, r, e) \wedge A_{i^*}|_{D_{i^*}}(s, a, r, e)$ for every s, r, and e in the domain D. By interpreting 'true' as 'grant' and 'false' as 'deny,' the formal definition of globally composed policy corresponds to the combination of policies described above.

As a final observation, recall the principle of *autonomy* (i.e. if an access is permitted within an individual system, it must also be permitted under secure interoperation) and that of *security* (if an access is not permitted within an individual system, it must not be permitted under secure interoperation) introduced in [10] for federated systems. From the discussion above, it is easy to see that both principles hold for $\bigwedge_{i=1}^{n} A_i|_{D_i}$, but this is not the case for G because of the presence of the policy A of the cloud provider. This means that each access control policy A_i can be administered independently in the access control domain D_i but the policy A of the cloud provider shall always be applied (thus sacrificing autonomy of the whole system) because it is ultimately responsible for the application of regulations and laws about smart metering data.

4   Selective Release of Data in the E@H Scenario

As described in Sect. 2.1, the (Telecom Italia) CDC is responsible to store consumers smart metering data and to guarantee later access to the stored information by the consumer owning it, and possibly to make the data available to third-party operators depending on the release conditions specified by consumers. Additionally, the CDC can host the data produced by the third-party operators and mediate access between the resources produced by them and the consumers. In this scenario, we identify three access control domains: that of the CDC (D_{CDC}) consisting of all possible subjects, resources, and environments of the cloud, that of Consumers (D_C) consisting of all subjects who are users of the CDC to store their own smart metering data, and one domain per third-party Operator p (D_{TPO_p}) consisting of the subjects who are users of both the CDC and the third-party operator p, and the resources of the users and possibly those produced by the third-party operator p. Let us now consider some FOL assertions that characterize the domains introduced above for some representative situations.

The access control domain of CDC should contain any subject and its related resources; thus, it does not constrain the values of the s and r. However, the CDC may need to perform administrative operations (e.g., back-up) during which standard activities are not possible. To model this situation, we can imagine that the environment has an attribute *mode* that can take values *normal*, *administrative*, etc. with the obvious meanings:

$$D_{CDC}(s, r, e) := (e.mode = normal).$$

In this way, any access control policy that will be enforced in the CDC will have to check that the operation mode of the cloud infrastructure is *normal*.

The access control domain of a consumer should contain all his/her smart metering data (resources):

$$D_C(s, r, e) := (s.role = consumer \wedge r.owner = s.id),$$

where we assume that subjects have an attribute *id* storing a unique identifier and an attribute *role* specifying whether the subject is a consumer, a third party operator, etc.; we also assume that a resource (containing some smart metering data) has an attribute *owner* carrying the identifier of the subject owning it. So, the FOL assertion above requires D_C to identify every subject labelled as consumer (e.g., after signing a contract with the CDC) with the owned smart metering data.

The access control domain of a third-party operator p may contain all the consumers with some features that are essential for its business. For instance, consider the case in which the third-party service p is an energy social network (recall the discussion at page 5 in Sect. 2.1) interested in collecting information about energy consumption of families with at least three members. The access control domain can be defined as follows:

$$D_{TPO_p}(s, r, e) := \begin{pmatrix} s.role = consumer \wedge s.occupant \geq 3 \, \wedge \\ member(s.id, p) \wedge r.owner = s.id \end{pmatrix},$$

where we assume that—besides the attribute *role* introduced above—subjects have also attribute *occupant* storing the number of people leaving in a house with subject $s.id$ that we require to be a non-negative integer larger than 3. We also assume the availability of a predicate *member* that checks whether a subject is a member of the Third Party Operator p. So, the FOL assertion above requires D_{TPO_p} to contain all subjects that have been labelled as consumer, that are also member of the third-party service p (e.g., because they signed a contract with p), and share the house with 2 or more people, and the resources owned by them.

We now consider some examples of ABAC policies that can be used in the domains discussed above. In the access control domain D_{CDC}, any resource can be read by its owner:

$$A_{CDC}(s, a, r, e) := (r.owner = s.id \wedge a.name = read).$$

When considering $A_{CDC}|_{D_{CDC}}$, it is easy to realize that the right to *read* their own resources is granted to any subject when the CDC infrastructure is working normally. Similarly, the smart metering data of a consumer should be updated by the consumer himself/herself (in reality by a program doing this on his/her behalf). This can be expressed by the following ABAC policy:

$$A_C(s, a, r, e) := (r.owner = s.id \wedge a.name = update),$$

where we assume that actions have attribute *name* that uniquely identifies them and can take the usual values *read, write, update*, etc. When considering $A_C|_{D_C}$, it is easy to realize that the right to *update* their own resources is granted only to (the smart metering applications on behalf of) consumers. We observe that, in most cases, the policy adopted by a consumer will not be designed by him/her but rather will be provided by the CDC and proposed to the consumer when signing the contract.

In the access control domain D_{TPO_p}, smart metering data of a consumer can be read by the third-party operator p provided that the consumer has labeled them as releasable to p. This can be expressed by the following ABAC policy:

$$A_{TPO_p}(s, a, r, e) := \begin{pmatrix} s.role = consumer \wedge r.owner = s.id \wedge \\ releasableto(r.id, p) \wedge a.name = read \end{pmatrix},$$

where we assume the availability of a predicate *releasableto* that checks whether the user has marked as releasable to p that data. When considering $A_{TPO_p}|_{D_{TPO_p}}$, it is easy to realize that the right to read consumer smart metering data is granted to p only if the consumer is registered with p.

As explained in Sect. 3.1, the global policy used by the CDC is the composition (conjunction) of $A_{CDC}|_{D_{CDC}}$, $A_C|_{D_C}$, and $A_{TPO_p}|_{D_{TPO_p}}$ for each third-party provider p provided that D_{CDC}, D_C, and $\{D_{TPO_p}\}_{p \in P}$ is a partition for the set of identifiers P of third-party services. The access control domains give the CDC the ability to limit the scope of applicability of the policies developed by the various stakeholders of the E@H scenario. While the policies discussed above have been simplified for simplicity, we believe that they provide a good idea of the kind of authorization constraints that can be expressed in the proposed approach. In fact, since our approach is based on the ABAC model, we inherit all its good features with respect to expressiveness. These allow for expressing, combining, and supplementing all the authorization constraints supported by classical access control models (e.g., Discretionary, Mandatory, Role-Based, etc.) [7]. For this reason, we believe our approach to be complete in terms of expressivity.

Another advantage of our approach is given by the "separation of concerns" principle supported by the notion of access control domain together with the proposed combination mechanism. First, access control domains allow for a clear separation between the condition for defining the scope of applicability of a policy and that for authorization in the pre-defined scope. For example, despite their simplicity, consider policies A_C for consumers and the consumer access control domain D_C. Second, the simple mechanism to combine the policies of the stakeholders makes it clear that the policies of the various stakeholders do not interfere—as their scope of applicability is limited to pairwise disjoint collections of subjects, resources, and environments—except for that of the CDC, which should always be applied because of its role of security supervisor, as pointed out at the end of Sect. 2.1. Finally, our combination mechanism streamlines the implementation of the centralized enforcement mechanism as will be discussed in the next section.

5   Implementation

As a proof of concept, we implemented a prototype of the proposed framework for the E@H platform. Recently, the E@H Association announced the release of JEMMA[6] (Java-based Energy Management Application framework), an open-source project that facilitates the development of home energy management applications. JEMMA is fully written in Java and it implements the E@H technical specifications. Thus, for our security solution we chose a Java technology. We use Spring[7], a powerful open source framework for the Java community, and its popular extension Spring Security, designed to support security related implementations. Since Spring Security did not yet directly support ABAC—and, as far as we know, no implementation of ABAC in Spring Security is currently available—we have augmented the framework to support it. We implemented a

---

[6] More details can be found on the official website of the JEMMA project: http://jemma.energy-home.org.

[7] http://projects.spring.io/spring-framework/

flexible and dynamic framework, compatible with the Spring MVC design architecture, and thus providing the Spring community with a reference implementation of the framework described. We have used the following tools and utilities while implementing ABAC: Maven as a project building and management tool, Apache Tomcat as a servlet container, hibernate as an object relational mapping (ORM) tool used for implementing our data access object (DAO), and MySQL as our database.

The goal of CDC is to offer a number of functionalities to access the resources through a Java API. This API must be used by all the stakeholders in order to access available resources. Clearly, this API can be directly invoked by Third Party Operators, while a (user-friendly) web interface can be supplied to mediate the invocations of consumers. Therefore, we use method level security to implement ABAC, securing method invocations by using the `@PreAuthorize` Spring annotation. As a policy specification language, we used the powerful Spring Expression Language (SpEL) [11], created by the Spring framework community to work with all the Spring framework products. We have implemented a custom expression evaluator that parses our policy rules (written in SpEL) from a resource bundle, invokes the SpEL evaluator, and passes the Boolean result to `@PreAuthorize`. According to this result of the evaluation the method can actually be invoked or not.

As a final remark, we observe that our prototype features a dashboard to permit consumers (usually not experts in writing authorization conditions and thereby using the policies provided by the CDC when signing the contract) to customize their policies. To understand how this works, consider policy A_{TPO_p} (towards the end of page 10) and recall that *releasableto* checks whether the user has marked a resource r as releasable to the third-party service p. The dashboard permits consumers to change the result returned by *releasableto* for all the resources they own so that authorization decisions for each resource can be tuned while leaving the policies unmodified. We believe this dashboard or similar mechanisms will play a crucial role in making our access control mechanism more widely usable.

The prototypical implementation described above has been developed in the context of the EIT ICT Labs activity "SecSES Secure Energy Systems" in close collaboration with Telecom Italia. It will represent a reference implementation for the future extensions of the E@H platform so as to enable more complex services, e.g., to support the energy social network scenario described at the end of Sect. 2.1.

6   Related Work

A huge amount of work has been done in the field of access control; the interested reader is pointed to [12] for an overview. In particular, several papers considered the problem of combining access control policies by means of a collection of operators that form an algebra; see, e.g., [13,14]. Our combination method can be recast in many of the rich algebras proposed in the literature (for instance, our notion of constrained policy is similar to the external scoping operation of [14]). However, our proposal has the advantage of simplicity with respect to the complexity of available solutions. In particular, we do not need to define complex resolution strategies for handling conflicts in policies. Being easy to grasp, its implementation on top of standard security frameworks (such as the Spring framework, as discussed in Sect. 5) is also easier. Additionally, since our framework is independent of the particular language used to write access control domains and ABAC policies by adopting the semantic approach to specifications in [9] (recall their definitions in Sect. 3.1), it seems possible to allow the various stakeholders to their language of choice to write their specifications (e.g., SpEL rather than XACML) provided that policy decision points are available at the cloud provider. Some proposals for access control mechanisms dedicated to grids have been put forward; see, e.g., [15–17]. However, to the best of our knowledge, none takes into account a cloud-based architecture as we do here although some (e.g., [16]) develop mechanisms based on ABAC.

In [18], a simple-to-use mechanism is proposed, allowing consumers to control the access of their data collected by devices and sensors. It enables a layperson, using a privacy dashboard, to tune the granularity of the consumption information accessed by value added services. This input is automatically translated into a given policy language (i.e. XACML) and used by a policy decision point to decide on access requests. This mechanism can be easily integrated in our framework. Indeed, the input provided by consumers via a dashboard can be used to specify the policies described in the previous sections.

To demonstrate the increasing attention on the smart metering solutions, a number of projects and initiatives has been put forward in the last years. Among them, we mention the EEBus Initiative e.V.[8] It is a German registered association including big companies like ABB, B/S/H, E-on, Miele, Vaillant, and others. It networks the leading companies, associations and stakeholders in the German and international energy, telecommunications and electrical industry. Energy@home and EEBus Initiative collaborate for the benefit of a common pan-European Smart Home approach.

7   Conclusions and Future Work

We have analysed the access control mechanisms to the cloud data center responsible to store smart metering data of the consumers and to guarantee later access to the stored information. We have identified the different stakeholders and access control domains involved, and thus described a framework for a selective release of smart metering data in this multi-domain environment. Finally, we have applied our framework to the Energy@Home scenario, implementing an ABAC mechanism in the Spring Security framework.

For simplicity, in the paper, we have only marginally discussed privacy issues that are indeed of great importance for any smart metering infrastructure. For instance, in Sect. 4, we have touched on the problem by considering the release

---

[8] http://www.eebus.org/

of personal smart metering data to third-party services with the ABAC policy A_{TPO_p}. This is an instance of the more general problem of how to regulate the use of personal information in secondary applications. We believe that our proposal can be extended with the privacy-aware access control system in [19] by integrating authorization protocols such as OAuth. We leave this as a very interesting and promising line of research as future work. Another interesting issue is to design automated techniques to verify security properties (e.g., safety) of the policies in our framework. By exploiting the use of FOL assertions, we believe that several policy analysis problems can be reduced to (decidable) theorem proving problems as done, e.g., in [20] for a similar attribute-based framework. We envisage to exploit the separation among the various policies and their limited interaction to decompose the proof obligations into smaller and hopefully easier to solve theorem proving problems.

Acknowledgments. This work has partially been supported by the activity "SecSES Secure Energy Systems" of the action line ASES Smart Energy Systems of the EIT ICT Labs, and by the MIUR PRIN 2010-11 project "Security Horizons." We are grateful to Jorge Cuéllar, the participants, and the reviewer of the "Second Open EIT ICT Labs Workshop on Smart Grid Security" for their remarks and comments that helped to improve the paper.

References

1. Skopik, F.: Security is not enough! on privacy challenges in smart grids. Int. J. Smart Grid Clean Energy **1**(1), 7–14 (2012)
2. Simmhan, Y., Kumbhare, A.G., Baohua, C., Prasanna, V.: An analysis of security and privacy issues in smart grid software architectures on clouds. In: IEEE International Conference on Cloud Computing (CLOUD), pp. 582–589 (2011)
3. Accenture in collaboration with WSP. Cloud Computing and Sustainability: The Environmental Benefits of Moving to the Cloud. White paper (2010). http://download.microsoft.com/download/A/F/F/AFFEB671-FA27-45CF-9373-0655247751CF/CloudComputingandSustainability-Whitepaper-Nov2010.pdf
4. Murrill, B.J., Liu, E.C., Thompson II, R.M.: Smart meter data: privacy and cybersecurity. Congressional Research report, R42338 (2012)
5. Cloud Security Alliance (2013). https://cloudsecurityalliance.org/download/the-notorious-nine-cloud-computing-top-threats-in-2013
6. Yuan, E., Tong, J.: Attributed based access control (ABAC) for web services. In: Proceedings of the IEEE International Conference on Web Services, ICWS '05, pp. 561–569. IEEE Computer Society, Washington, DC (2005)
7. NIST. Guide to Attribute Based Access Control (ABAC) Definition and Considerations (2013). http://csrc.nist.gov/publications/drafts/800-162/sp800_162_draft.pdf
8. Jin, X., Krishnan, R., Sandhu, R.: A unified attribute-based access control model covering DAC, MAC and RBAC. In: Cuppens-Boulahia, N., Cuppens, F., Garcia-Alfaro, J. (eds.) DBSec 2012. LNCS, vol. 7371, pp. 41–55. Springer, Heidelberg (2012)
9. Zave, P., Jackson, M.: Conjunction as composition. ACM Trans. Softw. Eng. Methodol. **2**(4), 379–411 (1993)

10. Gong, L., Qian, X.: Computational issues in secure interoperation. IEEE Trans. Softw. Eng. **22**(1), 43–52 (1996)
11. Spring. Spring Expression Language (2013). http://docs.spring.io/spring/docs/3. 2.x/spring-framework-reference/html/expressions.html
12. De Capitani di Vimercati, S., Foresti, S., Jajodia, S., Samarati, P.: Access control policies and languages. Int. J. Comput. Sci. Eng. **3**(2), 94–102 (2007)
13. Bonatti, P., De Capitani di Vimercati, S., Samarati, P.: An Algebra for Composing Access Control Policies. ACM Trans. Inf. Syst. Secur. (TISSEC) **5**(1), 1–35 (2002)
14. Wijesekera, D., Jajodia, S.: A propositional policy algebra for access control. ACM Trans. Inf. Syst. Secur. **6**(2), 286–325 (2003)
15. Jung, M., Hofer, T., Dobelt, S., Kienesberger, G., Judex, F., Kastner, W.: Access control for a smart grid SOA. In: 2012 International Conference for Internet Technology and Secured Transactions, pp. 281–287 (2012)
16. Lang, B., Foster, I., Siebenlist, F., Ananthakrishnan, R., Freeman, T.: A flexible attribute based access control method for grid computing. J. Grid Comput. **7**(2), 169–180 (2009)
17. Kim, J., Kwon, Y., Lee, Y., Seo, J., Kim, H.: Access control mechanism supporting scalability, interoperability and flexibility of multi-domain smart grid system. In: Information Science and Industrial Applications ISI (2012)
18. Ebinger, P., Hernández Ramos, J.L., Kikiras, P., Lischka, M., Wiesmaier, A.: Privacy in smart metering ecosystems. In: Cuellar, J. (ed.) SmartGridSec 2012. LNCS, vol. 7823, pp. 120–131. Springer, Heidelberg (2013)
19. Ardagna, C.A., Cremonini, M., De Capitani di Vimercati, S., Samarati, P.: A privacy-aware access control system. J. Comput. Secur. (JCS) **16**(4), 369–392 (2008)
20. Armando, A., Oudkerk, S., Ranise, S., Wrona, K.: Formal modelling of content-based protection and release for access control in NATO operations. In: Danger, J.-L., Debbabi, M., Marion, J.-Y., Garcia-Alfaro, J., Heywood, N.Z. (eds.) FPS 2013. LNCS, vol. 8352, pp. 227–244. Springer, Heidelberg (2014)

KEDS: Decentralised Network Security for the Smart Home Environment

Justin King-Lacroix$^{(\boxtimes)}$ and Andrew Martin

Department of Computer Science, University of Oxford,
Wolfson Building, Parks Road, Oxford OX1 3QD, UK
{Justin.King-Lacroix,Andrew.Martin}@cs.ox.ac.uk

Abstract. The increasingly wide deployment of smart grid technologies in the home has resulted in home automation networks becoming multi-stakeholder, with the number of stakeholders increasing over time.

However, the technologies underpinning these networks universally feature a heavily centralised security model, with policy data held on privileged machines that are both security- and availability-critical. On a multi-stakeholder network, no single stakeholder can be trusted with the authority to operate such privileged machines.

This paper presents a novel network architecture for multi-stakeholder networking. It also proposes a set of modifications to ZigBee, an emerging industry standard in the smart grid domain, that would cause it to conform to this architecture. These are used as the basis for an example application: the smart home.

1 Introduction

The term smart grid refers to the increasing instrumentation of electricity infrastructure with Internet-connected sensors. These sensors report energy consumption data in real time to utility providers, in order to aid both prediction and management of electricity demand. However, this real-time reporting raises security and privacy concerns [1], especially as the granularity of the reported data approaches the level of individual homes.

Sensors in the home for measuring electricity consumption are referred to as smart meters. They contain embedded microprocessors, and are usually connected to a dedicated backhaul network operating alongside electrical distribution lines. These meters are at the hub of the smart home environment introduced by the widely-cited NIST Framework and Roadmap for Smart Grid Interoperability Standards [2]. Newer home automation solutions are able to integrate into this environment, in order to exchange energy-management data, potentially including per-device energy consumption information, with the electricity provider (via the smart meter). Other utilities, such as gas and water, are also beginning to deploy smart meters for real-time monitoring. These meters must somehow report information to their respective operators; the consumer's Internet connection and the electricity provider's backhaul are the two primary means of achieving this.

© Springer International Publishing Switzerland 2014
J. Cuellar (Ed.): SmartGridSec 2014, LNCS 8448, pp. 63–78, 2014.
DOI: 10.1007/978-3-319-10329-7_5

Smart home networks are thus multi-stakeholder networks of a novel kind. The stakeholders involved cannot completely trust each other, and yet the devices they control must exchange high-level services in order to fulfil their operational goals. Additionally, each stakeholder controls only one or a handful of devices, and so the network cannot be decomposed into stakeholder-specific subnetworks.

1.1 Contributions Made in this Paper

The contributions of this paper are:

- To highlight the challenge presented by multi-stakeholder networking.
- To describe a key-exchange protocol, KEDS, for low-power embedded networks.
- To describe a network architecture for multi-stakeholder networks, with no central control points, based on KEDS.
- To combine the preceding two contributions into a set of changes to ZigBee, with a view towards its application in a smart home setting.

1.2 Structure of this Paper

The remainder of this paper is structured as follows: In Sect. 2, we outline existing approaches to network security and multi-stakeholder networking, and examine why these are inappropriate for the smart grid case. We then outline the security model and relevant features of ZigBee, an emerging industry standard for smart grid home networks.

In Sect. 3, we highlight the key security and performance requirements of a multi-stakeholder network, and propose a network architecture and security model for network-layer protocols which respects those requirements. We then outline a series of modifications to ZigBee in order to implement that architecture. Section 4 evaluates the architecture and protocol presented, discussing its implications for the security and performance of the network, as well as its potential operational overhead.

In Sect. 5, we return to the smart grid, remarking upon the feasibility of the complete removal of trusted third-parties in this context. Finally, Sect. 6 concludes the paper, and outlines our next steps.

Throughout this paper, terminology from the well-known OSI model for communication systems will be used.

2 Background

2.1 Existing Approach to Network Security

Network security has generally assumed a strict separation between insiders – people and machines within the network perimeter – and outsiders – those external to it. Network security technologies deployed in the home – in particular, those underlying Wi-Fi [3] and ZigBee [4] – are built on the assumption that outsiders should be entirely denied network access, while insiders are admitted and treated identically.

Furthermore, such access-control decisions are based on information in central, privileged directories of security principals and authentication metadata. The machines hosting these directories – the Access Point in the Wi-Fi case, or the Trust Center for ZigBee – exercise total control over the network; their owner is assumed to be its owner.

2.2   Existing Approaches to Multi-stakeholder Networking

Multi-stakeholder networking has seen implementation in two contexts: Internet Network Access Points, and military systems. In both cases, the focus has been on interconnecting a small number of large networks controlled by mutually-distrusting entities. The technologies in use were developed specifically for this purpose, and do not generalise to other application domains.

Network Access Points. Internet Network Access Points, and their equivalents in large data centres, have always had a single purpose: the routing of traffic across the Internet. The Border Gateway Protocol [5] operates at these junction points to interconnect the networks of the various organisations present. Participants in these systems make a strong trust assumption: that it is in each stakeholder's best interests to maximise the efficiency of the routing infrastructure. More recent developments [6] weaken this trust assumption by cryptographic means, introducing a trusted third-party certificate issuer which validates route announcements. However, again, this is a solution specific to the use case: a third-party authority already exists for the assignment of Internet addresses, the Internet Assigned Numbers Authority, IANA.

Military Systems. Relevant military research focuses on three areas: the routing of packets across hostile (or potentially-hostile) terrain [7], the interconnection of networks with multiple levels of security [8,9], and the formation of ad-hoc wireless networks in a disaster-relief scenario [10]. In all cases, the basic problem is the same as for Network Access Points: the routing of packets over an internetwork [11]. The issue of higher-level services is rarely considered.

In disaster-relief, some work has been done on information exchange between participating organisations. However, this work addresses mainly the policy concerns surrounding the exchange of information between civilian and military stakeholders [12], with little done on the security architecture of the networks being used.

2.3   ZigBee

ZigBee [4] is a network protocol specification designed for low-power wireless mesh networking in the embedded space, and is an emerging industry standard for smart grid home networks. It covers the network layer of the stack, and above (excluding the application layer), with little division between layers. IEEE802.15.4 [13] provides the link layer and below.

Its security model is based on symmetric cryptography, with key distribution the responsibility of a central Trust Center. In high-security mode, packets are encrypted and integrity-protected with keys of two types: the *network key*, a network-wide secret which all nodes must possess, and *link keys*, which are used for pairwise communication between nodes. At network join time, each node must be provisioned with a Trust Center Link Key, which is used for all communication with the Trust Center, including distribution of further keys for communication with the rest of the network.

Nodes are arranged in a tree structure, with each router a node in the tree, and end-devices at its leaves. The root node is known as the Coordinator; the Coordinator is also usually (though not necessarily) the Trust Center. Joining a ZigBee network is a complex operation: the join protocol has multiple branches, and requires a large number of network round-trips (12, in the worst case). The specification mandates that the Trust Center keep a registry of currently-active devices, kept up-to-date by information messages from routers as nodes join and leave. It may at any time instruct a router to eject a node from the network.

Clearly, the Trust Center is a single point of failure for the entire network. It possesses all keys currently in use, and so is capable of decrypting all traffic and impersonating any node, and additionally has the right to admit nodes to or exclude them from the network. Thus, in a multi-stakeholder context, whichever stakeholder controls the Trust Center controls all communications on the network.

ZigBee Smart Energy Profile. The ZigBee Smart Energy Profile [14] (SEP) specification introduces a requirement for each node to possess a key pair for use in elliptic-curve cryptographic (ECC) protocols, serving as its cryptographic identity. Link keys can thus be negotiated pairwise between nodes, without potential for eavesdropping by the Trust Center. However, not all SEP operations are mandated to use link keys for security.

3   Modern Multi-stakeholder Networks

Multi-stakeholder networks are characterised by the presence of multiple entities with disparate and *potentially competing* interests. In such an environment, if one such entity is granted administrative control of the infrastructure, necessarily that entity gains the ability to prioritise its interests over those of the others, potentially to their detriment. Such a network therefore should not contain any single points of control, since such a point of control would give administrative control of the network infrastructure to its owner.

The introduction of a trusted third party is a natural solution to this problem. However, this presupposes the existence of an entity whose interests do not compete with the other stakeholders on the network, which is unlikely to be the case the smart grid context. Moreover, devices controlled by such trusted third-parties present an obvioustarget for attack.

The most robust solution, therefore, is to distribute security responsibilities over all stakeholders. Since, in the smart home environment, each stakeholder only controls one (or a small number) of nodes, security responsibilities must therefore be distributed over all nodes in the network. In general, this can be done by ensuring all traffic is encrypted with keys known only to its sender and receiver.

On the wider Internet, this is done by means of public-key cryptography. However, prior to the advent of ECC, public-key operations consumed too much CPU power to be usable on the resource-constrained embedded systems that dominate the smart grid. ECC is now a mature and widely-deployed technique, and has been implemented on very low-power devices [15], permitting high-security communications even under strict resource constraints.

Structure of this Section. The remainder of this section will describe our proposal. We begin with its position in the software stack, with some mention of interfaces upwards and downwards. We then describe the network-wide key management structure, along with its consequences.

Following this description, we introduce two novel mechanisms to support the key management structure we present: key-exchange with data stapling, and cryptographic delegation. We then apply our proposal to ZigBee, outlining a series of modifications that we propose to make.

3.1   Proposed Architecture

Network Stack Model and Interfaces. Our proposal covers the network layer of the software stack. IEEE802.15.4 will provide the data link and physical layers, given its wide deployment in the smart grid domain.

We expect implementations to adhere to a mostly-open trust model: all code on a given node should trust the network (and below) layers with unencrypted data. The reason for this is simple: encryption of packets will be done by the data link layer. A minor exception is that the network layer need not expose encryption keys to higher layers.

Key Management. Our key management architecture is straightforward:

1. Each node must possess an ECC key pair, which forms its identity.
2. A pair of nodes wishing to communicate must first establish a shared secret (for use in encryption and integrity-protection) using those ECC keys.
3. There are no network-wide shared secrets.

We mandate that all key management be done at the network layer; higher layers should delegate this task downwards where possible. As a result, all communication between the same pair of nodes will use the same key to communicate.

Finally, we require that all network traffic use encryption and integrity protection, using the aforementioned pairwise keys; it is the responsibility of the network layer to arrange for this to occur, with the actual cryptographic work done by the data link layer.

There is an important subtlety related to item 2 above: a new key must be established for *each pair of communicating devices*, whether those devices are neighbours or not. The KEDS protocol below is designed both for use as a fast network join protocol, and for bootstrapping secure channels between nodes several routing hops apart. If key establishment is restricted only to neighbouring routing hops, communications will be vulnerable to attack by intervening routing nodes, and end-to-end security is lost.

Broadcast/Multicast Traffic. In this rigid pairwise keying model, broadcast and multicast messages present a challenge. The naïve message broadcast protocol in this environment has router nodes re-encrypt a message once for each neighbouring node to which it is retransmitted. In order to protect against modification by intervening routers, messages are required to be digitally signed by their originators.

This protocol is only suitable for infrequent broadcasts, due both to the processor and radio overhead it imposes on routers, and the large number of public-key transactions required by the rest of the network. For more frequent broadcasts, and any multicasts, an alternative mechanism is necessary. The TESLA [16] protocol is ideally-suited to this use, with initialisation data distributed using the naïve protocol for broadcasts, or unicast transmissions in the multicast case.

3.2 Key-Exchange with Data-Stapling (KEDS)

Communication between nodes must always begin with a key-agreement phase. Diffie-Hellman (DH) is the oldest and most popular protocol for this purpose. We have selected one of its ECC-based descendents, ECMQV (as described in the ZigBee SEP specification [14]) for our purposes here, due to the low computational requirements of ECC algorithms.

DH-based protocols consist of four messages (see Fig. 1). We propose a data stapling extension to the protocol: in each key-agreement message, we introduce a field for additional data, which is encrypted and integrity-protected using the resultant key.

The first message is a special case: since neither side yet possesses enough information to derive the resulting key, data cannot be encrypted. However, integrity-verification data can be generated and included in the second message, alongside its stapled data. The SD1DV (for 'Stapled Data 1 Delayed Verification') field is included for this purpose.

3.3 Cryptographic Delegation

There may still remain classes of devices for which the frequency of public-key transactions in KEDS is too high. For these devices, we introduce the following

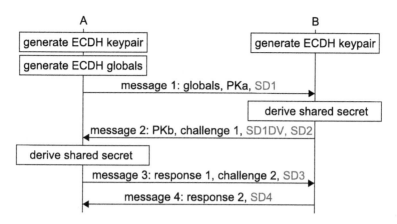

Fig. 1. The ECMQV protocol. Fields in red are added by KEDS. Note that SD1 is necessarily unencrypted.

feature: *cryptographic delegation*. A node may issue a digital certificate designating another (presumably computationally stronger) node as its *cryptographic delegate*. This certificate confers upon the delegate the right to conduct key-agreement transactions on its delegator's behalf, and can be sent to a prospective communication partner at the time it issues a key-agreement request (KEDS message 1).

Delegation clearly leaves the delegator vulnerable to eavesdropping and impersonation attacks: a delegate necessarily possesses all keys it negotiates on its delegate's behalf. A node can therefore issue a *revocation certificate* for a delegate it no longer trusts. This certificate can be transmitted immediately to existing peers, which must, upon its reception, immediately begin negotiating new keys.

Cryptographic delegation has been previously applied in grid computing [17], where X.509 proxy certificates allow users to issue a time-limited permission for jobs to execute on their behalf without requiring explicit authorisation for every run. However, the approach to revocation – that of timed expiry of certificates – assumes globally synchronised clocks, which is not a safe assumption for a network of embedded systems.

3.4   Modifications to ZigBee

The ZigBee Smart Energy Profile already introduces many of the elements in our protocol, chiefly the use of elliptic-curve cryptography to negotiate pairwise keys between nodes. However, security responsibilities are still largely centralised, since link keys are negotiated at the application layer, and only used for certain operations (with many transactions still using the network key), and the Trust Center additionally still exercises control over admissions to the network.

The KEDS architecture requires security responsibilities to be fully distributed. The following modifications are thus necessary to ZigBee to produce a protocol that conformed to it:

1. All current group keying – particularly the network key – are eliminated. A *multicast* key type is added to support TESLA operations.
2. The ECMQV key-agreement protocol introduced by SEP becomes the sole and mandatory key-exchange mechanism, to be used both with neighbouring nodes (during a network-join) and distant nodes (after the network-join is complete).
3. The Trust Center is entirely removed.
4. Of the various frame security levels supported by ZigBee, all except AES-CCM-128 (which is mandatory in IEEE802.15.4) are disallowed.
5. The ZigBee join protocol is deprecated in its entirety. Instead, the KEDS mechanism would be used, using data stapling to transmit network configuration information.
6. The broadcast and multicast mechanisms from Sect. 3.1 are added.

Backwards-Compatibility. As presented, KEDS breaks compatibility with existing ZigBee software. This is deliberate, since the ZigBee security model is incompatible with that of KEDS. However, backwards-compatibility could be implemented in the following way: a KEDS node could act as the ZigBee Trust Center for a network subtree of which it is the root. It would also act as KEDS cryptographic delegate for all devices in that subtree.

ZigBee devices need not join as end-devices; routers are also easily supported. However, only some of the possible branches of the ZigBee join protocol can be allowed: MAC-layer associations would not, only the ZigBee NWK join. Naturally, the KEDS frame security requirements would also necessarily be extended to ZigBee nodes.

4   Implications

In this section, we discuss the implications for the security, performance, and energy consumption of a network based on KEDS, as well as examining ease of administration and development. For this purpose, it is worth remarking on a similarity between smart home and wireless sensor networks: both network types consist largely of embedded devices under similar constraints, permitting discussion of one to be applied easily to the other. We will therefore borrow the rich set of terminology available for the evaluation of wireless sensor networks from an overview of the field by Lee *et al.* [18]. The definitions from that paper that we will be reusing are reproduced in Table 1.

4.1   Security

Much of this paper has been devoted to highlighting security issues, since these are a driving force in the design of KEDS. Much of the security impact of what we have proposed has therefore already been covered.

Table 1. Definitions from Lee et al. [18]

Term	Definition
Confidentiality	Nodes should not reveal any data to unintended recipients
Integrity	Data should not be changed between transmissions due to the environment or malicious activities
Data freshness	Old data should not be used as new (i.e., prevent replay attacks)
Authentication	Data used in decision-making processes must originate from the correct source
Robustness	When some nodes are compromised, the entire network should not also become compromised. The quantitative value with which this requirement should be satisfied depends on the application
Self-organization	Nodes should be independent and flexible enough to be self-organizing (autonomous) and self-healing (failure tolerant)
Availability	The network should not fail frequently
Time synchronization	Collaborative node applications need time synchronization. Time synchronization protocols should not be manipulated to produce inaccurate time
Secure localization	Nodes should be able to accurately and securely acquire location information

Distributing security responsibilities requires security policy decisions to be made and enforced on each device, since there is by design no longer a central decision or enforcement point on the network. The removal of this single point of failure is clearly an improvement in robustness, but also in self-organisation.

Pairwise keying is beneficial from the standpoints of confidentiality, integrity, and authenticity: no node is capable of altering or forging messages, and all messages are confidential to the nodes exchanging them.

The lack of global secrets (or, indeed, global policy) or central control nodes to compromise creates an equivalence between insider and outsider attacks, and makes both difficult.

Network-layer key management has a subtle privacy advantage over the application-layer management favoured in ZigBee: packets need no longer indicate which key they are using (since the source and destination node addresses uniquely determine this). As a result, an observer cannot determine the application to which the packet belongs, eliminating a class of traffic-analysis attack.

4.2   Performance

Evaluation of the performance of a network of embedded devices centers on the consumption of various resources in a limited environment. Most important are CPU time, memory, and energy; it is these three which we consider here.

Pairwise keying has a substantial disadvantage compared to group keying: its memory requirement scales linearly with the size of the network. Put another way, each node must have sufficient key storage to hold one key (plus associated metadata) for each other node with which it will communicate. This memory must also be powered, creating an associated energy overhead.

Each public-key transaction also incurs an energy cost. Since one such transaction must be performed for each pair of communicating devices, the network-wide energy cost of key agreement scales as the square of the size of the network, in the worst case.

Encryption and integrity-protection of every packet also costs resources: both the CPU time of actually performing the cryptographic operations, and the energy required to power it during those operations. Integrity-protection additionally reduces the available application data per packet, potentially requiring more packets to be transmitted, at a cost of yet more energy.

Broadcasts have a particularly high cost. In the naïve protocol, each broadcast packet transmission requires re-encryption by every intervening router, for every peer to which they are to be retransmitted; this costs both processor time, for the large number of cryptographic operations, and energy, for both that processor time and the large number of packet retransmissions. TESLA operations are slightly different: once the protocol has been bootstrapped, each TESLA message requires two packet broadcasts (the first being the message itself, and the second its TESLA key). However, unlike in the naïve case, these broadcasts need not be re-encrypted; the energy cost is almost entirely due to radio transmission. Additionally, the total number of radio transmissions is reduced compared to the naïve protocol, since routers need only retransmit each packet once.

ZigBee already incurs some of these costs: the Smart Energy Profile requires all packets to be encrypted and integrity-protected, and introduces ECC protocols (including ECMQV) to ZigBee networks. TESLA is being considered for use in vehicular networks [19], although was originally designed for wireless sensor networks.

Despite requiring public-key cryptography, use of KEDS has the potential to reduce energy consumption. The ZigBee network join protocol requires 12 round-trips in the worst case. By contrast, a network join using KEDS requires three round-trips, and a security association with another node once joined only two. Additionally, data-stapling can reduce the total number of data packets that need to be transmitted. Finally, the cryptographic delegation mechanism can permit particularly low-powered devices to offload most of their KEDS processing to a more powerful neighbour.

4.3 Operational Overhead

Development for and administration of distributed networks is generally considered more complex and difficult than their centralised counterparts. This is, however, not always the case. In particular, the cryptographically-strong node identities afforded by public-key cryptography permit both developers and administrators to reason about the identities of those nodes with a high degree of confidence: unlike MAC addresses, private keys cannot be forged or spoofed (although they can be stolen). Additionally, nodes can be deployed without pre-loading of symmetric keys, since those keys can be safely sent over the network.

The combination of KEDS and a single security mode vastly simplifies development and deployment. Mismatches between supported cipher suites can no longer occur, and the KEDS network join protocol is vastly simpler than that of ZigBee. Application programmers are no longer required to manage cryptographic keys, since this responsibility is delegated to the network layer; they need only implement their application's access-control policy.

The removal of the Trust Center eliminates the central registry of devices it would otherwise maintain. This may actually be a benefit: the currency of such a registry must be enforced at network join points, which in the case of ZigBee are at every router. This requires all routers to be trusted; the elimination of the registry thus also eliminates this requirement.

Finally, the cryptographic delegation feature has a more subtle advantage: on a multi-stakeholder network, it indicates strongly that the delegating node trusts the target node, and thus that the stakeholders involved trust each other in a similar way. This can be used as a form of vouching [20].

5   A Note on the Smart Grid

Much of the work in this paper has been devoted to removing the need for trusted third-parties in order to bootstrap security. However, on the smart grid, contact with devices of unknown provenance or type are expected to be commonplace. There must be some way, therefore, for two nodes to be able to assert their hardware capabilities to each other in a trustworthy manner. As a result, we expect that there will be some kind of certification of device characteristics, either by national or supranational regulatory authorities, industry bodies, or agreements between stakeholders.

Note that while these entities are trusted third-parties, they are of a different kind to the ones hitherto discussed. The protections that we introduce to the network environment defend against device-impersonation and man-in-the-middle attacks launched from active participants on the network. The certification required in the smart grid case, and the credentials digitally expressing that certification, do not come from such active participants, but from external entities, and the range of attacks they can launch is different: their certificates can make arbitrary assertions about the *capabilities* and *properties* of a device, but no more (and in particular, they cannot impersonate a device, nor compromise the secure channels to which it is party).

5.1   An Illustrative Example

To make these ideas concrete, let us consider an example home automation network. In this example, we will make the following simplifying assumptions:

– Each device belongs to a single stakeholder. This allows us to neglect issues of operating system security, which would otherwise be relevant towards isolating colocated stakeholders from each other.
– The home is free-standing (that is, not a flat or apartment). This eliminates the building administrator as a potential stakeholder, as well as possible interactions between flats in the same building.
– Its owner is its sole resident. This eliminates other residents as potential competing stakeholders.

It is important to note that the cases eliminated from this example are *not* outside the scope of our protocol; they are simply excluded from this example for the purpose of clarity.

Our example network will consist of the following devices: (see Fig. 2)

An Internet router/gateway device (IGD): a mains-powered device which connects the automation network to the Internet.
Smartphone: a battery-powered device with a powerful CPU and a rich user interface.
Electricity meter: a mains-powered device with some processing power, but little or no user interface. It reports power usage to the electricity provider, via a dedicated connection to the grid's backhaul.
Water meter: a battery-powered device with a low-power CPU and little or no user interface. It reports water usage to the water provider over the Internet, via the IGD.
Gas meter: a battery-powered device with a low-power CPU and little or no user interface. It reports gas usage to the gas provider over the Internet, via the IGD.
Hot water tank: a mains-powered device which attempts to heat water when electricity prices are lowest. The electricity provider can toggle this device for demand-shedding purposes.
Washing machine: a mains-powered device which reports maintenance data to its manufacturer, attempts to heat water when prices are low, without delaying the washing too long. The electricity provider can toggle this device for demand-shedding purposes, but only during certain phases of cycle, and only for so long.
Heating system: a mains-powered device whose main energy source is burning gas. It runs on a schedule, though can be toggled by the electricity provider for demand-shedding purposes, provided the house stays close to the set temperature.
Lights and light switches throughout the house: all mains-powered, but with low-power CPUs and no user interface.

Table 2 shows the stakeholder considered to 'own' each device, as well as notes on other stakeholders with an interest in its function. Where a stakeholder can control a device it does not own, it is assumed to do so via one that it does – so, for example, commands from the electricity provider to toggle the hot water tank or washing machine should originate from the electricity meter.

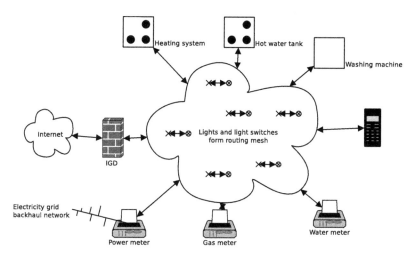

Fig. 2. Our example home network.

The homeowner is a partial exception: she is the only stakeholder with a human presence in the home. She can thus operate devices via their physical control panels as well as via her smartphone. She is also capable of bringing devices temporarily into close physical proximity to one another (for example, tapping her smartphone on an NFC pad on the hot water tank), which may be necessary for some authentication/KEDS sequences.

Security associations between devices are relatively clear: lights and light switches must be paired with each other; the hot water tank, heating system, and washing machine must be paired with the electricity meter; and the water meter, gas meter, and washing machine must be paired with the IGD. Some or all of these devices may also be paired with the smartphone, depending on the status information they expose to the user.

Each such pairing requires different information to be supplied, during the KEDS exchange, to authenticate the channel. Pairings involving the electricity meter might require it to present some certificate asserting its presence at and control over the relevant address or electrical connection point (if there are several electrical providers acting at the same address). That between the heating system and the electricity provider might require some similar certificate from the systems manufacturer, asserting that it can actually respond to load-shedding commands and indicating the maximum load that can be shed. The connection between the heating system and smartphone might not need any certificates at all, instead relying on some assertion of physical proximity (such as an NFC pad) to pair. The smartphone could then even issue a certificate vouching for the physical presence of that heating system in the home during some other KEDS transaction (such as the aforementioned between heating and power meter).

Table 2. 'Stakeholder map' of our example network.

Device	Owner	Notes
IGD	Homeowner	
Smartphone	Homeowner	
Electricity meter	Electrical provider	
Water meter	Water provider	
Gas meter	Gas provider	
Hot water tank	Homeowner	
Washing machine	Manufacturer	Operated by homeowner, partial control by electricity provider
Home heating system	Homeowner	Partial control by electricity provider
Lights	Manufacturers	Operated by homeowner
Light switches	Manufacturers	Operated by homeowner

Security associations also allow for find-grained access control: the IGD could be configured to only allow the washing machine, water meter, and gas meter access to the Internet, refusing any KEDS association requests from other devices. Equally importantly, the confidentiality and integrity requirements on all communications mean that irrespective of the path through the mesh that any given message takes, its contents remain both secret and unalterable, either by a malicious or faulty device.

6   Conclusions and Future Work

We have presented a novel network architecture for multi-stakeholder networks. This architecture distributes security responsibilities among the nodes that make up the network, rendering insider attacks as difficult as attacks by outsiders by eliminating trusted third-parties on the network. We have also discussed how we expect this architecture to be implemented by modifying ZigBee, an emerging industry standard in smart grid networks. This discussion included the implications of such a network from the perspectives of security and performance, with some additional discussion on administrative and development complexity. This discussion ended with some comments specific to the smart grid, including an example application to the smart home; one comment is that trusted third-parties may still be necessary, but only in order to lend weight to devices' assertions of their hardware capabilities.

Our next step will be to implement the proposed protocol, and perform real-world power, resource-consumption, and throughput measurements, to support the predictions made in this paper.

References

1. Paverd, A.: Trustworthy remote entities in the smart grid. In: Proceedings of the ACM Symposium On Applied Computing (SAC) Student Research Competition, pp. 9–10 (2013)
2. National Institute of Standards and Technology (NIST). NIST special publication 1108R2: NIST framework and roadmap for smart grid interoperability standards, release 2.0. Technical report (2012)
3. IEEE: Standard for Local and metropolitan area networks, Part 11: Wireless LAN Medium Access Control (MAC) and Physical Layer (PHY) Specifications. IEEE Std 802.11-2012
4. Alliance, Z.: ZigBee Specification (2008)
5. Gregori, E., Improta, A., Lenzini, L., Rossi, L., Sani, L.: BGP and inter-AS economic relationships. In: Domingo-Pascual, J., Manzoni, P., Palazzo, S., Pont, A., Scoglio, C. (eds.) NETWORKING 2011, Part II. LNCS, vol. 6641, pp. 54–67. Springer, Heidelberg (2011)
6. Butler, K., Farley, T., McDaniel, P., Rexford, J.: A survey of BGP security issues and solutions. Proc. IEEE 98(1), 100–122 (2010)
7. Gohari, A.A., Pakbaz, R., Melliar-Smith, P.M., Moser, L.E., Rodoplu, V.: RMR: reliability map routing for tactical mobile ad hoc networks. IEEE J. Sel. Areas Commun. 29(10), 1935–1947 (2011)
8. Gibson, T.: An architecture for flexible multi-security domain networks. In: Proceedings of the Network and Distributed Systems Security Symposium, San Diego, February 2001
9. Schumacher, H.J.J., Ghosh, S., Lee, T.S.: Top secret traffic and the public ATM network infrastructure. Inf. Syst. Secur. 7(4), 27–45 (1999)
10. Mason, A.R.: Exploring of wireless technology to provide information sharing among military, United Nations and civilian organizations during complex humanitarian emergencies and peacekeeping operations. Master's thesis, Naval Postgraduate School, March 2003
11. Hughes, B., Sharpe, T.: NATO Tacoms. In: MILCOM, IEEE, pp. 1–7 (2006)
12. Wentz, L.: An ICT primer: Information and communication technologies for civil-military coordination in disaster relief and stabilization and reconstruction. Technical report, National Defense University Center for Technology and National Security Policy, Washington, DC, USA (2006)
13. IEEE: Standard for Local and metropolitan area networks, Part 15.4: Low-Rate Wireless Personal Area Networks. IEEE Std 802.15.4-2011
14. Alliance, Z.: ZigBee Smart Energy Profile Specification (2011)
15. Gupta, V., Millard, M., Fung, S., Gura, N., Eberle, H.: Sizzle: a standards-based end-to-end security architecture for the embedded Internet. In: IEEE International Conference on Pervasive Computing and Communications, pp. 247–256 (2005)
16. Perrig, A., Song, D., Canetti, R., Tygar, J.D., Briscoe, B.: Timed Efficient Stream Loss-Tolerant Authentication (TESLA): Multicast Source Authentication Transform Introduction. RFC 4082 (Informational), June 2005
17. Welch, V., Foster, I., Kesselman, C., Mulmo, O., Pearlman, L., Gawor, J., Meder, S., Siebenlist, F.: X.509 proxy certificates for dynamic delegation. In: Proceedings of the 3rd Annual PKI R&D Workshop (2004)

18. Lee, J., Leung, V., Wong, K., Chan, H.: Key management issues in wireless sensor networks: current proposals and future developments. IEEE Wirel. Commun. Mag. **14**(5), 76–84 (2007)
19. Hartenstein, H., Laberteaux, K.: A tutorial survey on vehicular ad hoc networks. IEEE Commun. Mag. **46**(6), 164–171 (2008)
20. Li, F., Mittal, P., Caesar, M., Borisov, N.: SybilControl. In: Proceedings of the 7th ACM Workshop on Scalable Trusted Computing, pp. 67–78, October 2012

Redactable Signatures to Control the Maximum Noise for Differential Privacy in the Smart Grid

Henrich C. Pöhls[1][(✉)] and Markus Karwe[2]

[1] Chair of IT-Security, University of Passau, Passau, Germany
hp@sec.uni-passau.de
[2] Institut für Informatik und Gesellschaft, Universität Freiburg, Freiburg, Germany
karwe@iig.uni-freiburg.de

Abstract. The Smart Grid is currently developed and fundamental security requirements like integrity and origin authentication need to be addressed while minimizing arising privacy issues. This paper balances two opposing goals: On the one hand, we mitigate privacy issues raised by overly precise energy consumption values via data perturbation mechanisms, e.g., add noise. On the other hand we limit the noise's range and keep a verifiable level of integrity of consumption values from the Smart Metering Gateway by using a redactable signature. We propose to use the value obtained by calculating the worst case guarantee of differential privacy as a metric to compare and judge a Smart Grid application's privacy invasiveness.

Keywords: Smart grid · Differential privacy · Redactable signature schemes

1 Introduction

The transition from nuclear to renewable energy is still in progress and brings stakeholders the burden to improve the overall energy management in order to keep net stability as well as reasonable prices [10, 30]. The Smart Grid (SG) is still in the development phase and can be seen as information overlay network for the traditional energy grid which enables stakeholders to improve the management. While the outlook for SG seems very promising it introduces new challenges like privacy for residential customers.

Corner stones of the SG are the Smart Meter (SM) and the Smart Meter Gateway (SMGW) as depicted in Fig. 3. Note that both devices are trusted and installed by a SG stakeholder, i.e., the power grid provider. A SM sends energy consumption values via the SMGW to a collecting SG stakeholder. Further note, we always assume that the SM produces accurate and timely readings. This allows

The research leading to these results has received funding from the European Union's Seventh Framework Programme (FP7/2007–2013) under grant agreement n° 609094.

The research leading to these results has received funding from the European Union's Seventh Framework Programme (FP7-SMARTCITIES-2013) under grant agreement n° 608712.

J. Cuellar (Ed.): SmartGridSec 2014, LNCS 8448, pp. 79–93, 2014.
DOI: 10.1007/978-3-319-10329-7_6

the stakeholder to get a fine resolution picture of the energy consumption at customer's premises, which can be used for purposes like demand forecasting or creating energy profiles [30]. To counter act malicious tampering, both SM and SMGW protect the integrity and authenticity of the transmitted data. All communication between the SM within a household and the SMGW is secured for wired as well as for wireless connections. Classical digital signatures offer such a protection: they allow detecting any change that occurred after the signature's generation. Cryptographically, a digital signature scheme is said to be *unforgeable*, e.g., RSA-PSS [4]. Hence, data requested by SG stakeholders is encrypted and signed by the SMGW before being sent [12].

Having tampering solved by digital signatures, one problem remains: The fine grained values impose a privacy threat to the residential customer. Several works show that too fine-grained energy values allow detecting appliances within the household [23], detecting the use mode of the appliances [11] as well as deducting the residential customers' behaviour [20]. To mitigate those threats current research and governmental organizations suggest using Privacy Enhancing Technologies (PET). For example, the German "Bundesamt für Sicherheit in der Informationstechnik (BSI)" is using pseudonymization as a privacy protecting mechanism [12]. In [17] it has been shown that de-pseudonymization is feasible in the Smart Grid and pseudonymization is vulnerable to linkage attacks. However, pseudonymization is only one tool from the PET toolbox. PET is rather a holistic concept than one technical solution. One main principle of PET is to reduce the amount of information to a minimum required for a specific application, i.e., data minimization. Another PET tool is the reduction of the data's accuracy or timeliness. However, the application of such a PET would result that in one way or another the data needs to be modified for privacy preserving reasons by a party other than the SM or the SMGW.

1.1   Problem #1: Balancing Data Utility (incl. Integrity and Authenticity) and Privacy

We see one problem in the opposing goals: On the one side the SG stakeholder needs access to integrity protected values gathered by a trusted untampered SM. On the other side consumer requires some trusted privacy component to perform data perturbation to protect the consumer's privacy. The main point we would like to raise is that the entity trusted to generate data is controlled and trusted by the SG stakeholder. With its goals and incentives to gather fine-grained data, this entity is untrusted to maintain the consumer's privacy. Vice versa, the SG stakeholder will not be able to rely on data gathered by an untrusted consumer-controlled device. Figure 1 depicts this situation.

1.2   Problem #2: Judging and Comparing Privacy Invasiveness

There is no debate that certain applications of the smart grid will need more data than others. At the moment exact nature of such future smart grid applications is unsure, so is the required data utility. This paper remains open towards future

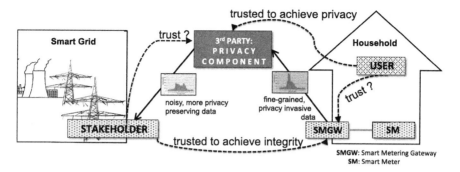

Fig. 1. Trust towards components by SG stakeholders and privacy-aware household

SG applications' need for data utility and future individual consumers' privacy-tolerances. However, we envision the need for a metric to compare and by this also judge the privacy-invasiveness of different applications. We believe that with an informed choice the user's willingness to participate in SG-applications will increase and that SG-applications will hence respect consumer's privacy preferences. Figure 2 shows that participation in applications are possible, if they require a data quality that is below the consumer's privacy preference. Privacy preserving mechanisms or unwillingness to participate limit the maximum data utility.

1.3   Contribution

This paper describes a technology that allows balancing the conflicting interests of privacy and integrity[1]. We follow an approach called data perturbation, which is widely used in the field of privacy preserving data mining and differential

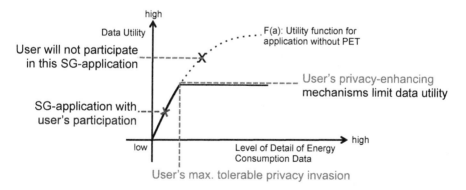

Fig. 2. Data-utility might be hindered by PET, but consumers will participate in applications within consumer's privacy preferences

---

[1] which here includes accuracy.

privacy [9]. Data perturbation based mechanisms preserve privacy of distinct customers by letting an entity tamper with the data. We will call this entity the *privacy gateway* (PGW). The downsides of data perturbation are twofold: First it obviously must result in a reduced data utility and second the data tampering entity must be trusted. The first is an inherent problem of PET whereas the impact on utility needs to be limited to a level where the application is still executable. We counter the latter by applying a redactable signature instead of a classical digital signature at the SMGW.

The contribution of this paper is to provide a differential privacy guarantee in the BSI Smart Metering Setting (see Fig. 4) and to control the amount of integrity violations needed to achieve the privacy: We achieve control, integrity protection and origin authentication for the SG stakeholder by letting the SMGW sign a *range of values* around actual energy consumption using a redactable signature scheme ($\mathcal{RSS}$). The residential customer's *privacy gateway* (PGW) still has the possibility 'tamper' with the data to increase privacy by choosing *one value* out of the signed range.

We gain all the advantages of data perturbation combined with those of redactable signatures:

(1) data perturbation still allowing the stakeholders to address customers individually allowing for applications like providing energy efficiency recommendations;

(2) data perturbation gives an ad omnia privacy guarantee of differential privacy with a small computational overhead;

(3) redactable signatures allow the verifier to gain reassurance that the SMGW actually signed this value. Hence, the signer limits allowed values according to maximum tolerable reduction of data utility;

(4) redactable signatures allow third parties to do the choosing without any interaction with the signer, hence the customer does not need to trust a third party like a Smart Metering Operator (SMO) or the Smart Metering Gateway Administrator to protect her privacy.

2   System Description and Integrity Requirements

The BSI proposed a technical guideline [12] for intelligent metering systems. While this technical guideline is controversial discussed in literature due to its broad as well as expensive security and its slim privacy concept [28], it allows for a controlled data communication between a household and SG stakeholders. The concept is depicted in Fig. 3.

SMGW checks whether a requesting stakeholder like a Distribution System Operator (DSO) or a Demand Side Manager (DSM) are allowed to access values like energy consumption or to send commands to the Controllable Local Systems (CLS). SMGW communicates via the residential Home Area Network (HAN) with CLS. In Addition the SMGW provides over the HAN data for the end consumer as well as the service technician. Within the Local Metrological Network (LMN) SMs for electricity, heat, gas and water are installed. SMs communicate consumption values to SMGW via the LMN.

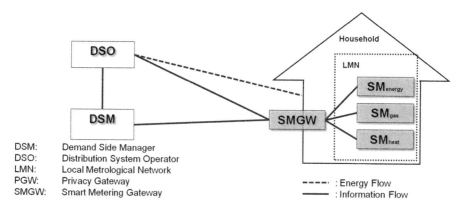

Fig. 3. BSI system structure

Stakeholders like the DSO can ask the SMGW to get consumption data. The time interval between the gathering may vary but in the UK a collection rate once every 15 min is discussed and considered to be sufficient to guarantee net stability. Even finer grained consumption values are advantageous for forecasting.

3 Privacy Threats

Service providers in the SG like DSO or DSM need to collect data from individual households for their services. This data allows to infer information about households. The general research focus for privacy incursion has been about energy consumption values which are considered the household's output channel. Note that research barely considers the other direction, the input channel to the household. Inferred information of energy consumption values can be structured in the following three categories: First, appliance detection, second, use mode detection, and third, behavior detection. Note that all these attacks are possible for any party that has access to the plain data. Hence, encryption will help to protect the confidentiality during transmission of data, i.e., achieve privacy against third-parties, but will not mitigate privacy attacks by the party finally receiving and decrypting the plain data.

In the first category an analyzer tries to find out which appliances run in a household site. This information can be used for advertising purposes. In the second category an analyzer tries to find out how those devices are used. Experiments with high frequency data shows that even the TV channel can be deduced with a high percentage rate [15]. In the third category data is used to investigate how many people live in a household and what those people do. In [20] wake and sleep cycles as well as presence and absence have been deduced.

The information transmitted over the channel from SG service providers to the household bears privacy risks which depend on the application. Demand Response (DR) application allow to infer incentive sensitivity as well as a customer's preferences. In a simple version of DR the DSM ask the customer to reduce the amount of consumed energy in a certain time frame. In return the customer gets a financial compensation. To measure the compensation amount the DSM needs to know the energy consumption of this time as well as data to compare in order to determine the real reduction. This data can be the consumption from former periods. With this data and to know when the customer accepts and executes DR requests, the DSM can infer incentive sensitivity information of the customer.

To mitigate privacy threats appliance and use mode detection as well as behaviour deduction, several privacy enhancing technologies have been introduced. PET are based upon the principle of data minimization and concealing. The main drawback of those techniques are that either customers can not be addressed individually or that fine granular data is not available.

4 Differential Privacy: Perturbation to Protect Privacy

A different approach than data minimization and concealing is the addition of noise to consumption data. While the outlook from the standpoint of privacy protection is very promising, the effect of the introduced error to data utility in SG is still in research. Data perturbation done in a right way, allows to reach the differential privacy ad omnia guarantee. The data perturbation is in general defined as the function $k()$. The following definitions are from [9].

Definition 1 (ϵ-differential privacy). *Be k a sanitizing algorithm, D_1 and D_2 two Databases which differ in at most one element, ϵ a privacy parameter which can be chosen and $S \subseteq Range(k)$.*

$$\frac{Pr(k(D_1) \in S)}{Pr(k(D_2) \in S)} \leq e^\epsilon$$

We use differential privacy as the basis for our metric. Especially, we use the calculation for the guarantee that if a single data record joins a dataset, the worst information leakage is e^ϵ. This rigid notion can be reached with limited computational overhead.

As an instantiation of using k to achieve privacy consider a DSO asking SMGW for current consumption data. The SMGW is retrieving this information and uses a function k, that adds noise taken from a Laplace distribution.

Definition 2 (Sanitizing Mechanism k). *The Sanitizing Mechanism k is :* $k(D) = f(D) + \mathfrak{L}(\frac{\Delta(f)}{\epsilon})$. *The mechanism is ϵ-differential private for all functions $f : D \rightarrow R^x$, where $\mathfrak{L}(\frac{\Delta(f)}{\epsilon})$ denotes the noise which is taken from the Laplace distribution, $\Delta f = max||f(D_1) - f(D_2)||$ and where D_1, D_2 differ in exactly one single dataset.*

Addition of noise as well as function f performed over the data base are done by a trusted entity, known as curator. In the SM case, the database needs to hold stored consumption values for specific points in time.

5 Redactable Signatures ($\mathcal{RSS}$): Fine Control of Integrity

Assume the message to be signed is a set which contains ℓ values as elements: $\mathcal{M} = \{m_1, \ldots, m_\ell\}$. This paper uses a set-like notation without loss of generality.[2] The fundamental difference to classic signatures is that a $\mathcal{RSS}$ allows anyone to *redact* an element from the signed list, such that the signature still verifies. Basically, a redacted list no longer contains all elements from $\mathcal{M}$. Assume $\mathcal{R} \subseteq \mathcal{M}$, than removing elements in $\mathcal{R}$ from $\mathcal{M}$ leaves a subset $\mathcal{M}' = \mathcal{M} \backslash \mathcal{R}$. The most important differentiator between a classical signature is that a redactable signature scheme allows deriving an adapted signature σ', which still verifies. This action is called *redaction* and can be performed by anyone; the secret signing key is not required. Hence the original signer is not involved. However, a secure $\mathcal{RSS}$ is unforgeable comparable to classic digital signature schemes; this ensures that each element $m_i \in \mathcal{M}$ is protected against modifications other than complete removal. To continue the example, assume you redact all the other $\ell - 1$ elements, leaving only one value m_i in the signed set: $\mathcal{M}' = \{m_i\}$. Due to the $\mathcal{RSS}$ you can adjust the signature to σ'. A positive consecutive verification of the signature σ' over $\mathcal{M}'$ means that all elements in $\mathcal{M}'$ are authentic. In other words without use of the secret signing key you can produce a valid signature for remaining unchanged elements. Hence m_i that remained in $\mathcal{M}'$ can be verified to having not been altered and originating from the original signer, which remains identifiable via its public key.

Algorithmic Description of $\mathcal{RSS}$. The following notation is derived from [25], which is based of Brzuska et al. [5].

Definition 3 (Redactable Signature Schemes). *An $\mathcal{RSS}$ consists of four efficient algorithms* $\mathcal{RSS} := (\mathsf{KeyGen}, \mathsf{Sign}, \mathsf{Verify}, \mathsf{Redact})$:

KeyGen. *The algorithm* KeyGen *outputs the public key* pk *and private key* sk *of the signer, where* λ *denotes the security parameter:*
$$(\mathrm{pk}, \mathrm{sk}) \leftarrow \mathsf{KeyGen}(1^\lambda)$$

Sign. *The algorithm* Sign *gets as input the secret key* sk *and the message* $\mathcal{M} = \{m_1, \ldots, m_\ell\}$, $m_i \in \{0,1\}^*$: $(\mathcal{M}, \sigma) \leftarrow \mathsf{Sign}(1^\lambda, \mathrm{sk}, \mathcal{M})$

Verify. *The algorithm* Verify *outputs a decision* $d \in \{\mathtt{true}, \mathtt{false}\}$, *indicating the validity of the signature* σ, *w.r.t.* pk, *protecting* $\mathcal{M} = \{m_1, \ldots, m_\ell\}$, $m_i \in \{0,1\}^*$: $d \leftarrow \mathsf{Verify}(1^\lambda, \mathrm{pk}, \mathcal{M}, \sigma)$

Redact. *The algorithm* Redact *takes as input the message* $\mathcal{M} = \{m_1, \ldots, m_\ell\}$, $m_i \in \{0,1\}^*$, *the public key* pk *of the signer, a valid signature* σ *and a set of elements* $\mathcal{R}$ *to be redacted. It returns a modified message* $\mathcal{M}' \leftarrow \mathcal{M} \backslash \mathcal{R}$ *(or* $\perp$, *indicating an error):* $(\mathcal{M}', \sigma') \leftarrow \mathsf{Redact}(1^\lambda, \mathrm{pk}, \mathcal{M}, \sigma, \mathcal{R})$

---

[2] Set-like notation eases understanding of the decomposition of a message as mathematical notions like intersection and union become applicable.

We require the correctness properties for $\mathcal{RSS}$s to hold: Hence, every genuinely signed or redacted message will verify. A formal definition is given in [5].

Security of $\mathcal{RSS}$. This section describes the required security properties and models on an informal level, the formal properties are described and proven in [5, 6, 14, 25]. A secure $\mathcal{RSS}$ must be unforgeable and private to be meaningful [5]. Unforgeability allows detecting Integrity violations, e.g., only the genuine signed message or a valid redaction thereof can bear a valid signature created by the owner of the secret signing key. A public verification key linked to a known entity and an unforgeable signature allows authentication of origin.

Unforgeability. No one should be able to compute a valid signature on a message not previously issued without having access to any private keys [5].

This is analogous to the unforgeability requirement for standard signatures [13], except excluding all valid redactions from the set of forgeries. The attacker can generate genuinely signed messages using an oracle, but has no access to the secret key. He has breached unforgeability if and only if he is able to compute a signature on a 'fresh' message, which is valid under the corresponding public verification key fixed at the beginning. A message is considered 'fresh' if it either has not previously queried from the oracle and if it can not have been created by one or more redaction(s) from a message queried from the oracle.

Privacy (weakly and a strongly). A *private* $\mathcal{RSS}$ prevents everyone except the signer from recovering any information (esp. the original value) about elements redacted, given the redacted $\mathcal{M}'$ and a valid signature σ' over $\mathcal{M}'$.

Note that information leakage through the modified message itself is out of scope. A weakly private $\mathcal{RSS}$ allows a third party to derive that elements have been redacted without gathering more information about their contents. Assume that each redacted element's value being replaced with $\square$ remains a visible element of $\mathcal{M}'$ [16]. The definition of a strongly private $\mathcal{RSS}$ is very similar, but redacted elements are considered *not* being visible as elements of $\mathcal{M}'$.

6   Solution: Signing a Range of Values with an $\mathcal{RSS}$

Solution Towards Problem #1. We allow the SMGW to provide the Smart Grid stakeholders like DSO and DSM with signed and henceforth trustable SM values, e.g., energy consumption values. At the same time, we allow the customer to achieve a desired level of privacy, by allowing the energy consumption value to be tampered with, e.g., adding noise. The party running PETs to achieve the consumer's privacy is termed Privacy Gateway (PGW). Our solution is depicted in Fig. 4. We assume that all information between the SMGW and the DSO and the DSM are running over the curator termed 'Privacy Gateway' (PGW).

Note that it is the SG stakeholder who knows and requests a desired level of data utility. This means in case of perturbation by noise to limit the maximum allowed noise. Of course, the SMGW could run privacy preserving algorithms

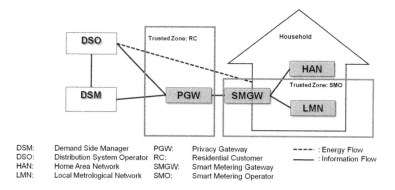

Fig. 4. System structure with PGW

directly and add noise to keep the customer's differential privacy. However this solution would require that the residential customer trusts the SM operator (SMO) to protect her privacy. The same problems occurs if the PGW is placed before the SMGW and would directly tamper with the readings from the SM. However, our solution allows the party doing the addition of noise to be trusted to preserve the customer's privacy, as the customer remains in full control. The task of the PGW is to tamper energy consumption values in order to protect the privacy of residential customers. The task of the SMGW is to sign the energy consumption values and the maximum tolerable perturbation in order to protect the integrity and trustworthiness of the SM readings. Both parties act on behalf of different stakeholders and hence are in different trust zone. Our solution uses redactable signatures to solves this conflict.

Solution Towards Problem #2. For brevity, we will now focus only on the transmission of a consumption value, other information that the SMGW sends alongside, like timestamps, are not considered.

The SMGW must make sure that values are not tampered in an unauthorized malicious way. Depending on the application DSO and DSM can tolerate a certain level of inaccuracy, e.g., allow that a certain amount of noise degrades their data utility. We denote the maximum amount of noise that can be added to an accurate reading by δ_{max}. Assuming SM measures the actual consumption value v DSO/DSM will accept any reading in the range $[v - \delta_{max}, v + \delta_{max}]$ as valid. If the SMGW applies a classical signature scheme on v PGW can not tamper with data signed by SMGW without invalidating the signature. An invalid signature would indicate towards the DSO/DSM that the received value is not trustworthy, as it could have been maliciously tampered with in an arbitrary way. Henceforth, we assume that the SMGW will be instructed by the SMGW's operator about the tolerable noise, on behalf of the SG stakeholder. The tolerable noise depends on the required accuracy level for SG stakeholder's application. The actual values depend on the DSO or DSM application needs.

Note that fixing $\Delta = 2\delta_{max}$ in Definition 1 allows calculating the maximum differential privacy that can be achieved. The PGW must be instructed by the consumer which level of privacy is tolerable for which optional applications. In this paper we assume that the consumer is free to not participate in an application for which his own personal privacy preference can not be achieved, i.e., PGW will not sent privacy-invasive data to a requesting SG stakeholder. However, we are fully aware that some communication must always be allowed for mandatory applications, e.g., net stability. For those mission critical mandatory SG applications we assume that the tolerable perturbation should be fixed by regulators.

6.1 Protocol Description

We propose the following phases: Setup, Signing, Adding Noise and Verification.

Setup:
1. Let $\mathcal{RSS} := (\mathsf{KeyGen}, \mathsf{Sign}, \mathsf{Verify}, \mathsf{Redact})$ be a secure (unforgeable and weakly private) redactable signature scheme.
2. After running KeyGen distribute the keys: SMGW gets a secret signing key sk and verification key vk, PGW and DSO/DSM get just the public SMGW's verification key vk.
3. SMGW is instructed by SMO which amount of noise it tolerates, and which accuracy is required.

Signing:
1. On receiving the actual consumption value v the SMGW calculates a range of discrete noisy values $\mathcal{M} = \{v - \delta_{max}, \ldots, v, \ldots, v + \delta_{max}\}$.
2. SGM signs $\mathcal{M}$ with an $\mathcal{RSS}$: $(\mathcal{M}, \sigma) \leftarrow \mathsf{Sign}(1^\lambda, sk, \mathcal{M})$.
3. SMGW sends $(\mathcal{M}, \sigma)$ to PGW.

Adding Noise:
1. On receiving $(\mathcal{M}, \sigma)$ PGW uses its database of historic values and the actual consumption value, which must be at the center of the range in $\mathcal{M}$, PGW runs the differential privacy algorithms to identify the value n in $\mathcal{M}$ which should be sent to DSO/DSM in order to satisfy $\frac{Pr(k(D_1) \in S)}{Pr(k(D_2) \in S)} \leq e^\epsilon$ where ϵ is a user predefined minimum required privacy parameter. The application execution is denied, if ϵ can not be reached.
2. PGW calculates $\mathcal{R} = \mathcal{M} \backslash n$.
3. PGW obtains a signature on $\mathcal{M}' = n$: $(\mathcal{M}', \sigma') \leftarrow \mathsf{Redact}(1^\lambda, pk, \mathcal{M}, \sigma, \mathcal{R})$.
4. PGW sends $(\{n\}, \sigma')$ to the DSO/DSM.

Verification:
1. On receiving $(\{n\}, \sigma')$, DSO/DSM uses the SMGW's verification key vk to verify if the signature on n is valid.

The amount of elements in $\mathcal{M}$ depends on the maximum noise and the accuracy, as $\mathcal{M}$ must contain concrete values, e.g., $\mathcal{M} = \{0.99, 1.00, 1.01, 1.02, 1.03, \ldots, 1.48, 1.49, 1.50, \ldots, 1.96, 1.97, 1.98, 1.99\}$ for an accuracy of two decimals, $\delta_{max} = 0.50$ and $v = 1.49$. The $\mathcal{RSS}$ limits the PGW only to redactions based on provided values, e.g., for $\mathcal{M} = \{1.11\}$. The PGW could generate a valid signature facilitating the algorithm Redact. However, the PGW can not generate valid signatures on values outside the range, e.g., $\mathcal{M} = \{0.98\}$ or $\mathcal{M} = \{2.00\}$. To do so would be as hard as forging the signature scheme of the $\mathcal{RSS}$, e.g., breaking the signature scheme like RSA-PSS [4,24]. To counter replaying or repressing messages, the SMGW can just add a timestamp as an additional element into $\mathcal{M}$ requiring this to be fresh and present during verification.

6.2 Security and Privacy Properties

We assume: SM is trusted to perform correct readings, can not be attacked, and transmits the reading securely to SMGW.

Theorem 1. *Our protocol is unforgeable, if the $\mathcal{RSS}$ is unforgeable.*

SG stakeholders can detect any subsequent malicious manipulation of information while it is travelling through the network. Additionally they can use the SMGW's verification key to identify the origin of noisy data.

Theorem 2. *Our protocol achieves the highest differential privacy possible for $\Delta = 2\delta_{max}$, if the $\mathcal{RSS}$ is at least weakly private.*

Proof Intuition for Theorem 1. If the $\mathcal{RSS}$ applied by the SMGW is unforgeable, than neither PGW nor attackers can forge a valid signature on a value $n^* \notin \mathcal{M}_i$, where $\mathcal{M}_i$ denotes all sets signed and sent by the SMGW. Any such forgery would be a forgery in the $\mathcal{RSS}$.

Proof Intuition for Theorem 2. Assume all communication from SMGW will always pass through PGW, see Fig. 4. The $\mathcal{RSS}$ allows PGW to be a separate entity acting as instructed by the residential customer. PGW is limited by the range defined within the SMGW's signature but can run the algorithm Redact to select any suitable value out of the range. So seeing a valid $(\mathcal{M}, \sigma)$, which verifies using Verify under the trusted public verification key of a SMGW, that no malicious modification has taken place. Privacy of the underlying $\mathcal{RSS}$ guarantees that attackers can not identify the actual value of removed elements. Hence attackers can not know the actual consumption. We distinguish two cases:
(1) If the $\mathcal{RSS}$ is strongly private, i.e., elements are completely removed during redaction, then the attacker sees a set $\mathcal{M}$ with exactly one element, i.e., $|\mathcal{M}| = 1$.
(2) If $\mathcal{RSS}$ is weakly private, i.e., original values are hidden behind a special symbol ($\square^r$), then the attacker sees a set $\mathcal{M}$ with exactly one element being an actual value and $2\delta_{max}$ symbols, i.e., $|\mathcal{M}| = 2\delta_{max} + 1$.
Hence, if $\mathcal{RSS}$ is weakly private attackers can infer δ_{max}. However, attackers do never learn the actual values of removed elements, nor their position because its a set. Using the differential privacy mechanism described in Sect. 4, PGW adds noise within the range guaranteeing a differential privacy of ϵ.

7   Related Work

Techniques like group signatures [18] are based on the idea to hide the identity of household within a group. This prevents to address customers individually and thus limits potential SG applications to provide energy efficiency recommendations [2]. Another approach applies modifications inside the customers power circuit, e.g., consuming additional or less power from the grid by using a re-chargeable battery [3]. The downside of this approach are sever costs of the battery purchase as well as the maintenance effort. Those types are not optimal, due to the loss of addressing customers individually or the very high costs.

The concept of $\mathcal{RSS}$ was introduced by *Steinfeld* et al. [27] as "content extraction signatures" and almost at the same time by *Johnson* et al. as "homomorphic signatures" [19]. From their initial work many RSS constructions emerged in the last years [8, 21, 22]. Extensions working on more complex structures, e.g., trees [5], have been proposed, but a set is enough for the solution discussed in this paper. In [5] *Brzuska* et al. presented a formal security model. Note that according to this model many schemes are not secure, as they do not fulfil their notion of *Privacy* [5, 25]. Also note, that many schemes proposed are also only weakly private, i.e., one can see that a third party redacted something [16, 19, 22, 27, 29]. This generally gives more information to an outsider as already noted in [21]. In this paper we will not require transparency, thus we leak the range of noise, but the actual values of redacted elements stay private.

Several works try to identify which privacy relevant information can be inferred by analyzing energy consumption values [11, 20, 23]. It is shown that appliances, how the appliances are used and the behavior of the residential customers can be deduced by the energy consumption values. DR Application data holds additionally information about the incentive sensitivity. PET have been developed to minimize the amount of information which is sent by the SM [18, 26]. To the best of our knowledge only pseudonymization is considered to be applied. The minimization of information is either spatial or temporal [7, 18]. Temporal data minimization techniques provide only gross granular data, while spatial based data minimization do not allow to allocate energy consumption values to certain single households. While pseudonymisation allows to address single households, it is shown that this technique can be sidestepped by linkage attacks [17]. Data perturbation do not minimize data, but tamper it to protect privacy. The downside is the direct and severe impact on the data utility. This concept allows to obtain the differential privacy guarantee for consumption values [1, 9] as well as addressing customers individually.

8   Discussion and Open Questions

For any application of smart metering it is vital that the SG stakeholders receive *reliable* and trustworthy information. In this case *reliable* means that the SG stakeholder, e.g., a power grid provider, gets this information as (1) timely and as (2) accurate as needed for the SG application. The exact level of accuracy and timeliness will vary depending on the application itself, but also on the actual contractual, regulatory and installation setting, and is beyond the scope of this paper. In our construction the SM operator (SMO) limits the range in which data perturbation, in our case the addition of noise, is considered acceptable by applying a redactable signature ($\mathcal{RSS}$) at the SMGW over a range of the SMO's choosing. Knowing the allowed level of accuracy allows the customer's privacy gateway (PGW) to calculate the differential privacy guarantee that it could achieve using the data perturbation mechanisms it could deploy. With this information the PGW can independently judge if the allowed perturbation is enough to keep a sophisticated level of privacy for the customer. If not, it can withhold the information until the customer explicitly consents to this leaking of PII. If the PGW has enough freedom it will adjust the data accordingly and forward it after the modification. A $\mathcal{RSS}$ allows this alteration of signed data and the SG stakeholder can verify if the change was within his defined limits.

The presented idea differs slightly from the general idea of differential privacy. In differential privacy ϵ is chosen under the perspective to protect privacy. Our idea is to regard the application side and limit the noise to its needs. This allows calculating the ϵ depending on the maximum amount of noise that the data perturbation mechanism k is allowed to apply. The amount of noise is defined by the max. Error which is acceptable for a SG application.

This approach can be criticised for its weak privacy protection. Very small noise will allow appliance detection and behaviour deduction. It remains unclear to which extent this small noise prohibits use mode detection. Due to the need of very fine grained data to get an acceptable quality level for use mode detection we assume the reduced accuracy by noise will limit invasiveness. It can also be argued that as the SG stakeholder controls the amount of noise, it can limit the privacy protection by setting a too low limit. Further investigation and discussion for concise applications with known data quality needs is required.

However, our approach creates a metric for the privacy loss, which can be used to compare privacy invasiveness of different applications from different SG stakeholders. The metric is to compare the maximum differential privacy (ϵ) that can be achieved if the allowable noise, and by this the data utility, has been fixed. As in general, several applications will be provided in the smart grid, each application and each application provider can in theory require a different degree of data utility, e.g., data precision. With the given metric, the consumer is able to compare the privacy invasiveness of any given application. Henceforth, we envision the customer to exercise an informed choice and either accepts or rejects to participate in the application. To illustrate the idea consider a SM which solely gathers consumption values for net stability. This is an essential and required basic application in SG. The data quality needed for those mission critical mandatory SG applications must follow data protection's principal of data minimization, probably under a close watch by regulators. Here, the user needs to accept this privacy loss, there is no real choice other than to participate. Given the maximum amount of noise for this application leads to a worst case privacy loss of $\epsilon_{netstab}$. Now, a new demand-response (DR) application is advertised to the customer. We assume the DR application tolerates only a smaller amount of noise, the worst case privacy loss is denoted as ϵ_{DR}. The consumer is now able to use the calculated worst case privacy losses for comparison. For example, a comparison value $\frac{\epsilon_{DR}}{\epsilon_{netstab}}$ greater than 1 will indicate that the optional DR-application will result in a decrease of privacy compared to net stability. This comparison can also be done to choose from different DR applications. Further research must show and define the needed accuracy for certain SG applications. While the value proposed for a privacy metric in this paper itself is still abstract, further research could use it to compare the privacy guarantees for concrete applications. Furthermore, user studies could help to show which loss of privacy is accepted by users and craft privacy endangerment statements depending on several ϵ, e.g., a traffic light system. Finally, we remark that current research barely considers the privacy impact of the input channel to the household.

References

1. Ács, G., Castelluccia, C.: I Have a DREAM! (DiffeRentially privatE smArt Metering). In: Filler, T., Pevný, T., Craver, S., Ker, A. (eds.) IH 2011. LNCS, vol. 6958, pp. 118–132. Springer, Heidelberg (2011)
2. Allcott, H.: Social norms and energy conservation. J. Public Econ. **95**(9–10), 1082–1095 (2011). (Special Issue: The Role of Firms in Tax Systems)
3. Backes, M., Meiser, S.: Differentially private smart metering with battery recharging. IACR Cryptology ePrint Archive **2012**, 183 (2012)
4. Bellare, M., Micciancio, D.: A new paradigm for collision-free hashing: incrementality at reduced cost. In: Fumy, W. (ed.) EUROCRYPT 1997. LNCS, vol. 1233, pp. 163–192. Springer, Heidelberg (1997)
5. Brzuska, C., et al.: Redactable signatures for tree-structured data: definitions and constructions. In: Zhou, J., Yung, M. (eds.) ACNS 2010. LNCS, vol. 6123, pp. 87–104. Springer, Heidelberg (2010)
6. Brzuska, C., Fischlin, M., Freudenreich, T., Lehmann, A., Page, M., Schelbert, J., Schröder, D., Volk, F.: Security of sanitizable signatures revisited. In: Jarecki, S., Tsudik, G. (eds.) PKC 2009. LNCS, vol. 5443, pp. 317–336. Springer, Heidelberg (2009)
7. Chan, T.-H.H., Shi, E., Song, D.: Privacy-preserving stream aggregation with fault tolerance. In: Keromytis, A.D. (ed.) FC 2012. LNCS, vol. 7397, pp. 200–214. Springer, Heidelberg (2012)
8. Chang, E.-C., Lim, C.L., Xu, J.: Short redactable signatures using random trees. In: Fischlin, M. (ed.) CT-RSA 2009. LNCS, vol. 5473, pp. 133–147. Springer, Heidelberg (2009)
9. Dwork, C.: Differential privacy. In: Bugliesi, M., Preneel, B., Sassone, V., Wegener, I. (eds.) ICALP 2006. LNCS, vol. 4052, pp. 1–12. Springer, Heidelberg (2006)
10. Earle, R., Kahn, E.P., Macan, E.: Measuring the capacity impacts of demand response. Electricity J. **22**(6), 47–58 (2009)
11. Enev, M., Gupta, S., Kohno, T., Patel, S.N.: Televisions, video privacy, and powerline electromagnetic interference. In: ACM CCS, pp. 537–550. ACM (2011)
12. Bundesamt für Sicherheit in der Informationstechnik. BSI TR-03109 @ONLINE (2011)

13. Goldwasser, S., Micali, S., Rivest, R.L.: A digital signature scheme secure against adaptive chosen-message attacks. SIAM J. Comput. **17**, 281–308 (1988)
14. Gong, J., Qian, H., Zhou, Y.: Fully-secure and practical sanitizable signatures. In: Lai, X., Yung, M., Lin, D. (eds.) Inscrypt 2010. LNCS, vol. 6584, pp. 300–317. Springer, Heidelberg (2011)
15. Greveler, U., Justus, B., Löhr, D.: Identifikation von Videoinhalten über granulare Stromverbrauchsdaten. In: Sicherheit. LNI, vol. 195, pp. 35–45. GI (2012)
16. Haber, S., Hatano, Y., Honda, Y., Horne, W.G., Miyazaki, K., Sander, T., Tezoku, S., Yao, D.: Efficient signature schemes supporting redaction, pseudonymization, and data deidentification. In: ASIACCS, pp. 353–362 (2008)
17. Jawurek, M., Johns, M., Rieck, K.: Smart metering de-pseudonymization. In: ACSAC, pp. 227–236 (2011)
18. Jeske, T.: Privacy-preserving smart metering without a trusted-third-party. In: SECRYPT, pp. 114–123. SciTePress (2011)
19. Johnson, R., Molnar, D., Song, D., Wagner, D.: Homomorphic signature schemes. In: Preneel, B. (ed.) CT-RSA 2002. LNCS, vol. 2271, pp. 244–262. Springer, Heidelberg (2002)
20. Lisovich, M.A., Mulligan, D.K., Wicker, S.B.: Inferring personal information from demand-response systems. IEEE Secur. Priv. **8**(1), 11–20 (2010)
21. Miyazaki, K., Hanaoka, G., Imai, H.: Digitally signed document sanitizing scheme based on bilinear maps. In: Proceedings of the ASIACCS '06, pp. 343–354. ACM, New York (2006)
22. Miyazaki, K., Iwamura, M., Matsumoto, T., Sasaki, R., Yoshiura, H., Tezuka, S., Imai, H.: Digitally signed document sanitizing scheme with disclosure condition control. IEICE Trans. **88−A(1)**, 239–246 (2005)
23. Molina-Markham, A., Shenoy, P., Fu, K., Cecchet, E., Irwin, D.: Private memoirs of a smart meter. In: Proceedings of the 2nd ACM BuildSys '10, pp. 61–66. ACM (2010)
24. Rivest, R.L., Shamir, A., Adleman, L.: A method for obtaining digital signatures and public-key cryptosystems. Commun. ACM **26**(1), 96–99 (1983)
25. Samelin, K., Pöhls, H.C., Bilzhause, A., Posegga, J., de Meer, H.: Redactable signatures for independent removal of structure and content. In: Ryan, M.D., Smyth, B., Wang, G. (eds.) ISPEC 2012. LNCS, vol. 7232, pp. 17–33. Springer, Heidelberg (2012)
26. Shi, E., Chan, T.-H.H., Rieffel, E.G., Chow, R., Song, D.: Privacy-preserving aggregation of time-series data. In: NDSS. The Internet Society (2011)
27. Steinfeld, R., Bull, L., Zheng, Y.: Content extraction signatures. In: Kim, K. (ed.) ICISC 2001. LNCS, vol. 2288, pp. 285–304. Springer, Heidelberg (2002)
28. von Oheimb, D.: IT security architecture approaches for smart metering and smart grid. In: Cuellar, J. (ed.) SmartGridSec 2012. LNCS, vol. 7823, pp. 1–25. Springer, Heidelberg (2013)
29. Wu, Z.-Y., Hsueh, C.-W., Tsai, C.-Y., Lai, F., Lee, H.-C., Chung, Y.: Redactable signatures for signed CDA documents. J. Med. Syst. **36**(3), 1795–1808 (2012)
30. Ziekow, H., Goebel, C., Strüker, J., Jacobsen, H.-A.: The potential of smart home sensors in forecasting household electricity demand. In: SmartGridComm (2013)

A Threat Analysis Methodology for Smart Home Scenarios

Kristian Beckers[1]($\boxtimes$), Stephan Faßbender[1], Maritta Heisel[1],
and Santiago Suppan[2]

[1] paluno - The Ruhr Institute for Software Technology – University
of Duisburg-Essen, Essen, Germany
{kristian.beckers,stephan.fassbender,
maritta.heisel}@paluno.uni-due.de
[2] Siemens AG, Munich, Germany
santiago.suppan.ext@siemens.com

Abstract. A smart grid is envisioned to enable a more economic, environmental friendly, sustainable and reliable supply of energy. But significant security concerns have to be addressed for the smart grid, dangers range from threatened availability of energy, to threats of customer privacy. This paper presents a structured method for identifying security threats in the smart home scenario and in particular for analyzing their severity and relevance. The method is able to unveil also new threats, not discussed in the literature before. The smart home scenario is represented by a context-pattern, which is a specific kind of pattern for the elicitation of domain knowledge [1]. Hence, by exchanging the smart home pattern by a context-pattern for another domain, e.g., clouds, our method can be used for these other domains, as well. The proposal is based on Microsoft's Security Development Lifecycle (SDL) [2], which uses Data Flow diagrams, but proposes new alternatives for scenario definition and asset identification based on context-patterns. These alleviate the lack of scalability of the SDL. In addition, we present Attack Path DFDs, that show how an attacker can compromise the system.

Keywords: Smart grid · Attack pattern · Threat analysis · Requirements engineering · Context

1 Introduction

A smart grid provides energy on demand from distributed generation stations of energy suppliers to prosumers that buy energy and also sell small amounts of energy. Prosumers live in smart homes, which use information technology to control smart appliances, e.g., heaters via end points such as smart phones. This is

Part of this work is funded by the German Research Foundation (DFG) under grant number HE3322/4-2 and the EU project Network of Excellence on Engineering Secure Future Internet Software Services and Systems (NESSoS, ICT-2009.1.4 Trustworthy ICT, Grant No. 256980).

© Springer International Publishing Switzerland 2014
J. Cuellar (Ed.): SmartGridSec 2014, LNCS 8448, pp. 94–124, 2014.
DOI: 10.1007/978-3-319-10329-7_7

one possible example of the two-way communication between technical elements ans stakeholders, such as the prosumers, his/her smart appliances, energy suppliers, etc., which the smart grid relies on. Significant security concerns have to be addressed for smart grids, due to the possible dangers of missing availability of energy for customers, as well as threats to the integrity and confidentiality of customer's data. These concerns are of particular relevance, because energy grids have a significantly longer lifespan than, e.g., telecommunication networks [3]. In addition, privacy threats, e.g., the possibility of creating behavioral profiles of prosumers, if their energy consumption data is transmitted over the grid in small time intervals [4]. These concerns have been analyzed by several organizations such as NIST [5] and even tools for penetration testing of Smart Meters exist[1].

However, all of these analyses investigate either the entire grid or focus on one particular element, e.g., a Smart Meter. We present a focused threat analysis for the smart home scenario in particular, because it is vital for the acceptance of smart grids to show the Prosumer that a secure operation of the grid is possible. A report from the security darkreading blog[2] states that the smart grid vendor Itron in the U.S., as well as the MidAmerican Energy Company have made the Microsoft's Security Development Lifecycle (SDL)[3] mandatory for the development of all software products. Furthermore, the government of India endorses practices of the SDL. Thus we rely on Microsoft's SDL in our analysis, as one of the best known security-development-life-cycle methodologies [6]. This will facilitate the adoption of our method among software requirements engineers. From a security perspective, Microsoft's SDL is very thorough in architectural threat analysis [7] and thus, recommended [8] and sometimes mandatory, as mentioned above. In particular, we improve the threat analysis of the SDL with a pattern based description for scenarios and refine some of its steps. Our contributions are a specific context-pattern for the smart home scenario that can be instantiated for any smart home scenario and re-use the results of our threat analysis. Our smart home context-pattern helps to elicit domain knowledge by describing common structures, stakeholders, and their relations. In [1], we described our smart home pattern which is based on smart grid context descriptions of standards and technical documents, and the experience of the industrial partners of the NESSoS[4] project. The usage of our smart home context-pattern has several benefits in comparison to the textual approach of Microsoft's SDL. The information about the scenario can be captured in a structured way by instantiating all elements of the pattern. The instantiation can be checked for completeness automatically and for soundness by a domain expert. The graphical representation

---

[1] The termineter homepage: https://code.google.com/p/termineter/ (last visited on: 8-1-2014).

[2] A report from the darkreading security blog: http://www.darkreading.com/applications/scadasmart-grid-vendor-adopts-microsofts/240000526?itc=edit_in_body_cross (last visited on: 8-1-2014).

[3] Note the SDL is an evolving concept even at Microsoft, but for simplicity's sake we consider only the SDL described in [2] for the remainder of this paper.

[4] The Network of Excellence on Engineering Secure Future Internet Software Services and Systems (NESSoS) homepage: http://www.nessos-project.eu.

of all elements helps to elicit external dependencies by analyzing the relations in the pattern. The graphical pattern helps also to discuss with the stakeholders if an element of the scenario is missing.

We aim to improve the SDL's threat analysis via turning it into a completely model-based method, meaning that every step of the method relies on models. Models are an abstraction of reality and contain relevant parts for our threat analysis. Models allow us to iterate over the elements and answer certain questions such as if an element presents value to the customer of the threat analysis, meaning: is it an asset? In addition, models help us to achieve completeness of a threat analysis, because we can check if all elements are considered or not. However, if an element is missing in the model, the threat analysis will not consider it. In order to prevent the threat analysis from analyzing an incomplete data flow diagram (abbreviated: "DFD"), we propose to use a model for the initial steps (steps 1 to 4 see Sect. 2.2) of the SDL threat analysis, as well. In particular, we propose to use the smart home context-pattern introduced previously. The information in the smart home pattern can be mapped to a DFD with little effort. Furthermore, the smart home pattern contains structural information and the DFD refines this information with data flows of the scenario. This information is vital for the threat analysis of smart home systems, because a major security issue is to restrict the flow of energy consumption data. The reason is that energy consumption data is considered personal information, as behavioral profiles can be derived from it, e.g., when inhabitants take a shower.

A fundamental difference between Microsoft's SDL and our method is that we do not categorize every element of a DFD as an asset. We define assets as everything that has value to a stakeholder in the scope of the analysis. We consider elements outside the scope, e.g., for external dependencies. Moreover, we analyze threats by identifying assets an attacker wants to harm, identify entry points of the attacker, identify vulnerabilities the attacker can exploit and define attack paths from entry points to assets. The attack paths are modeled in specific DFDs that show the data flows caused by a certain attacker type, e.g., network attacker from all entry points to the assets in so-called *attack path DFDs*.

Moreover, our threat analysis methodology is based on (1) context-pattern for model-based, high level, and re-usable scenario description and (2) DFDs for design level analysis. We assume that these basis of our methodology can be adapted to other security development lifecycle approaches such as the Comprehensive, Lightweight Application Security Process (CLASP) by the Open Web Application Security Project (OWASP) [9], as well. CLASP contains definitions of process phases. In particular, CLASP contains one phase called *Perform security analysis of system requirements and design (threat modeling)*. The input for this phase are security, business, and functional requirements, while the output of this phase are documented system threats, refined security requirements, and an architectural impact analysis. We can imagine that the security, business, and functional requirements can each refer to elements of the smart home pattern to ensure that their statements refer to the smart home scenario. Our mapping from the smart home pattern to the DFDs can be used to analyse and describe threats in relation to the architecture. Hence, we assume that our methodology can be adapted to other security development lifecycle approaches.

The remainder of the paper is organised as follows. Section 2 presents background knowledge on smart grids, and Microsoft's SDL, and discusses the difference of our research to the related work. Section 3 describes our structured threat analysis method. Section 4 shows an example application of our method to a industrial smart home scenario. Finally, Sect. 5 concludes this work. In addition, we present an extended version of this paper in a technical report, which is available for the interested reader[5].

2   Background and Related Work

We introduce background on smart grids in Sect. 2.1, describe Microsoft's security development lifecycle in Sect. 2.2, and discuss related work in Sect. 2.3.

2.1   Background on Smart Grids

Based on the definitions of the European Commission [10], the European Smart Grid Task Force[6], and the Office of Electricity Transmission and Distribution[7], the smart grid can be described as a large, flexible, self-monitoring, self-balancing, and self-regulating electricity infrastructure which uses two-way digital communication to gather and respond to information in an automated manner in order to improve the efficiency, reliability (meaning safety and security), and sustainability of the production and distribution of energy. This new infrastructure will be able to efficiently integrate the behavior and actions of all users connected to it. This means generators, consumers, those that do both, and other third parties that provide services besides energy generation.

The European Network and Information Security Agency provides a brief overview of basic ICT components, which are: (i) operational systems, (ii) classic IT systems, (iii) communication and network protocols and (iv) end points. Each of these components has well known security threats, which facilitate to identify their possible weaknesses in the future electrical grid. However, the combination of these components and their interaction will create further, yet unknown security issues. In a smart grid every stakeholder will have the capability to remotely interact with every component of the grid, in an authorized or in a maliciously way. Security of the smart home and its information assets will prove to be critical for the grid's security. For example, Smart Meter measurements is the key information on which automated energy load estimation is based on. If data integrity is comprised and meter measurements are changed, energy supply

---

[5] Technical report: http://www.uml4pf.org/publications/smarthome.pdf.

[6] http://ec.europa.eu/energy/gas_electricity/smartgrids/taskforce_en.htm
   (last visited on 15-12-2013).

[7] http://energy.gov/oe/technology-development/smart-grid
   (last visited on 15-12-2013).

switch offs of a house or a sector could happen, for safety reasons, if one or several compromised meters report a dangerously high consumption rate [11].

2.2   Threat Analysis in Microsoft's Security Development Lifecycle

We propose a threat analysis based on the Microsoft Security Development Life-cycle (SDL) [2], because of its widespread application. Threat analysis is part of the risk analysis stage of the SDL and consists of the following steps, which concern a software that we call System-under-Analysis (SuA):

(1) **Define use scenarios** to identify all relevant information about the scenarios in which the SuA is used, e.g., types of stakeholders and to define key threat scenarios, e.g., theft of a device or insider threat scenarios.

(2) **Gather a list of external dependencies** means to identify essential software and hardware elements on which the SuA depends e.g. an operating system or a database.

(3) **Define security assumptions** about the environment in which the SuA is located. The environment means the elements of the external dependencies and further elements defined in the scope. An assumptions could be, that databases stores authentication information in an encrypted way.

(4) **Create external security notes** that constrain stakeholders or technical elements that interact with the SuA, e.g., only an IT administrator is allowed to change the configuration of the SuA.

(5) **Create one or more data flow diagrams (DFDs) of the application being modeled**, which is the SuA and its environment is modeled in DFDs (see Table 5 for an overview on DFD elements). The DFD with the highest abstraction level is called the context diagram. Complex processes of the context diagram are refined in separate DFDs.

(6) **Determine threat types** by using the STRIDE threat taxonomy [2]. STRIDE categorizes different actions conducted by an attacker. These actions are assigned to DFD elements defined in Step (5).

(7) **Identify the threats to the system** by listing all DFD elements. Howard and Lipner [2] simply define all DFD elements as assets. Complex processes can be refined in further DFDs. In this case, the processes in the refined DFDs are the assets and not the complex processes. Note that data flows connected to a complex process are always assets.

(8) **Determine risk** with a risk level from 1 to 4, with risk level 1 being the highest. Risks are the chance of an attack multiplied with its damage potential. All threats are labeled with a risk level depending on the chance of an attack and the potential damages. An exception are repudiation threats that are difficult to assess, because they refer to actions that are not noticed. The authors state that these risks are usually assigned the risk level of a corresponding tampering threat.

(9) **Plan mitigation** refers to the possible mitigations of risks and proposes the following mitigation strategies: *do nothing, remove the feature, turn off the feature, warn the user,* and *counter the threat with technology.*

2.3   Related Work

Related work on threats affecting the smart grid exist, but is often too general, as the whole smart grid information network is the scope of the threat analysis, which includes several stakeholders, and technologies. The following list of related work provides an overview and outlines structural benefits for our subsequent work, but also drawbacks from generalization or high level descriptions.

The Public Interest Energy Research Program (PIER)[8] is a project report on smart grid cyber security. The report describes threats for the smart grid. The reported security issues are derived from Wikipedia and the Open Smart Grid shared documents. There is a total number of 26 threats listed (page 26) and mapped to 9 smart grid security issues, security goals and threat levels. The result is a mostly general overview, which neither employs a clear methodology for threat derivation, nor provides concrete information on the endangered assets and therefore, cannot be used as basis for requirements elicitation.

The European Network and Information Security Agency (ENISA) provides in the annex to their smart grid report insight on ICT components and vulnerabilities in the smart grid[9]. A threat classification is given, which comprises: (1) accidental/inadvertent threats, which can be divided into (2) safety failures, (3) equipment failures, (4) carelessness, (5) natural disasters and (6) deliberate threats. Several threats are subsequently assigned to the threat classes in form of an overview table, but it remains unclear why these threats were chosen and why they are assigned to each class. The document neither provides further description on the classification, nor does it link to the source of threat identification. The incomprehensible classification of several threats, e.g., "propaganda" as a "technical threat", hinder the use of its threat catalog for future work.

Aloul et al. survey literature on smart grid complexity, vulnerabilities, attacks and proposed solutions [3]. Their work is based on the smart grid architecture proposed by the National Institute of Standards and Technology (NIST). The authors conduct a threat and attacker analysis. However, attacks are only briefly related to vulnerable ICT components, but without addressing the smart grid architecture presented previously. As a result, vulnerabilities and attacks cannot be linked to our scenario directly considered in this work. scenarios as well.

Wang et al. detail cyber security threats and requirements related to high-level "security objectives" [12, p. 1348], which is the CIA-triad. Wang et al. use well know technologies and metrics from the Internet as a comparison, and derive threats and requirements according to the security protection goals of the triad. Future work can profit from their structured approach, although the authors themselves describe the results at high and non-technical level. In addition, Yang et al. introduce a graphical impact analysis model for the smart grid.

---

[8] http://www.energy.ca.gov/2012publications/CEC-500-2012-047/
CEC-500-2012-047.pdf (last visited on 15-12-2013).

[9] https://www.enisa.europa.eu/activities/Resilience-and-CIIP/
critical-infrastructure-and-services/smart-grids-and-smart-metering/
ENISA_Annex%20II%20-%20Security%20Aspects%20of%20Smart%20Grid.pdf
(last visited on 15-12-2013).

Yang et al. [13] apart form the model description, general aspects considering threats and requirements can be found. In the future, the proposed impact analysis can be used subsequently after our structured threat elicitation. It will be useful when we broaden our scope, but as it is defined right now it does not concern the details of our smart home scenario. Moreover, McDaniel et al. [14] give a high-level introduction on security and privacy challenges. But they highlight and discuss the challenges without going into detail. Thus, the work is not providing any foundation for future work.

SINTEF [15] surveys and analyses security threats associated with the deployment of an Advanced Metering Infrastructure (AMI) in the Demo Steinkjer demonstration project. The derived threats focus on energy supplier communication. The method SINTEF uses is also based on Microsoft's SDL, which provides a complementary view of threats outside the scope of this paper. In addition, the authors enlist vulnerabilities based on a DFD and afterwards identify assets and draw attack trees for attacker goals such as "Compromise meter". In contrast, our method identifies assets first and focuses our threat analysis on modeling attacker behavior via identifying possible entry points and identifying vulnerabilities that can be exploited to harm the assets.

Dhillon [16] models the flow of information in a system and investigates possible interaction points of an attacker with the system. The author proposes to use annotations on the models for security relevant information, e.g., authentication data flows. These annotations are used to check, for example, that a database is the entry point for possible threats. These annotations can complement our work in the future and improve the vulnerability analysis. However, this work is not specific to smart grids.

3 A structured Method for Smart Grid Threat Analysis

We show our method in Fig. 1 and explain it in the following. For simplicity's sake, we do not consider the determination risk and plan mitigation steps in our method.

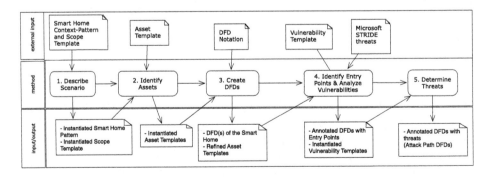

Fig. 1. A Structured Method for Smart Grid Threat Analysis

Step 1. Describe Scenario - The scenario description shall include all relevant elements of the scope and its environment. The description begins with the scope and focus of the analysis, modeling the target of analysis at an adequate level of abstraction, identifying stakeholders and relevant technical elements. Afterwards, stakeholders and relevant technical elements outside the scope (in the environment) are determined. A thorough description of the environment is essential, because stakeholders and technical elements in the environment can be external dependencies for assets (c.f., Sect. 4) in the scope of the analysis. We base these descriptions on the smart home pattern (c.f., Sect. 4) and instantiate it for the particular smart home scenario. Meaning all stakeholders and technical elements have to be labeled with the particular names in the particular scenario. The pattern can be extended with further stakeholders and technical elements for a particular scenario. If these extensions appear in multiple instantiations (scenarios), a discussion should decide if these elements shall even become part of the pattern itself. The pattern is accompanied by a scope template (c.f., Sect. 4). This template lists the elements of the scope and the elements that are not part of it, and a reasoning *why* they are left out. Moreover, we use the instantiated indirect environment of the smart home pattern to consider relevant laws and regulations. We list the relevant legal demands in the scope template.

Step 2. Identify Assets - The Microsoft SDL is lacking a precise definition of an asset. Thus, we use the definition of the ISO 27001 standard. The ISO 27001 standard defines an asset [17, p. 2] as follows: "anything that has value to the organization". The organization in our case are the stakeholders in the scope of our analysis. We identify assets in the smart home pattern by analyzing the instantiated scope template and the instantiated smart home pattern. The associations (vertices between the stakeholders) in the scope are a starting point. We check if the elements at the end of the associations potentially have value to the stakeholders and, thus, are assets. We describe the assets in asset templates. For each asset, we have to define external dependencies. The analysis of the external dependencies leads to security assumptions and to security notes for the environment. The asset templates are refined during method each time further information, e.g., due to refinement of scope elements, becomes available. Key threat scenarios are also considered in the SDL to conclude this step, but their additional benefit is left unclear compared to the effort of their identification. Thus, key threat scenarios are omitted in this method.

Step 3. Create DFDs - At this point, we have described the scenario and identified the assets of our threat analysis. We base our threat analysis on DFDs as proposed by the SDL. In addition, DFDs help to refine the technical details in the smart home pattern. Hence, we need to map the smart home pattern elements to the DFDs. Note that we only map elements of the direct environment of the pattern (see Fig. 2), because the indirect environment only contains laws and regulations, which have been considered in the first step. We map the domain knowledge in the smart home pattern to DFDs (c.f., Sect. 4). Moreover, we have more details in the DFD than in the smart home pattern. Hence, we refine the asset templates with additional information and if necessary instantiate further asset templates.

Step 4. Identify Entry Points and Analyze Vulnerabilities - The next step is to model the attackers. In particular, this step conducts an identification of possible entry points of an attacker as suggested by [18]. We elicit possible *entry points* (c.f., Sect. 4) of attackers that want to harm the previously identified assets. We suggest to use basic attacker types as proposed in our previous work [19,20]: *Physical Attackers* threaten the physical elements of the system, e.g., hardware or buildings that host computers; *Network Attackers* threaten *network connections* within the target of analysis; *Software Attackers* threaten software components of the system, e.g., the application configuration inside the *Smart Meter*; *Social Engineering Attackers* threaten humans, e.g., Prosumers[10]. We specify all possible entry points for an attacker in an annotated DFD. The DFD contains a symbol of a red triangle with an exclamation mark in the middle to illustrate the entry points (see Fig. 6). We use the previously defined entry points and specify concrete threats for each entry point using the STRIDE threat taxonomy. We use a vulnerability template to document the STRIDE threat type, attacker type, and a description of a possible exploit. Section 4 provides examples for these activities.

Step 5. Determine Threats - We use the entry points to elicit *attack paths*, which are based on Microsoft Threat Modeling. An attack path is a description of an attack from an entry point to an asset [18]. Hence, we propose so-called *Attack Path DFDs* to describe threats an attacker possibly causes towards an asset. These are DFD diagrams with an attacker process that illustrate possible ways from all entry points the attacker can use to arrive at the location of the asset and ways to harm it. The diagram is created by trying to reach one asset from all entry points. All relevant entry points and all relevant elements from the previous DFDs are part of an *Attack Path DFD*. It is also possible to exclude an entry point for an asset via reasoning. For example, if there is no path using data flows from an entry point to an asset, that entry point is not relevant for that asset. The possible use of exploits documented in the previous step are modeled in the DFD, as well (see Sect. 4 for details). The *Attack Path DFDs* are used to discuss and document the relevant threats towards the system-to-be.

4 Application of Our Method

Step 1. Describe Scenario

For the elicitation of the context, we introduced so called *context-patterns* in earlier works of ours [21–24]. We also published the initial steps towards a pattern language for context-patterns [1]. We created a *Smart Home* context-pattern that is specifically based on a particular scenario NeSSoS industrial partners are considering.

---

[10] Note that a Prosumer is an energy consumer, who also sells small amounts of energy to the energy provider.

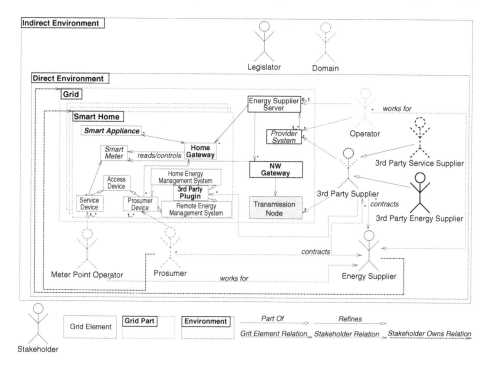

Fig. 2. Smart Home General Pattern

This context-pattern is a refinement of our general smart grid pattern, which was described based on a in deep analysis of several documents like the CC protection profiles for Smart Meters [25,26], the documentation of the OpenNode project [27,28], the documentation of the OpenMeter project [29], the industry case studies from the NESSoS project, and the Canadian smart grid implementation program [30,31]. The general pattern is available in one of our publications [1].

We depict our smart home context-pattern in Fig. 2. The pattern is divided into four major parts. The first part is the *grid* in which the smart home will be integrated. The *direct environment* contains all the *direct stakeholders*, who have a direct relation to one or more parts of the grid. Hence, they are able to directly influence the grid. In contrast, the *indirect stakeholders* of the *indirect environment* have no influence and, in most cases, also no interest in the grid parts and elements themselves. But they have an influence on the direct stakeholders, and therefore they are important for the system-to-be. The *Smart Home* contains the system to be built. This does not necessarily mean that all parts of the smart home are object of an development project, but at least one will be the machine to be built. The grid, the direct environment, the indirect environment, and the smart home are object to be described to get an understanding of the system-to-be and its context.

Note that all stakeholders are represented by stick-figures. To distinguish the different types of stakeholders in an smart home pattern later on, each type's stick-figure representation has its own line style. There are two kinds of important indirect stakeholders. First, the *domain* which represents further specific domains, beside the smart grid domain, for which the system-to-be is developed. The domains influence is based on self-regulations of a domain, standards for this domain and so forth. Second, the *legislator* describes the government of a country for example. A legislator enacts and enforces different regulations which the system-to-be has to be compliant to.

For the direct stakeholders there are five kinds of importance. The *Prosumer* *contracts* the *Energy Supplier* and/or the *3rd Party Energy Supplier* to buy energy and grid services. In addition, the *Prosumer* can also sell small amounts of energy to the *Energy Supplier* and/or the *3rd Party Energy Supplier*, which is a *3rd Party Supplier*. The amount of bought and sold energy is measured by the *Smart Meter*. The *Prosumer* reads the energy values using a *Prosumer Device*. Two special Prosumer devices are the *Home Energy Management System* and the *Remote Energy Management System*, which allow, besides the viewing of energy values, the configuration of *Smart Appliances*. *Smart Appliances* are configurable devices such as heaters, which can be configured to turn on at a specific time or when certain conditions arise, for example, a certain temperature. To extend the functionality of the remote/Home Energy Management Systems, the Prosumer can buy *3rd Party Plugins* from different *3rd Party Service Providers*. This can be simple GUi services for viewing information, but also complex new functionality, which e.g. requires a permanent internet access to get information from the environment like weather data. All the communication between the smart home elements is coordinated via the *Home Gateway*. One exception are *Service Devices* used by the *Meter Point Operator*.

The meter point operator *works for* the energy supplier. His/Her tasks are installing and maintaining the devices at the consumer side, in particular, the Smart Meter via service devices. They are a type of *Access Devices* like the Prosumer devices, but with special abilities. Access Devices are directly connected to the Smart Meter.

The *Operator* also *works for* the energy supplier and executes different tasks, e.g., maintenance or billing using legacy *Provider Systems* and the *Energy Supplier Server*. The provider system and the energy supplier server connect to the smart home using a dedicated channel provided by the *NW (Network) Gateway* or directly via the internet. The NW Gateway also communicates with a *Transmission Node*. We marked the transmission node in gray in this pattern, because we will not consider it for the remainder of this paper. The other technical grid elements are described in more detail in Table 7.

We illustrate our *scope template* in Table 1. The first column states the name of the stakeholders or grid elements, the next column states if the stakeholders or grid element is part of the scope, and the last column defines why a stakeholders or grid element is part of the scope or not.

Table 1. Scope template

Smart home pattern element	Part of scope	Reasoning
Stakeholder		
State the name of the stakeholder	Yes or No	Explain why the stakeholder is part of the scope or not
Grid elements		
State the name of the grid element	Yes or No	Explain why the grid element is part of the scope or not

Example Smart Home Scenario[11] - We illustrate a Smart Home scenario that industrial partners of the NeSSoS project are considering in Fig. 3. In our example, the threat analysis is conduced by an energy provider called *Tesla AG* and it is conducted on behalf of the *Tesla Prosumer*. Tesla wants to find out if the equipment and operations they apply to the Tesla Prosumer's Smart Home is secure to operate and does not harm the Tesla Prosumer's privacy concerns. Tesla excludes any equipment that they did not recommend or provide from the scope of the threat analysis. The elements in the scope are listed in Table 2.

This scenario considers the German Law as the binding law, because it concerns a release of a Smart Grid specifically tailored to German Prosumers. Hence, we instantiate the legislator *Germany* and since privacy concerns are relevant, we refer to the German Federal Data Protection Act (BDSG). Moreover, regulations for the *Energy* domain have to be obeyed, such as the electricity- and gas-supply act (Energiewirtschaftsgesetz, EnWG), as well as laws regarding the protection of the environment (*Nature Protection*), like the German Renewable Energy Act (Erneuerbare-Energien-Gesetz, EEG).

Tesla uses a *Tesla Server* for the electronic communication with the smart home and in particular the *Wan+WLan+Lan Router* hardware of the Tesla Prosumer. The Tesla server is maintained by the *Tesla Service Staff Member* and it is connected with the *Sunshine System*, the server of the *Sunshine Inc*, which is a subcontractor of the Tesla AG. In addition, the *Energy Meter* that is provided by Tesla also communicates directly with the *Tesla NW Gateway*. The Tesla Prosumer uses several Smart Appliances: A *Thermostat*, a *Smart TV*, and a *Solar Collector*. The Energy Meter is maintained by the *SmartSpecialist KG* using a *Meter Display & Interface* and a *Meter Calibration Tool*. The Tesla Prosumer uses a *Home Energy Management System* to control his/her Smart Appliances when he/she is at home. When the Tesla Prosumer is not at home he/she uses the *Remote Energy Management System* to control his/her Smart Appliances. Furthermore, the Tesla Prosumer uses a *Weather Controlled Heating Plugin* for the Home Energy Management System to automate the temperature regulation of the smart home. This plugin is provided by the *Smart Apps* company.

---

[11] All organizations appearing in this work are fictitious. Any resemblance to real organizations, companies or persons is purely coincidental.

Table 2. Scope template instance

Smart home pattern element	Part of scope	Reasoning
Stakeholder		
Smart Specialist KG	No	Only visits the smart home for maintenance
Tesla Prosumer	Yes	
Tesla AG	No	Does not reside in the smart home
Tesla Service Staff Member	No	Does not reside in the smart home
Sunshine Inc.	No	Does not reside in the smart home
Smart Apps	No	Does not reside in the smart home
Grid Elements		
Tesla Server	No	Is outside the smart home
Tesla NW Gateway	No	Is outside the smart home
Sunshine System	No	Is outside the smart home
Wan+Wlan+LAN+Router	Yes	The router is provided by the *Tesla AG*
Solar Collector	No	Not provided or recommended by *Tesla AG*
Smart TV	No	Not provided or recommended by *Tesla AG*
Thermostat	No	Not provided or recommended by *Tesla AG*
Energy Meter	Yes	Is inside the smart home and provided by *Tesla AG*
Meter Display and Interface	Yes	Is inside the smart home and provided by *Tesla AG*
Meter Calibration Tool	No	It is only inside the smart home when the *SmartSpecialistKG* conducts maintenance on the *Smart Meter*
Home Energy Management System	Yes	Is inside the smart home and provided by *Tesla AG*
Remote Energy Management System	Yes	Is inside the smart home and provided by *Tesla AG*
Weather Controlled Heating Plugin	No	Is inside the smart home, but not provided by *Tesla AG*

Step 2. Identify Assets

We identify the assets in our scope and use our asset template (see Table 3) to document them.

We show an instantiated asset template for the *Home Energy Management System* (see Table 4) and refer for the remaining instantiations to our technical report (see Footnote 5).

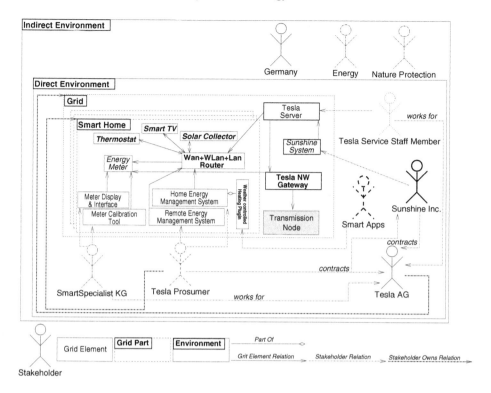

Fig. 3. Smart Home Instantiation Pattern

Step 3. Create DFDs

The DFD model helps to analyze the scenario and to identify crucial data flows for the definition of entry points, security requirements, possible threats (not only by external attackers but also by insiders or normal participants of the system). The Data Flow Diagram (DFD) depicts which information flows between which

Table 3. Asset template

Asset	State the name of the asset
Reasoning	Argue why this asset has a value for a stakeholder in the scope
External dependency	State the external system or stakeholder on which the asset depends
Security assumptions	State security assumptions about the environment of the asset
Security notes	State security notes for the environment of the asset
Contains assets	Are other assets part of this asset?

Table 4. Instantiated asset template for the Home Energy Management System

Asset	Home Energy Management System
Reasoning	The Home Energy Management Systems controls Smart Appliances and is the communication terminal for the Prosumer with *Tesla* and other energy providers
External dependency	The Home Energy Management Systems relies on the *Wan+Wlan+LAN+Router* to provide the communication infrastructure and to support proper confidentiality and authentication mechanisms
Security assumptions	The *Wan+Wlan+LAN+Router* is configured and maintained reliably
Security notes	The *Remote Energy Management System* and the *Wan+Wlan+LAN+Router* are configured to use proper confidentiality and authentication mechanisms
Contains assets	Remote Energy Management System

Table 5. Description of DFD elements according to [2]

DFD element type	Description
A double circle is a *Complex Process*	A representation of a process that performs different operations
A circle is a *Process*	A representation of a process that performs one discrete task
A rectangle is an *External Entity*	Something the SuA requires, but does not control
Parallel lines are a *Data Store*	Persistent data storage that the SuA uses
An arrowed line is a *Data Flow*	Means of data transmission throughout the SuA
A dotted line is a *Privilege Boundary*	Privilege Boundary represent data moving between different trust levels

interfaces. Figure 5 represents the information flow between the identified assets, including processes, storage, interfaces and elements of a smart home. Elements are depicted as described in Table 5.

For creating the DFD we use the smart home pattern instance (Fig. 3) as an input. The DFD is then created in two phases: the *mapping of the smart home pattern instance* to a generic DFD, and the *refinement of the generic DFD* with information about data storage and specific, additional processes. Note that the DFDs focus on technical elements, and thus, all stakeholders are left out, and the relations between stakeholders are not considered in DFDs. Hence, the resulting DFD will be a refinement of the smart home pattern instance showing only a technical point of view, adding the information about involved data and its flows.

Table 6. Mapping context-pattern elements to DFD elements

Smart Home Pattern Element	Part of Smart Home	Part of Scope	DFD Element
Stakeholder			Not Mapped
Grid Element	☑	☑	Complex Process
Grid Element	☑	☐	External Entity
Grid Element	☐		External Entity
Grid Element Relation		☑	Data flow
Grid Element Relation			Data flow
Stakeholder Relation			Not mapped

☑ : yes, ☐ : No, : not relevant

Mapping of the Smart Home Pattern Instance. For the general mapping of the smart home pattern instance to the generic DFD, we use a mapping table (see Table 6). We leave out all stakeholders and stakeholder relations for the aforementioned reasons. Thus, there is no mapping for them.

Note: Starting from this point, we exemplify our method on only the most important elements (see Fig. 4) of the scenario (see Fig. 3). A more complete mapping and analysis of the scenario is presented in the extended technical report[12].

As a **first step**, we focus on those grid elements of the DFD, which are clearly part of the scope. They are represented as complex processes. Table 7 contain suggestions on how to model an element of the smart home pattern instance, depending on which element of the smart home pattern it instantiates. For example, Table 7 suggests to add the Smart Meter instance as a complex process with three data stores (*Measurement (Billing) Data, Keystore*, and *Configuration*) and the corresponding data flows. Hence, the instantiated element "Energy Meter" of the smart home pattern instance (see Fig. 3), is represented in the DFD as a complex process called *Energy Meter* with the data stores *Energy Meter Keystore, Energy Meter Application Data, Energy Meter Measurement (Billing) Data* (see Fig. 5).

The **second step** is to consider elements inside the smart home, which are relevant in a security perspective, but cannot be actively changed, because they are provided by external third parties. They are modeled as external entities inside the smart home. All elements added in this step have to be separated from the elements added in Step 1 using privilege boundaries. The reason is, that the smart home has several stakeholders. We analyze the core components of the smart home, which are usually provided by one party and related subcontractors, such as the energy provided and meter point operators. The level of trust for parts that cannot be managed actively by those, is thus different to elements, that interact within the smart home, but are provided by external, heterogeneous parties. For example, the Smart TV, which is an element in the smart home (see the pattern instance in Fig. 3), is an element that interacts with other components, but is not part of the scope, as it is provided by an external

---

[12] The technical report can be found at: http://www.uml4pf.org/publications/smart-home.pdf.

Table 7. Suggestion for modeling elements in scope

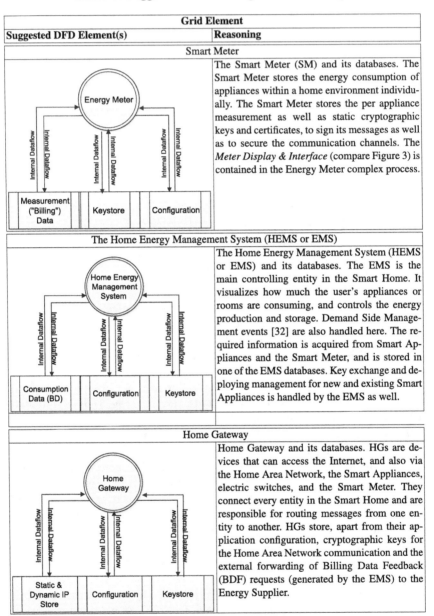

Grid Element	
Suggested DFD Element(s)	**Reasoning**
Smart Meter	
(diagram: Energy Meter process with Internal Dataflow connections to Measurement ("Billing") Data, Keystore, Configuration)	The Smart Meter (SM) and its databases. The Smart Meter stores the energy consumption of appliances within a home environment individually. The Smart Meter stores the per appliance measurement as well as static cryptographic keys and certificates, to sign its messages as well as to secure the communication channels. The *Meter Display & Interface* (compare Figure 3) is contained in the Energy Meter complex process.
The Home Energy Management System (HEMS or EMS)	
(diagram: Home Energy Management System process with Internal Dataflow connections to Consumption Data (BD), Configuration, Keystore)	The Home Energy Management System (HEMS or EMS) and its databases. The EMS is the main controlling entity in the Smart Home. It visualizes how much the user's appliances or rooms are consuming, and controls the energy production and storage. Demand Side Management events [32] are also handled here. The required information is acquired from Smart Appliances and the Smart Meter, and is stored in one of the EMS databases. Key exchange and deploying management for new and existing Smart Appliances is handled by the EMS as well.
Home Gateway	
(diagram: Home Gateway process with Internal Dataflow connections to Static & Dynamic IP Store, Configuration, Keystore)	Home Gateway and its databases. HGs are devices that can access the Internet, and also via the Home Area Network, the Smart Appliances, electric switches, and the Smart Meter. They connect every entity in the Smart Home and are responsible for routing messages from one entity to another. HGs store, apart from their application configuration, cryptographic keys for the Home Area Network communication and the external forwarding of Billing Data Feedback (BDF) requests (generated by the EMS) to the Energy Supplier.

(non-trusted) manufacturer. Hence, it is added as external entity separated by a privilege boundary (see Fig. 5).

The **third step** is to add the grid elements, which external to the smart home, but are still relevant in a security point of view. Note that we introduce the

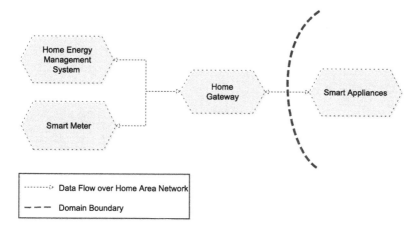

Fig. 4. Generic DFD for Smart Home

generic DFD with generic placeholders for the elements inside the smart home (see Fig. 4), and do not substitute them yet by the instatiations suggested in Table 7. However, the elements inside the smart home, that are provided by third parties, are shown as external entities and will remain so throughout the analysis. In a latter step, all this elements will be substituted by their instantiations. For example the *Home Gateway* in Fig. 4 is replaced with the *WLAN, LAN, WAN Router* from Fig. 3.

The **fourth step** is to add the grid element relations contained in the smart grid pattern instance to the DFD and the grid elements, which are not part of the smart home. Basically, each grid element relation, which is part of the scope, is mapped to at least one data flow. A grid element relation is part of the scope, if at least one of the connected grid elements is part of the scope. It is mapped to one data flow, if it is unidirectional. Otherwise, it is mapped to two data flows. Figure 4[13] comprises all elements in their first, generic representation and their mapped relations (Table 9).

Refinement of the Initial DFD. The initial DFD as modeled in Step 1 to 4 can be refined further where ever needed. Data stores can be split up to refine assets, or central processes are added. For example, we added the process Internet Routing to the DFD shown in Fig. 5 (see Footnote 13). From the intersection of elements in Figs. 3 and 5, a list of refined assets can be derived. One refined asset is detailed in Table 8. The representation of the refined assets corresponds to the asset template presented in Step 4. The Prosumer interaction with the EMS in his/her premises. The data flow diagram already captures some aspects of security, which helps to further identify possible assets. Every component has a cryptographic keystore, which stores any cryptographic information needed

---

[13] Note that we simplified the model for readability purposes. The interested reader can find the complete model in our technical report (see Footnote 5).

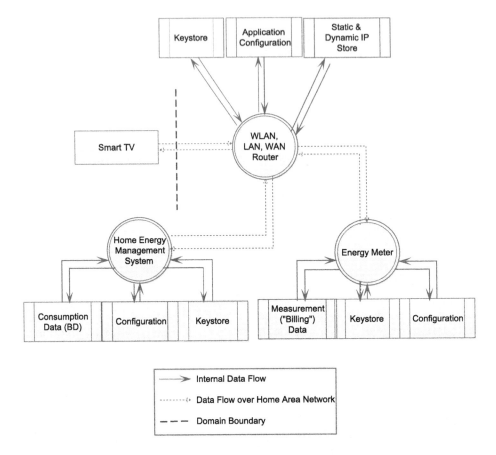

Fig. 5. DFD for a Smart Home Scenario

for signing messages and securing communication channels. Personally identifiable information such as Billing Data and customer profile data is also depicted (see Fig. 5). It should be noted that underlying protocols such as key exchange, pairing and other protocols are not further discussed in this paper (Table 10).

Step 4. Identify Entry Points and Analyze Vulnerabilities

From the perspective of an attacker, the assets identified in the previous steps represent valuable targets. With all assets in mind, different *entry points* can be identified. Entry points describe a certain vulnerability, which can be exploited, creating an *attack tree* from the entry point to one or several assets. Figure 6 gives insight into the different entry points. It should be noted that entry points are elicited considering the security assumptions of each individual asset defined in the refined asset descriptions (e.g., see Table 8, "Security Assumptions").

Whether an element is possibly an entry point or not depends highly on attackers, their different motives and expertise. Different attacker classifications

Table 8. Asset: Home Energy Management System

Asset	Home Energy Management System
Reasoning	The Home Energy Management System controls Smart Appliances, processes & visualizes real-time Billing Data, reacts to Demand Side Management events and is the communication terminal for the prosumer with the Energy Supplier and other third parties
External dependency	The Home Energy Management System relies on the *Home Gateway* to provide the communication infrastructure and to support proper confidentiality and authentication mechanisms. Additionally, it has to rely on the Smart Meter's Billing Data and its correct energy measurement for energy management
Security assumptions	The *Home Gateway* and the *Smart Meter* are configured and maintained reliably. The Energy Management System does only allow the prosumer to interact with the user interface for energy management and does not allow to access or alter any other functionality. The EMS does only allow third party plugins to execute sandboxed algorithms, Demand Side Management does not allow direct load control (DLC)
Security notes	The Energy Management System should not be physically accessible by the prosumer. Solely the user interface (e.g., a touch screen) should be available
Contains assets	Cryptographic keys for authentication and communication with third parties, Billing Data in real-time frequency

Table 9. Asset: Smart Meter

Asset	Smart Meter
Reasoning	The Smart Meter's measurement affects the billing, energy management of the Prosumer, energy forecasts for individual sectors and value added services from third parties
External dependency	The *Smart Meter* relies partially on the *Home Gateway* for transmitting Billing Data to the Energy Management System
Security assumptions	The *Home Gateway* and the provides a stable connection and is a trusted device
Security notes	The *MPO* does not obtain any energy consumption data of the prosumer. The Smart Meter does not allow any interaction with the prosumer, Billing Data is acquired by means of the Energy Management System. The Smart Meter does not allow remote energy shutdown
Contains assets	Billing Data, cryptographic keys for message verification and for communicating with other parties

Table 10. Asset: Home Gateway

Asset	Home Gateway
Reasoning	The communication internally in the Smart Home and externally with the grid is based on the *Home Gateway*. Without the HG, the *Home Energy Management System* could neither receive Billing Data from the Smart Meter, nor manage Smart Appliance's behavior, nor send and receive Billing Data Feedback as well as react to Demand Side Management events
External dependency	The Home Gateway has to be available and configured properly by the supplier
Security assumptions	Proper configuration means that end point IP addresses are correct, that authentication is enforced and confidentiality of the data transmissions is adequate
Security notes	The Prosumer has to prevent that confidentiality of data transmissions are adequate and that authentication mechanisms are activated. Misbehavior needs to be notified to the MPO
Contains assets	Communication keys for the Home Area Network

Table 11. Assets: cryptographic keystores

Asset	Cryptographic Keystores
Reasoning	Cryptographic keystores were referenced in the sub assets section ("contains assets") of every asset described above. Cryptographic information assure message integrity, as well as confidentiality for the communication partners
External dependency	Cryptographic information depends on the underlying protocols for secret generation, key exchange and management
Security assumptions	Key storage is only accessible by internal data flows
Security notes	Billing Data and profile data should not be used for purposes other than contractual purposes
Contains assets	-

can be used in this step, e.g., classification by motivation as in [3]. An exemplifying set of expertise attackers is chosen here, namely the *network* and the *software attackers*, inside and outside the smart home. An exhaustive analysis of all attacker models, including *physical* and *social engineering* adversaries, will be considered in future work. **Network attackers** are adversaries that have access to a target network and can eavesdrop and modify its messages actively. They have limited computational capabilities, time as well as financial resources. They can be both, an authorized user or an external adversary. It is assumed that they cannot break any cryptographic challenges, nor are they

Table 12. Assets: personally identifiable information: customer profile data, billing data

Asset	Profile Data, Billing Data
Reasoning	Personally Identifiable Information (PII) like profile data (name, address, birthday, etc.) and Billing Data allow deep insight into the habits and affections of the PII's subject
External dependency	Billing Data depends on the Smart Meter measurement accuracy. Aggregated Billing Data depends on the aggregation process
Security assumptions	Smart Meter measurements are accurate. Aggregation algorithms are secure
Security notes	The cryptographic keystore is physically secured
Contains assets	-

able to penetrate physical locks nor break software security measures. **Software attackers** on the other hand, are able to analyze, reverse engineer and compromise software systems. They are not capable of interfering in network traffic, nor are they able to penetrate physical security. They have limited computational capabilities, time as well as financial resources and can be both, an authorized member of the system or an external adversary (Table 11).

For eliciting the possible entry points, we apply for each complex process a high level reasoning, if the aforementioned attacker types can access this particular process or not. If we cannot reject the assumption that any attacker can access the process at hand, it is marked as a general entry point. Next, we conduct for each process which is marked as general entry point, an entry point refinement. We check for each data flow from or to this process whether one of the possible attackers can potentially access it or not. If at least one attacker has access to the data flow at hand, we mark this data flow as an entry point. The result is shown in Fig. 6 (see Footnote 13). Warning triangles visualize each entry point in the Smart Home. An attacker will chose individual entry points depending on the asset(s) that he/she wants to compromise (Table 12).

With the elicitation of assets and entry points, vulnerabilities and possible threats can be derived. This is done in the following step by mapping entry points to assets and categorizing them according to the STRIDE taxonomy.

STRIDE stands for the following actions conducted by an attacker: *Spoofing*, e.g., the identity of a stakeholder; *Tampering* with data or code; *Repudiation* means plausible deniability of having performed an action; *Information disclosure* of access restricted data; *Denial of service* attacks; *Elevation of privilege* means an attacker gains an increased capability and gains admin (or root) capability. In Sect. 2.2, we introduced the identification of threats by mapping STRIDE threats to DFD elements. We use a vulnerability template (see Table 14) to describe the possible vulnerabilities associated with our entry points.

Table 13. Entry point elicitation table

Process	Possible Attackers	Reasoning
Wan+Wlan+LAN+Router	☑ Network Attacker ☐ Software Attacker	The router is connected to all kinds of networks of the smart home. Hence, the it is vulnerable to attacks against these networks. The software running on router cannot be changed or influenced without direct access.
Energy Meter	☑ Network Attacker ☐ Software Attacker	The Energy Meter is connected to the smart home using WLAN. Thus, it is accessible by an network attacker. The software cannot be changed and is tamper proofed.
Home Energy Management System	☑ Network attacker ☑ Software attacker	Is connected to the WLAN. Hence, accessible by the network attacker. And it is highly configurable and extensible with own code. Hence, it is prone to software attacks.

☑ : yes, ☐ : No

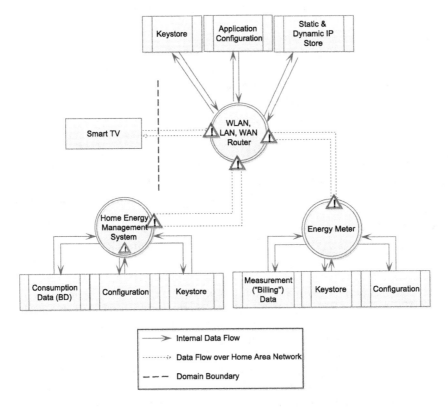

Fig. 6. Attacker Entry Points for the Smart Home

Table 14. Vulnerability template

Entry point	STRIDE threat	Attacker type	Reasoning
State the concerned entry point including relevant data flows and/or processes. For network attacker, data flows are always relevant and processes are optional, for a software attacker it's vice versa. The reason is that a network attacker considers the data flow first and afterwards can manipulate or use flows to manipulate a process. We add the process, if it is essential for this entry point to exist. For example, if a device provides root access rights to all incoming network connections it is essential for this entry point. In contrast, software attackers focus on exploits for source code, but may require data flows to, e.g., facilitate a data leak	State the considered STRIDE threat	State the concerned attacker type	Describe the threat instance

We illustrate one instantiated vulnerability templates for the *Home Energy Management System* (see Table 15). We refer for the remaining instantiations of our vulnerability template to our technical report (see Footnote 5).

Step 5. Determine Threats

In this final step of our threat analysis, we analyze how an attacker can possibly harm assets by using the entry points and their STRIDE threats elicited previously. For each asset we model at least one *Attack Path DFD*, which is a DFD that contains at least one threat caused by an attacker. All identified threats have to appear in at least one *Attack Path DFD*. The assets concerned in an *Attack Path DFD* are marked with a star symbol. The threat is modeled as a complex process that is marked in red and with the attacker symbol. This complex process exploits the entry points. We model these exploits using dotted lines

Table 15. Vulnerability template instance Home Energy Management System

Entry Point	STRIDE threat	Attacker type	Reasoning
Home Energy Management System (Process)	Spoofing	Software attacker	In a special scenario, Status & Control messages could be used to exploit the **EMS**. The attacker could analyze over a large period of time every message in the *HAN* and learn possible new ways to *spoof* other elements of the Home Area Network, e.g., the Smart Meter. This could lead to information disclosure and denial of service
Home Energy Management System (Process)	Tampering	Software attacker	An attacker can manipulate user policies, Status & Command messages and change the behavior of Smart Appliances at his will. In a worst case scenario, the attacker could physically harm a person inside the home
Home Energy Management System (Process)	Repudiation	Software attacker	An attacker can override non-repudiation mechanisms to gain advantage of e.g. third party services
Home Energy Management System (Process)	Information disclosure	Software attacker	An attacker has access to the EMS' databases. This enables the disclosure of all HAN traffic and Billing Data generated in real-time
Home Energy Management System (Process)	Denial of service	Software attacker	An attacker is able to deny any communication with the EMS, sabotaging Demand-Side-Management events, control over Smart Appliances, and the Prosumer's energy management
Home Energy Management System (Process)	Elevation of privileges	Software attacker	The EMS supports *third party plugins*, which are allowed a sandboxed space in the EMS' functionality. If a malicious plugin is able to find a backdoor to the full EMS functionality, several assets could be compromised: *Billing Data and customer profile data* that identify the customer, *cryptographic keys* which allow proper authentication against the *Energy Supplier*, other *third parties* and the *Smart Meter*. The *EMS* controls the physical behavior of *Smart Appliances* which might endanger the appliance itself or the well being of persons inside the house

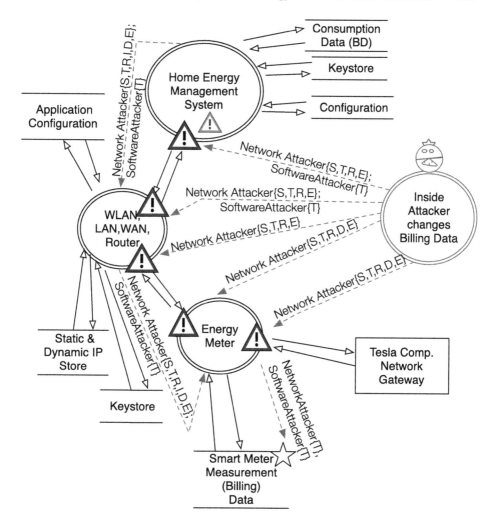

Fig. 7. Attack Path DFD: Inside attacker changes billing data

with filled arrows. The arrows are labeled with the attacker type followed by the exploited threat in curly brackets. If several attacker types have to be annotated on one exploit arrow, they are separated with a semicolon. In addition, we add exploit arrows at the processes containing the entry points to illustrate different paths towards the asset. Hence, the Attack Path DFD diagrams show multiple ways of how an attacker can harm an asset.

We present examples of an inside attacker that aims to change the billing data in Fig. 7 and an outside attacker in Fig. 8. An inside attacker in the smart home scenario is using only scope elements as entry points. In our example, an inside attacker could be an employee of Tesla or a resident of the smart home. Outside attackers are all other kinds of attackers.

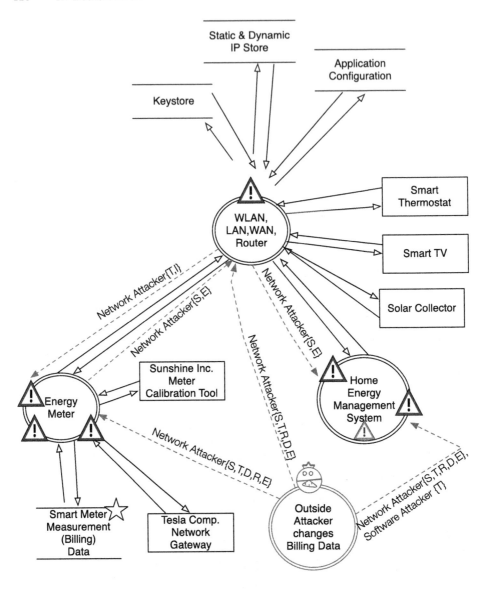

Fig. 8. Attack Path DFD: Outside attacker changes Billing Data

The attack path DFDs have to be analyzed for all possible attack paths. For example, the inside attacker with the goal to change billing data in the smart home (see Fig. 7) (see Footnote 13) can initiate spoofing by a network attacker at the entry point at the *Home Energy Management System* and pretend to be the *Energy Meter* that sends *Smart Meter Measurements*. Note that we did not show any STRIDE attacks that are not relevant for the attack process, such as information disclosure of *Smart Meter Measurements*. Tampering by a software attacker with the *Smart Meter Measurements* results in an exploit of the *Home Energy Management System*, such as cross side scripting (XSS). The attack executes malicious code in the *Home Energy Management System*. This causes the *Home Energy Management System* to display wrong *Smart Meter Measurements (Billing) Data*, which might lead to the false demand side management events, causing grid instability or enabling economic advantages for an attacker. In order to prevent the *Energy Meter* to send an update on *Smart Meter Measurements* the attacker could also initiate a denial of service attack to the meter. Another example is that the inside attacker could spoof the *Energy Meter* by pretending to be the *Tesla Comp. Network Gateway*. In this case the inside attacker would be an employee of Tesla, who has access to the keys for the encrypted communication between the *Tesla Comp. Network Gateway* and the *Energy Meter*. The employee could order the *Energy Meter* to reset the *Smart Meter Measurements (Billing) Data* and cause a loss of information. Another possibility would be that the attacker changes the measurements during the transmission to the *Tesla Comp. Network Gateway*. We propose to compile a list of attack paths that uses every entry point at least once.

We also provide examples concerning an outside attacker (see Fig. 8) (see Footnote 13). An outside attacker could use the *Internet Routing* to connect to the *WLAN,LAN,WAN, Router* process, e.g., via Spoofing as the *Tesla Comp. Server*. From there an attacker could try to move to the *Energy Meter* and pretend to be the *Tesla Comp. Server*. This could lead to a reset of the routing information, e.g., the IP-Address of the Tesla Comp. Network Gateway could be changed via a specific command. Normally this should only be possible via the *Sunshine Inc. Meter Calibration Tool*, however the attacker can conduct a denial of service attack on the flow between the Meter and the *Tesla Comp. Network Gateway*. When the Meter cannot contact the Tesla Comp. using the *Tesla Comp. Network Gateway* for more than 24 h, the *Energy Meter* accepts connections from the *Tesla Comp. Server* via the *WLAN,LAN,WAN, Router* with equal privileges.

5   Conclusion

We contribute a method for threat analysis of smart home scenarios. Our work is based on the threat analysis of the Microsoft Security Development Lifecycle (SDL), which is becoming a recognized best practice methodology. In particular, we provide patterns and templates that help to elicit and analyze domain knowledge and can be re-used for different projects. We illustrated our method on a smart home scenario that the industrial partners of the NESSoS project are considering.

The main benefits of our methods are as follows:

- A structured threat analysis method that refines the approach of the Microsoft SDL.
- Smart Home pattern for structured domain knowledge elicitation of different smart home scenarios.

- Scope and asset templates that refer to the elements of the smart home pattern and contain the demanded descriptions of the Microsoft SDL of these elements.
- A DFD pattern derived from the smart home pattern that can also be instantiated for different scenarios.
- Templates to describe assets and entry points into the system.
- Attack Path DFDs that illustrate how an attacker can move in the system from entry points to an asset in order to harm it.

In the future, we will formalize the threat analysis to enable computer-aided support for our threat analysis. Moreover, we want to conduct a controlled experiment with practitioners. Some of them shall use our method and some will apply the Microsoft SDL without our support. We will compare the results to figure out if our method reduces the workload of software engineers and at the same time enhances and/or refines threat findings.

References

1. Beckers, K., Faßbender, S., Heisel, M.: A meta-model approach to the fundamentals for a pattern language for context elicitation. In: Proceedings of the 18th European Conference on Pattern Languages of Programs (Europlop), ACM (2013) (Accepted for Publication)
2. Howard, M., Lipner, S.: The Security Development Lifecycle: SDL: A Process for Developing Demonstrably More Secure Software. Microsoft Press, Cambridge (2006)
3. Aloula, F., Al-Alia, A.R., Al-Dalkya, R., Al-Mardinia, M., El-Hajj, W.: Smart grid security: threats, vulnerabilities and solutions. Int. J. Smart Grid Clean Energy $1(1)$, 1–6 (2012)
4. Lin, H., Fang, Y.: Privacy-aware profiling and statistical data extraction for smart sustainable energy systems. IEEE Trans. Smart Grid $4(1)$, 332–340 (2013)
5. NIST: Guidelines for smart grid cyber security (2010)
6. Geer, D.: Are companies actually using secure development life cycles? Computer $43(6)$, 12–16 (2010)
7. Win, B.D., Scandariato, R., Buyens, K., Grégoire, J., Joosen, W.: On the secure software development process: Clasp, {SDL} and touchpoints compared. Inf. Softw. Technol. $51(7)$, 1152–1171 (2009). Special Section: Software Engineering for Secure Systems Software Engineering for Secure Systems
8. SANS: Sans - a member of the microsoft security development lifecycle (sdl) pro network (2014). http://www.sans.org/security-resources/microsoft-sdl
9. OWASP: CLASP (Comprehensive, Lightweight Application Security Process). Technical report, The Open Web Application Security Project (OWASP) (2011). https://www.owasp.org/index.php/Category:OWASP_CLASP_Project
10. Commission of the European communities.: Communication from the commission to the european parliament, the council, the European economic and social committee and the committee of the regions (2011)
11. Lu, Z., Lu, X., Wang, W., Wang, C.: Review and evaluation of security threats on the communication networks in the smart grid. In: Military Communications Conference, 2010 - MILCOM 2010, pp. 1830–1835 (2010)
12. Wang, W., Lu, Z.: Survey cyber security in the smart grid: survey and challenges. Comput. Netw. $57(5)$, 1344–1371 (2013)

13. Yang, Y., Littler, T., Sezer, S., McLaughlin, K., Wang, H.: Impact of cyber-security issues on smart grid. In: 2011 2nd IEEE PES International Conference and Exhibition on Innovative Smart Grid Technologies (ISGT Europe), pp. 1–7 (2011)
14. McDaniel, P., McLaughlin, S.: Security and privacy challenges in the smart grid. IEEE Secur. Priv. 7(3), 75–77 (2009)
15. Tøndel, I.A., Jaatun, M.G., Line, M.B.: Security threats in demo steinkjer - report from the telenor-sintef collaboration project on smart grids. Technical report, SINTEF/NTNU (2012)
16. Dhillon, D.: Developer-driven threat modeling: lessons learned in the trenches. IEEE Secur. Priv. 9(4), 41–47 (2011)
17. ISO/IEC: Information technology - Security techniques - Information security management systems - Requirements. ISO/IEC 27001, International Organization for Standardization (ISO) and International Electrotechnical Commission (IEC), Geneva, Switzerland (2005)
18. Swiderski, F., Snyder, W.: Threat Modeling. Microsoft Press, Redmond (2004)
19. Beckers, K., Côté, I., Hatebur, D., Faßbender, S., Heisel, M.: Common criteria compliAnt software development (CC-CASD). In: Proceedings 28th Symposium on Applied Computing, pp. 937–943. ACM (2013)
20. Beckers, K., Hatebur, D., Heisel, M.: A problem-based threat analysis in compliance with common criteria. In: Proceedings of the International Conference on Availability, Reliability and Security (ARES), pp. 111–120. IEEE Computer Society (2013)
21. Beckers, K., Küster, J.C., Faßbender, S., Schmidt, H.: Pattern-based support for context establishment and asset identification of the ISO 27000 in the field of cloud computing. In: Proceedings of the International Conference on Availability, Reliability and Security (ARES), pp. 327–333. IEEE Computer Society (2011)
22. Beckers, K., Faßbender, S.: Peer-to-peer driven software engineering considering security, reliability, and performance. In: Proceedings of the International Conference on Availability, Reliability and Security (ARES) - 2nd International Workshop on Resilience and IT-Risk in Social Infrastructures(RISI 2012), pp. 485–494. IEEE Computer Society (2012)
23. Beckers, K., Faßbender, S., Heisel, M., Meis, R.: Pattern-based context establishment for service-oriented architectures. In: Heisel, M. (ed.) Software Service and Application Engineering. LNCS, vol. 7365, pp. 81–101. Springer, Heidelberg (2012)
24. Beckers, K., Faßbender, S., Küster, J.-C., Schmidt, H.: A pattern-based method for identifying and analyzing laws. In: Regnell, B., Damian, D. (eds.) REFSQ 2011. LNCS, vol. 7195, pp. 256–262. Springer, Heidelberg (2012)
25. BSI: Protection Profile for the Gateway of a Smart Metering System (Gateway PP). Version 01.01.01(final draft), Bundesamt für Sicherheit in der Informationstechnik (BSI) - Federal Office for Information Security Germany, Bonn, Germany (2011). https://www.bsi.bund.de/SharedDocs/Downloads/DE/BSI/SmartMeter/PP-SmartMeter.pdf?_blob=publicationFile
26. BSI: Protection Profile for the Security Module of a Smart Meter Gateway (Security Module PP). Version 1.0), Bundesamt für Sicherheit in der Informationstechnik (BSI) - Federal Office for Information Security Germany, Bonn, Germany (2013). https://www.bsi.bund.de/SharedDocs/Downloads/DE/BSI/SmartMeter/PP_Security_%20Module.pdf?_blob=publicationFile
27. OPEN node project: Evaluation of general requirements according state of the art. Technical report, OPEN node project (2010)
28. OPEN node project: Functional Use cases. Technical report, OPEN node project (2011)

29. OPEN meter project: D1.1 Requirements of AMI. Technical report, OPEN meter project (2009)
30. Department of Energy and Climate Change: Smart metering implementation programme, response to prospectus consultation, overview document. Technical report, Office of Gas and Electricity Markets (2011)
31. Department of Energy and Climate Change: Smart metering implementation programme, response to prospectus consultation, design requirements. Technical report, Office of Gas and Electricity Markets (2011)
32. Mohsenian-Rad, A.H., Wong, V., Jatskevich, J., Schober, R., Leon-Garcia, A.: Autonomous demand-side management based on game-theoretic energy consumption scheduling for the future smart grid. IEEE Trans. Smart Grid 1(3), 320–331 (2010)

A Privacy-Friendly Framework
for Vehicle-to-Grid Interactions

Cristina Rottondi$^{(\boxtimes)}$, Simone Fontana, and Giacomo Verticale$^{(\boxtimes)}$

Dipartimento di Elettronica, Informazione e Bioingegneria, Politecnico di Milano,
P.zza L. da Vinci 32, 20133 Milano, Italy
{cristinaemma.rottondi,giacomo.verticale}@polimi.it

Abstract. In the next decades, Electric Vehicles (EVs) are expected to
gain increasing popularity and huge penetration in the automotive market, thanks to their potentialities for close interaction with the Smart
Grid ecosystem. Firstly, recharging EV's batteries with energy produced
by renewables will allow for a consistent reduction of pollution due to the
carbon emissions of traditional gasoline combustion; secondly, batteries
could be exploited to store/inject energy from/to the grid in order to
compensate the unpredictable fluctuations caused by Renewable Energy
Sources (RES). To this aim, a load aggregator is envisioned as a scheduling entity to plan the EVs' battery recharge/discharge according to the
user's needs and the current power generation of the grid. The main
drawback of the introduction of such load aggregator is a potential harm
of users' privacy: gathering information about the EVs' recharge requests
and plug/unplug events could make the scheduler able to infer the private travelling habits of the customers, thus exposing them to the risk of
tracking attacks and to other privacy threats. To address this issue, this
paper proposes a security infrastructure for privacy-friendly Vehicle-to-
Grid (V2G) interactions, which enables the load aggregator to schedule
the EV's battery charge/discharge without learning the current battery
level, nor the amount of charged/discharged energy, nor the time periods
in which the EVs are available for recharge. Our proposed scheduling protocol is based on the Shamir Secret Sharing scheme. We provide a security analysis of the privacy guarantees provided by our framework and
compare its performance to the optimal schedule that would be obtained
if the aggregator had full knowledge of the charging-related information.

1 Introduction

Electric Vehicles (EVs) such as battery powered automobiles and hybrid systems
combining electricity generators with gasoline engines [1,2] promise to reshape
the current concept of automotive industry [3,4], due to their low polluting emissions and their potential synergies with the future intelligent electricity network
(the so called Smart Grid). Transferring the energy demand from fuel/gasoline

The work in this paper has been partially funded by the Italian Ministry of Education, University and Reserach (MIUR) project ESPRESSo.

© Springer International Publishing Switzerland 2014
J. Cuellar (Ed.): SmartGridSec 2014, LNCS 8448, pp. 125–138, 2014.
DOI: 10.1007/978-3-319-10329-7_8

to electricity for transportation might significantly impact the overall power load experienced by the grid, thus challenging the power quality and stability of the energy distribution system. On the other hand, EVs' batteries could also represent a distributed storage resource, capable of absorbing surpluses in power generation (due e.g. to the intermittent and unpredictable production patterns of Renewable Energy Sources (RES)) and of injecting power into the grid during peak consumption periods [5,6].

Enabling such two-way energy exchanges between EVs and the power grid (named Vehicle-to-Grid (V2G) interactions) arises numerous issues in terms of suitable communication infrastructures [7], algorithms for intelligent energy management, and ancillary services to support the power transmission from sellers to purchasers. In particular, the new role of an aggregator devoted to the coordination of the charging/discharging process of a fleet of EVs has been speculated [8,9]: such new stakeholder will act as broker between the retail vehicle owners and the electrical utilities or grid operators, and various business models have already been proposed [10,11].

However, in order to make V2G interactions effective, details about the time periods in which the EVs are plugged-in at recharging station and about the expected amount of energy to be recharged in order to fulfill the user's traveling needs have to be communicated to the aggregator. Such data could potentially disclose private information (e.g. presence in a given location at a certain time), thus arising privacy concerns [12,13]: for instance, robbers could track people's movements before attempting burglaries, information about vehicle maintenance could be inferred and exploited for insurances and warranties, or companies could perform targeted marketing for car-related services.

This paper proposes a privacy-friendly infrastructure for V2G interactions which allows multiple Aggregators to cooperate in order to define the charging/discharging schedule of a fleet of EVs without learning the times of the vehicle's plug/unplug events, nor the amount of charged/discharged energy. All the data communicated by the EVs are shared among the Aggregators by means of the Shamir Secret Sharing (SSS) threshold cryptosystem, so that only a collusion of the whole set of Aggregators would be able to reconstruct the plain data.

The paper is organized as follows: Sect. 2 briefly overviews the related work, whereas some basics about the SSS cryptosystem are provided in Sect. 3. The privacy-preserving framework and the associated communication protocol for collaborative scheduling of the battery charge/discharge periods are presented in Sect. 4. The security analysis and the performance assessment of our infrastructure are discussed in Sects. 5 and 6, respectively. Section 7 concludes the paper.

2   Related Work

In the last years, the investigation of enabling technologies for (hybrid) electric automobiles has attracted increasing interest in the scientific community, and numerous issues concerning their integration within the power grid system have been addressed: Liu *et al.* [14] thoroughly analyse the impact of a massive introduction of EVs in the Smart Grid ecosystem, whereas Bessa *et al.* summarize the economical and technical models of aggregator agents for EVs proposed during the last decade.

Numerous studies on optimal strategies for EV's battery recharge have appeared: among those, Han et al. [15] formulate a game model for V2G interactions in presence of a profit-driven recharging station and two coexisting sets of EVs, behaving respectively as selfish or cooperative: the recharge of the former set of EVs is decided by the customers themselves according to the real-time energy selling price, while the station can directly control the charging/discharging process of the EVs belonging to the latter set. In our framework, we also consider two different priority levels: vehicles with high priority must necessarily be charged, while low-priority vehicles can be either charged or discharged according to the current grid power availability. Mets et al. [16] propose optimization strategies for the power consumption generated by PHEV charging in a residential use case, both in absence or presence of information about the trend of local and neighborhood power usage. Similarly, our scheduling algorithm assumes the knowledge of information about power generation provided by the grid, and vehicles learn whether the current power load experienced by the grid meets the current power supply trend. However, both paper do not focus on protecting user's recharge/travelling data, which are assumed to be known to all the nodes.

To the best of our knowledge, only a few papers investigated the security and privacy concerns which arise in the context of V2G interactions. Stegelmann and Kesdogan [17] list the security properties that a V2G network should satisfy, under assumption that the aggregator is an honest-but-curious entity. In their model the aggregator attempts to deduce the users' travel patterns by observing the EV's connections and disconnections at the recharging stations and matching them with possible itineraries, according to the corresponding estimated travelling times. A further refinement of such attacker model is presented by the same authors in [18], which supposes the aggregator to collect also auxiliary information about the current battery level of the EVs. Our attack scenario assumes the same adversary model, and our proposed protocol discloses to the aggregator no information regarding the recharging/discharging periods, the battery level and the amount of refilled energy.

An honest-but-curious aggregator is assumed also by Yang *et al.* [19], who design a two-layer infrastructure for EV monitoring and rewarding processes. The architecture comprises a set of local aggregators interfacing the EVs and a central aggregation entity which directly interacts with the market stakeholders, and ensures mutual authentication while preserving location and identity privacy and allowing for anonymous rewards. Our framework also assumes multiple collaborating aggregators and relies on the Shamir Secret Sharing threshold cryptosystem, which is computationally lighter.

Liu *et al.* [20] discuss a payment mechanism for V2G interactions ensuring anonymity, location privacy and allowing for car tracing in case of theft, whereas a pseudonym-based authentication protocol is proposed by Nicanfar *et al.* [21]. The protocol ensures location untraceability and relies on an external trusted entity that records the associations between pseudonyms and real identities to provide accountability for billing purposes. Though our framework is not aimed at billing, it could be easily integrated with such payment mechanisms.

3   Background on Shamir Secret Sharing Scheme

Shamir Secret Sharing (SSS) scheme [22] belongs to the family of threshold cryptosystems, which allow multiple collaborating entities to recover a secret previously divided in w *shares* and distributed among w participants. The secret can be reconstructed if at least t out of w participants cooperate, where $t \leq w$ is an arbitrary integer design parameter.

More specifically, the SSS scheme operates by choosing a prime number q, selecting $t-1$ integer random numbers $\rho_1, \rho_2, \cdots, \rho_{t-1}$ uniformly distributed in $[0, q-1]$, and splitting the secret $m \in Z_q$ in w shares (x_s, y_s) $(1 \leq s \leq w)$ by calculating the s-th share as $y_s = m + \rho_1 x_s + \rho_2 x_s^2 + \ldots + \rho_{t-1} x_s^{t-1} \bmod q$, where $x_s \in Z_q$ is arbitrarily chosen. The secret m can be recovered in presence of t or more shares, by means of an interpolation algorithm (e.g. the Lagrangian interpolator).

The SSS scheme provides homomorphic addition and multiplication, meaning that such operations can be computed directly on the shares, leading to the same result that would be obtained by operating on the secrets directly. However, while the sum of two shares can be autonomously performed by a single participant, multiplication requires an interactive and collaborative protocol, e.g. as the one described in [23]. It follows that any function containing only additions and multiplications can be calculated without directly accessing the secrets. In particular, numerous collaborative procedures to compare two secret values have been proposed (see e.g. [24,25]). In this paper, we will adopt the comparison protocol presented in [25], which works as follows: each party holding the s-th shares $(x_s, y_s), (x'_s, y'_s)$ of the secrets m and m' to be compared selects two big random numbers r_s, r'_s, which can multiplicatively hide $m - m'$, and a random bit $b_s \in \{0, 1\}$. The collaborative protocol enables each party to obtain a share of the quantity $c = (m - m') \prod_{s=1}^{t} (-1)^{b_s} r_s - \sum_{s=1}^{t} (-1)^{1-b_s} r'_s$. The result of the comparison can be computed by retrieving c, setting a bit e either to 0 in case $c > 0$ or to 1 otherwise[1], and calculating the result of the XOR operation $\xi = e \oplus b_1 \oplus \cdots \oplus b_t$. $\xi = 0$ indicates that $m > m'$, while $\xi = 1$ indicates that $m \leq m'$. The reader is referred to [25] for additional details about the collaborative procedure and the proof of the correctness of the comparison protocol.

---

[1] Note that in a modulo n field negative numbers are represented by the upper half of the range $[0, n-1]$.

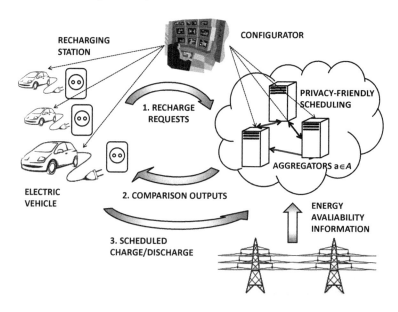

Fig. 1. The privacy-friendly scheduling infrastructure

4   The Privacy-Friendly V2G Communication Framework

Our proposed framework, which is depicted in Fig. 1, includes a set of EVs, $\mathcal{V}$, and set of Aggregators, $\mathcal{A}$, which cooperate to schedule the EVs' battery recharge/discharge.

We make the following assumptions:

1. Every EV can access the Internet both while travelling and being parked thanks to dedicated hardware and software (e.g. as proposed in [26]).
2. EVs and the Aggregators communicate over confidential and authenticated end-to-end channels.
3. The setup of the public-key infrastructure is performed by an external Configurator node.

We also assume that time is organized in a set of epochs $\mathcal{I}$ of duration T and that whenever a new epoch $i \in \mathcal{I}$ starts, the grid managers informs all the Aggregators about the maximum amount g_{i+1} of energy which is expected to be available for battery recharge during the next epoch, or which would be absorbed by the grid to balance the energy requests generated by other types of loads (e.g. emergency/critical services or must-run appliances). Moreover, each epoch i is divided in $|\mathcal{V}|$ time slots of duration $\tau \leq T/|\mathcal{V}|$.

The aim of the privacy-preserving infrastructure is to schedule the charge/discharge periods of each EV in order to fulfill the users' recharge needs without exceeding the grid overall power availability, while providing as much energy as possible to the grid by discharging batteries in case of power generation deficits.

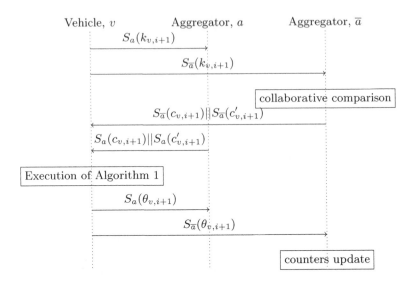

Fig. 2. Data exchange during the battery charge/discharge scheduling procedure

During an initial setup phase, a randomly chosen Aggregator $\bar{a}$ initializes a counter $d_v = 0$, which records the cumulative amount of charged/discharged energy for each Vehicle $v \in \mathcal{V}$ and which can be used for billing purposes, divides d_v in $|\mathcal{A}|$ shares using a (w, t)-SSS scheme with parameters $t = w = |\mathcal{A}|$ and distributes each share $S_a(d_v)$ to a different Aggregator $a \in \mathcal{A}$.

During the i-th epoch, the Aggregators initiate a polling cycle to schedule the charging/discharging processes of each EV for the successive epoch $i + 1$. The messages exchanged among Vehicles and Aggregators during the execution of the scheduling protocol are shown in Fig. 2. Let P_i be a variable recording the amount of power required for the charges/discharges scheduled during the current epoch i: positive values of P_i indicate that the grid must provide power to charge the batteries, while negative values indicate that the energy collected from the batteries is injected in the grid. Initially, the Aggregator $\bar{a}$ sets P_{i+1} to 0, divides it in shares and distributes the shares $S_a(P_{i+1})$ to the other Aggregators. Then, it randomly assigns to each vehicle $v \in \mathcal{V}$ one of the $|\mathcal{V}|$ time slots within epoch i. The assignment is refreshed at every epoch, in order to ensure fairness. During the time slot assigned to Vehicle v, the following steps are executed:

1. v initializes a parameter $k_{v,i+1}$ either to 0, in case it is unable or unwilling to be charged/discharged during the $i + 1$-th epoch (for instance because it is currently travelling or because its battery is already full) or to r_v, which indicates the Vehicle's charge/discharge rate. Further, v sets a priority bit $B_{v,i+1}$ to 1 if the Vehicle necessarily needs to be recharged during the next epoch (e.g. because the current battery level is extremely low), or to 0 otherwise. In the latter case, the battery of v could be either charged or discharged, according to the energy availability of the grid. Note that defining the policies

for the setting of $B_{v,i+1}$ is out of the scope of this paper, since it is influenced by multiple factors, including possible incentives in case of power injection from the battery to the grid, the travelling habits of the user, and the energy pricing. Then, v divides $k_{v,i+1}$ in $|\mathcal{A}|$ shares[2] $S_1(k_{v,i+1}), \dots, S_{|\mathcal{A}|}(k_{v,i+1})$ and distributes them among the $|\mathcal{A}|$ Aggregators, so that each Aggregator receives a different share.

2. Upon reception of the respective shares, in case $g_{i+1} > 0$ the Aggregators engage two collaborative procedures (see Sect. 3) to compare $P_{i+1} + k_{v,i+1}$ to g_{i+1}, and P_{i+1} to g_{i+1}. Conversely, in case $g_{i+1} < 0$, the Aggregators compare $P_{i+1} - k_{v,i+1}$ to g_{i+1}, and P_{i+1} to g_{i+1}. At the end of the comparison protocol, each Aggregator a obtains the shares of the two comparison results $S_a(c_{v,i+1}), S_a(c'_{v,i+1})$ and sends the message $S_a(c_{v,i+1})||S_a(c'_{v,i+1})$ to v.

3. v reconstructs the results of the two comparisons and schedules the battery recharge/discharge according to Algorithm 1, which produces the scheduling output $\theta_{v,i+1} \in \{-r_v, 0, r_v\}$. The scheduling principle is the following: if the priority bit $B_{v,i+1}$ is set to 1, v schedules the recharge of its battery during the $i + 1$-th epoch, regardless to the current grid conditions. Otherwise, the battery might be charged or discharged according to the grid energy availability/request, or no action is scheduled in case the grid power balancing has already been reached. Then, v divides $\theta_{v,i+1}$ in shares $S_1(\theta_{v,i+1}), \dots, S_{|\mathcal{A}|}(\theta_{v,i+1})$ and communicates each share to the respective Aggregator.

4. Each Aggregator a updates its own shares of d_v and P_{i+1} by adding $S_a(\theta_{v,i+1})$. Note that the counter d_v can be retrieved by any external entity in charge of providing the billing service by collecting the $|\mathcal{A}|$ shares of d_v from the Aggregators and interpolating them.

5   Security Discussion

In this Section we define the attacker model and the property of **blindness**, which we prove to be satisfied by our privacy-friendly scheduling framework.

Our attack scenario assumes that each Aggregator is *honest-but-curious*, meaning that it honestly executes the scheduling algorithm, but tries to obtain further information about the current battery levels of the EVs, the amount of refilled energy and the travelling patterns of the EVs by performing any desired elaboration on the received data. Moreover, it might collude with other Aggregators and access the messages they receive. Conversely, the EVs are supposed to behave honestly.

We say that the scheduling architecture provides $|\tilde{\mathcal{A}}|$-**blindness** if during any set of epochs $\tilde{\mathcal{I}} \subseteq \mathcal{I}$ a collusion of $\tilde{\mathcal{A}}$ Aggregators of cardinality $|\tilde{\mathcal{A}}| < |\mathcal{A}|$ learns

---

[2] For the sake of easiness, in this paper we set as SSS threshold $t = w$, meaning that all the Aggregators must collaborate to perform the charge/discharge scheduling procedure. However, to improve resiliency to faults and malfunctions, t could be lower than w. For a discussion on the correct choice of t and w, the reader is referred to [27].

Algorithm 1. The Privacy-Friendly Scheduling Algorithm

1: *On input of* $(S_1(c_{v,i+1}), \ldots, S_{|\mathcal{A}|}(c_{v,i+1}))$ *and* $(S_1(c'_{v,i+1}), \ldots, S_{|\mathcal{A}|}(c'_{v,i+1}))$
2: $\theta_{v,i+1} \leftarrow 0$
3: **if** $B_{v,i+1} = 1$ **then**
4:     $\theta_{v,i+1} \leftarrow r_v$ {recharge is scheduled regardless to the grid energy availability}
5: **else**
6:     **if** $g_{i+1} > 0 \wedge P_{i+1} + k_{v,i+1} < g_{i+1}$ **or** $g_{i+1} < 0 \wedge P_{i+1} < g_{i+1}$ **then**
7:         $\theta_{v,i+1} \leftarrow k_{v,i+1}$ {recharge is scheduled if the grid energy availability exceeds the current overall power load or if the total power injected into the grid exceeds the grid's energy request}
8:     **else**
9:         **if** $g_{i+1} > 0 \wedge P_{i+1} > g_{i+1}$ **or** $g_{i+1} < 0 \wedge P_{i+1} - k_{v,i+1} > g_{i+1}$ **then**
10:             $\theta_{v,i+1} \leftarrow -k_{v,i+1}$ {discharge is scheduled if the grid energy availability is not sufficient to serve the current load experienced by the grid or if the total power injected into the grid does not satisfy the grid's energy request}
11:         **end if**
12:     **end if**
13: **end if**

---

no additional information with respect to what is implied by the knowledge of $S_a(k_{v,i+1}), S_a(c_{v,i+1}), S_a(c'_{v,i+1}), S_a(\theta_{v,i+1})$ for each Aggregator $a \in \tilde{\mathcal{A}}$.

Definition 1. *We now define the* Blind *experiment, involving a challenger* $\mathcal{C}$ *controlling the set of Vehicles* $\mathcal{V}$ *and a probabilistic polynomial-time adversary* $\mathcal{D}$ *controlling the set of colluded Aggregators* $\tilde{\mathcal{A}}$:

1. $\mathcal{D}$ *selects two Vehicles* $v_1, v_2 \in \mathcal{V}$ *and the values* $k_{v_0,i}, k_{v_1,i}, \theta_{v_0,i}, \theta_{v_1,i}, g_i, P_i \, \forall i \in \tilde{\mathcal{I}}$ *and communicates them to* $\mathcal{C}$.
2. $\mathcal{C}$ *selects a random bit* $\bar{b}$ *and computes* $S_a(k_{v_{\bar{b}},i}), S_a(\theta_{v_{\bar{b}},i}) \, \forall i \in \tilde{\mathcal{I}}, a \in \tilde{\mathcal{A}}$, *runs the comparative procedure according to the value of* g_i *to obtain* $S_a(c_{v_{\bar{b}},i}), S_a(c'_{v_{\bar{b}},i})$ $\forall i \in \tilde{\mathcal{I}}, a \in \tilde{\mathcal{A}}$ *while storing two lists* $L_a(c_{v_b,i}), L_a(c'_{v_{\bar{b}},i})$ *of the messages received/ sent by each Aggregator* $a \in \tilde{\mathcal{A}}$ *during the execution, and gives all the results to* $\mathcal{D}$
3. $\mathcal{D}$ *outputs a bit* $\bar{b}'$.

The architecture provides $|\mathcal{A}|$-*blindness if:*

$$P(\bar{b}' = \bar{b} \mid S_a(k_{v_{\bar{b}},i}), S_a(\theta_{v_{\bar{b}},i}), L_a(c_{v_{\bar{b}},i}), L_a(c'_{v_{\bar{b}},i}), S_a(c_{v_{\bar{b}},i}), S_a(c'_{v_{\bar{b}},i})$$

$$\forall i \in \tilde{\mathcal{I}}, a \in \tilde{\mathcal{A}}) = P(\bar{b}' = \bar{b}) = \frac{1}{2} \quad (1)$$

Theorem 1. *The privacy-preserving scheduling described in Sect. 4 provides* $|\mathcal{A}|$-*blindness*.

Proof. The proof is a consequence of the property of *perfect secrecy* of the SSS scheme [28] and shows that the content of all the input/output messages received/sent by the collusion $\tilde{\mathcal{A}}$ during the scheduling procedure leaks no information about $\bar{b}$. For a single time epoch i, the proof can be constructed analogously to the one provided in [29, Theorem 3]: let $K_0, K_1, \Theta_0, \Theta_1$ be the random variables indicating the value of the parameters $k_{v_0,i}, k_{v_1,i}, \theta_{v_0,i}, \theta_{v_1,i}$ of Vehicles v_0, v_1. Since the values of K_0, Θ_0 are completely determined by knowledge of K_1, Θ_1, it follows that:

$$\Pr(\bar{b} = 0 \mid S_a(k_{v_{\bar{b}},i}), S_a(\theta_{v_{\bar{b}},i}), L_a(c_{v_{\bar{b}},i}), L_a(c'_{v_{\bar{b}},i}), S_a(c_{v_{\bar{b}},i}), S_a(c'_{v_{\bar{b}},i}))$$
$$\forall a \in \tilde{A} = \Pr(K_0 = k_{v_0,i}, K_1 = k_{v_1,i}, \Theta_0 = \theta_{v_0,i}, \Theta_1 = \theta_{v_1,i} \mid$$
$$S_a(k_{v_{\bar{b}},i}), S_a(\theta_{v_{\bar{b}},i}), L_a(c_{v_{\bar{b}},i}), L_a(c'_{v_{\bar{b}},i}), S_a(c_{v_{\bar{b}},i}), S_a(c'_{v_{\bar{b}},i})) \ \forall a \in \tilde{A}$$
$$= \Pr(K_0 = k_{v_0,i}, \Theta_0 = \theta_{v_0,i}, \mid S_a(k_{v_{\bar{b}},i}), S_a(\theta_{v_{\bar{b}},i}), L_a(c_{v_{\bar{b}},i}), L_a(c'_{v_{\bar{b}},i}),$$
$$S_a(c_{v_{\bar{b}},i}), S_a(c'_{v_{\bar{b}},i})) \ \forall a \in \tilde{A} \quad (2)$$

Since the random polynomials used to split each secret in $|\mathcal{A}|$ shares are independently generated, the knowledge of $S_a(k_{v_{\bar{b}},i}), S_a(\theta_{v_{\bar{b}},i})$ gives no information about $K_{1-\bar{b}}, \Theta_{1-\bar{b}}$. Further, we note that the messages listed in $L_a(c_{v_b,i}), L_a(c'_{v_b,i})$ are either shares of functions of the random numbers $r_s^{\bar{b},i}, r_s'^{\bar{b},i}, b_s^{\bar{b},i}$ utilized during the comparison protocol (see Sect. 3), or of intermediate results for the collaborative computation of $S_a(c_{v_{\bar{b}},i}), S_a(c'_{v_{\bar{b}},i})$, in which each share is in turn divided in w shares according to the procedure described in [23]. Therefore, by exploiting the perfect secrecy property of SSS (which states that the knowledge of less than t shares does not leak any information about the secret), we can write:

$$\Pr(K_0 = k_{v_0,i}, \Theta_0 = \theta_{v_0,i}, \mid S_a(k_{v_{\bar{b}},i}), S_a(\theta_{v_{\bar{b}},i}), L_a(c_{v_{\bar{b}},i}), L_a(c'_{v_{\bar{b}},i}),$$
$$S_a(c_{v_{\bar{b}},i}), S_a(c'_{v_{\bar{b}},i})) \ \forall a \in \tilde{A} = \Pr(K_0 = k_{v_0,i}, \Theta_0 = \theta_{v_0,i}) = \Pr(\bar{b} = 0) = \frac{1}{2} \quad (3)$$

The extension to a set of $|\tilde{\mathcal{I}}|$ epochs is straightforward, since the random polynomials used in the SSS scheme are also refreshed epoch by epoch.

Since in this paper we assume $t = w = |\mathcal{A}|$, information leakages can occur only in case all the $|\mathcal{A}|$ Aggregators are compromised and the infrastructure is $|\mathcal{A}|$-**blind**.

6   Performance Evaluation

We now evaluate our scheduling mechanism in terms of computational complexity, number and length of the messages, and compare its performance to the optimal results obtained by means of the ILP formulation proposed in [30].

6.1   Computational Complexity

We start evaluating the number of input/output messages at each node, for a single scheduling epoch. As shown in Table 1, the number of messages exchanged by the Vehicles exhibits a linear dependence on the number of shares $|\mathcal{A}|$, whereas for the Aggregators the dependence is linear in $|\mathcal{V}|$ and superlinear in $|\mathcal{A}|$

Table 1. Number of input/output messages per node for a single scheduling epoch

Node	Input	Output
Vehicle	$2|A|$	$2|A|$
Aggregator	$|\mathcal{V}|(2+3(|\mathcal{A}|-1)$ $+\sum_{j=1}^{\lfloor \log_2 |\mathcal{A}| \rfloor}(|\mathcal{A}|-1)\lfloor \frac{|\mathcal{A}|}{2^j} \rfloor)$	$|\mathcal{V}|(2+3(|\mathcal{A}|-1)$ $+\sum_{j=1}^{\lfloor \log_2 |\mathcal{A}| \rfloor}(|\mathcal{A}|-1)\lfloor \frac{|\mathcal{A}|}{2^j} \rfloor)$

Table 2. Computational load at each node for the scheduling of a single service request

Vehicle	$2C_s(q) + C_r(q)$
Aggregator	$|\mathcal{V}|(2C_s(q) + 2C_c(q) + 4C_a(q))$

see Table 3 for the cost details

(due to the collaborative comparison procedure discussed in [25], which is performed in a logarithmic number of interactions among the Aggregators). Note that, assuming that the values x_s used for the computation of the shares (x_s, y_s) are system parameters chosen in advance and thus do not need to be communicated to the nodes during the execution of the scheduling protocol, each message has size $L[q]$, where q is the modulo of the SSS scheme and $L[x]$ is a function which returns the length of x in number of bits.

Table 2 reports the operations per time epoch performed by each node. The computational cost of each operation is detailed in Table 3 based on [23, 25]. The most demanding procedure is the share collaborative comparison performed by the Aggregators in multiple rounds depending on $|\mathcal{A}|$.

6.2 Numerical Results

We compare the scheduling results obtained by our proposed protocol to the benchmark Integer Linear Program (ILP) proposed in [30], which assumes that the Aggregators have full knowledge of the time periods in which the EVs are plugged-in, the current battery charge level l_{vi} and the total amount of energy to be recharged in each battery. The policy used to determine the priority level of the EVs is the following: each Vehicle chooses a battery threshold level t_v: if in a given time epoch it holds that $l_{vi} < t_v$ and the Vehicle v will be available for recharge at epoch $i + 1$, then v sets $B_{v,i+1} = 1$, otherwise to 0. In case $B_{v,i+1} = 1$, v must be necessarily recharged in the next time epoch. The aim of the ILP is the maximization of the power consumption-to-power availability ratio δ, i.e. the ratio between the amount of power absorbed/injected by the EVs and the amount of power provided/requested by the grid. Note that δ ranges in $(-\infty : 1]$: 1 indicates that the EV fleet provides/absorbs the whole amount of power produced/requested by the grid, whereas negative values indicate that the scheduled battery recharge absorbs power even if the grid is experiencing power shortage.

We consider a scenario of a residential area of 1000 houses with peak power consumption of 3 kW [31], a windfarm (peak production of 8 MW [32]) and

Table 3. Detail of operation costs

$C_s(x)$	cost of the generation of $|\mathcal{A}|$ shares modulo x	$|\mathcal{A}|(|\mathcal{A}| - 1)$ additions modulo x
		$|\mathcal{A}|(|\mathcal{A}| - 1)$ multiplications modulo x $(|\mathcal{A}| - 1)$ random number generations modulo x
$C_a(x)$	cost of a share addition modulo x	1 addition modulo x
$C_l(x)$	cost of a share Lagrange interpolation modulo x	$O(|\mathcal{A}|^2)$ multiplications modulo x
$C_m(x)$	cost of a share collaborative multiplication modulo x	$C_s(x) + (|\mathcal{A}| - 1)C_a(x) +$ 2 multiplications modulo x, performed in 2 rounds
$C_c(x)$	cost of a collaborative comparison modulo x	2 random number generation modulo $x + 1$ random number generation modulo 2
		2 exponentiations modulo $x + 2$ multiplications modulo x
		$2C_s(x) + (|\mathcal{A}| + 1)C_a(x) + O(|\mathcal{A}|)C_m(x) + C_l(x)$, performed in $\lceil \log_2 |\mathcal{A}| \rceil$ rounds
$C_r(x)$	cost of a comparison result retrieval modulo x	$C_l(x) + |\mathcal{A}| - 1$ XOR operations over $\lceil \log_2 x \rceil$ bits

1000 EVs (battery maximum capacity between 12.75 and 17 kWh, charging rate of 0.75 or 1 kW [14], minimum recharge threshold between 1.5 and 2 kWh). The behavior of each Vehicle v in terms of departure time, arrival time and amount of energy required for the travel has been defined based on the TripChaining dataset [33].

Results averaged over 200 days (each day is divided in 96 epochs of 15 min duration, see Fig. 3 for an example of daily schedule) show that the running time of the privacy-friendly approach is significantly lower than the one of the ILP model (seconds vs. hours). The maximum δ provided by our algorithm is on average lower than the optimal one, which is due to the fact that, in case g_i is negative, the privacy-friendly approach always schedules the recharge of high priority EVs, while the ILP model might postpone it according to the knowledge of their future travelling behavior. However, the fraction of epochs in which $\delta \geq 0$, i.e. in which the overall energy absorption/injection due to the scheduled battery recharge/discharge compensates the grid's power supply/request trend, is not significantly lowered by the privacy-friendly approach w.r.t. the optimal solution provided by the ILP formulation (on average 99.7 % versus 99.86 %). Such behavior is confirmed when considering the degree of similarity (expressed in terms of Root Mean Square Error, normalized w.r.t. the overall grid power availability) between the curve of the grid power supply/request and the curve of the scheduled power usage: the privacy friendly algorithm leads only to a mild increase of the normalized RMSE w.r.t. the optimal scheduling (see Table 4).

Table 4. Comparison of the performance of ILP vs. privacy-friendly scheduling

Privacy-friendly scheduling					
Aver. δ	Max δ	Min δ	Epochs in which $\delta \geq 0$ (%)	Aver. Norm. RMSE	Time
−0.13	0.09	−14.02	99.70	2.84	0.4 s
ILP					
0.10	0.74	−1.05	99.86	1.99	3 h

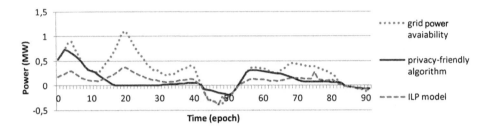

Fig. 3. Comparison of optimal vs privacy-friendly scheduled battery charges/discharges. Positive values indicate that the grid provides energy to recharge the EVs' batteries, while negative values indicate that energy provided by the batteries is injected into the grid.

7   Conclusion

This paper proposes a privacy-preserving Vehicle-to-Grid communication infrastructure which schedules the battery charge/discharge times of electric vehicles without exposing the users' travelling habits, the current battery level nor the amount of refilled energy. Performance in terms of computational times and gap w.r.t. the optimal schedule obtained by means of an Integer Linear Program shows the viability of the proposed privacy-friendly approach, which provides results not significantly dissimilar w.r.t. the optimal ones.

References

1. Chan, C., Bouscayrol, A., Chen, K.: Electric, hybrid, and fuel-cell vehicles: architectures and modeling. IEEE Trans. Veh. Technol. **59**(2), 589–598 (2010)
2. Offer, G., Howey, D., Contestabile, M., Clague, R., Brandon, N.: Comparative analysis of battery electric, hydrogen fuel cell and hybrid vehicles in a future sustainable road transport system. Energy Policy **38**(1), 24–29 (2010)
3. Parks, K., Denholm, P., Markel, A.J.: Costs and emissions associated with plug-in hybrid electric vehicle charging in the Xcel Energy Colorado service territory. National Renewable Energy Laboratory Golden, CO (2007)
4. Sioshansi, R., Denholm, P.: Emissions impacts and benefits of plug-in hybrid electric vehicles and vehicle-to-grid services. Environ. Sci. Technol. **43**(4), 1199–1204 (2009)

5. Kempton, W., Tomić, J.: Vehicle-to-grid power implementation: from stabilizing the grid to supporting large-scale renewable energy. J. Power Sources **144**(1), 280–294 (2005)
6. DeForest, N., Funk, J., Lorimer, A., Ur, B., Sidhu, I., Kaminsky, P., Tenderich, B.: Impact of widespread electric vehicle adoption on the electrical utility business-threats and opportunities. Center for Entrepreneurship and Technology (CET) (2009)
7. U.S. Department of Energy (DOE): Communication requirements for smart grid technologies (2010)
8. Kempton, W., Tomic, J., Letendre, S., Brooks, A., Lipman, T.: Vehicle-to-grid power: battery, hybrid, and fuel cell vehicles as resources for distributed electric power in california. In of Transportation Studies (UCD), U.D.I., ed.: Working Paper Series ECD-ITS-Rr-=1-03 (2001)
9. Brooks, A.: Integration of electric drive vehicles with the power grid-a new application for vehicle batteries. In: The Seventeenth Annual Battery Conference on Applications and Advances, p. 239 (2002)
10. Kempton, W., Marra, F., Andersen, P., Garcia-Valle, R.: Business models and control and management architectures for ev electrical grid integration. In: Garcia-Valle, R., Peas Lopes, J.A. (eds.) Electric Vehicle Integration into Modern Power Networks. Power Electronics and Power Systems, pp. 87–105. Springer, New York (2013)
11. Brooks, A.: Vehicle-to-grid demonstration project: grid regulation ancillary service with a battery electric vehicle. In: Research Report to CARB, AC Propulsion (2002)
12. Hoh, B., Gruteser, M., Xiong, H., Alrabady, A.: Enhancing security and privacy in traffic-monitoring systems. IEEE Pervasive Comput. **5**(4), 38–46 (2006)
13. Liao, L., Patterson, D.J., Fox, D., Kautz, H.: Learning and inferring transportation routines. Artif. Intell. **171**(5–6), 311–331 (2007)
14. Liu, R., Dow, L., Liu, E.: A survey of pev impacts on electric utilities. In: 2011 IEEE PES Innovative Smart Grid Technologies (ISGT), pp. 1–8 (2011)
15. Han, Y., Chen, Y., Han, F., Liu, K.: An optimal dynamic pricing and schedule approach in v2g. In: 2012 Asia-Pacific Signal Information Processing Association Annual Summit and Conference (APSIPA ASC), pp. 1–8 (2012)
16. Mets, K., Verschueren, T., Haerick, W., Develder, C., De Turck, F.: Optimizing smart energy control strategies for plug-in hybrid electric vehicle charging. In: 2010 IEEE/IFIP Network Operations and Management Symposium Workshops (NOMS Wksps), pp. 293–299, April 2010
17. Stegelmann, M., Kesdogan, D.: Design and evaluation of a privacy-preserving architecture for vehicle-to-grid interaction. In: Petkova-Nikova, S., Pashalidis, A., Pernul, G. (eds.) EuroPKI 2011. LNCS, vol. 7163, pp. 75–90. Springer, Heidelberg (2012)
18. Stegelmann, M., Kesdogan, D.: Location privacy for vehicle-to-grid interaction through battery management. In: 2012 Ninth International Conference on Information Technology: New Generations (ITNG), pp. 373–378 (2012)
19. Yang, Z., Yu, S., Lou, W., Liu, C.: p^2: privacy-preserving communication and precise reward architecture for v2g networks in smart grid. IEEE Trans. Smart Grid **2**(4), 697–706 (2011)
20. Liu, J.K., Au, M.H., Susilo, W., Zhou, J.: Enhancing location privacy for electric vehicles (at the *Right* time). In: Foresti, S., Yung, M., Martinelli, F. (eds.) ESORICS 2012. LNCS, vol. 7459, pp. 397–414. Springer, Heidelberg (2012)

21. Nicanfar, H., Hosseininezhad, S., TalebiFard, P., Leung, V.C.M.: Robust privacy-preserving authentication scheme for communication between electric vehicle as power energy storage and power stations. In: INFOCOM, pp. 3429–3434. IEEE (2013)
22. Shamir, A.: How to share a secret. Commun. ACM **22**, 612–613 (1979)
23. Bogdanov, D.: Foundations and properties of shamir's secret sharing scheme (2007). Research Seminar in Cryptography
24. Nishide, T., Ohta, K.: Multiparty computation for interval, equality, and comparison without bit-decomposition protocol. In: Okamoto, T., Wang, X. (eds.) PKC 2007. LNCS, vol. 4450, pp. 343–360. Springer, Heidelberg (2007)
25. Kerschbaum, F., Biswas, D., de Hoogh, S.: Performance comparison of secure comparison protocols. In: 20th International Workshop on Database and Expert Systems Application, pp. 133–136 (2009)
26. Bychkovsky, V., Hull, B., Miu, A., Balakrishnan, H., Madden, S.: A measurement study of vehicular internet access using in situ wi-fi networks. In: Proceedings of the 12th Annual International Conference on Mobile Computing and Networking, MobiCom '06, pp. 50–61. ACM, New York (2006)
27. Rottondi, C., Verticale, G., Capone, A.: Privacy-preserving smart metering with multiple data consumers. Comput. Netw. **57**(7), 1699–1713 (2013)
28. Stinson, D.: Cryptography Theory and Practice, 2nd edn. CRC Press, Boca Raton (2005)
29. Rottondi, C., Mauri, G., Verticale, G.: A protocol for metering data pseudonymization in smart grids to appear on Transactions on Emerging Telecommunications Technologies.doi:10.1002/ett.2760
30. Rottondi, C., Fontana, S., Verticale, G.: Enabling privacy in vehicle-to-grid interactions for battery recharging. Energies **7**, 2780–2798 (2014)
31. Barker, S., Mishra, A., Irwin, D., Cecchet, E., Shenoy, P., Albrecht, J.: Smart*: an open data set and tools for enabling research in sustainable homes. In: The 1st KDD Workshop on Data Mining Applications in Sustainability (SustKDD) (2011)
32. Global Energy Forecasting Competition 2012: Wind forecasting. http://www.kaggle.com/c/GEF2012-wind-forecasting/data
33. U.S. Department of Transportation, Federal Highway Administration: National household travel survey (2009)

Reactive Security for Smart Grids Using Models@run.time-Based Simulation and Reasoning

Thomas Hartmann[(⊠)], Francois Fouquet, Jacques Klein, Gregory Nain,
and Yves Le Traon

Interdisciplinary Centre for Security, Reliability and Trust (SnT),
University of Luxembourg, Luxembourg, Luxembourg
{thomas.hartmann,francois.fouquet,jacques.klein,
gregory.nain,yves.letraon}@uni.lu
http://wwwen.uni.lu/snt

Abstract. Smart grids leverage modern information and communication technology to offer new perspectives to electricity consumers, producers, and distributors. However, these new possibilities also increase the complexity of the grid and make it more prone to failures. Moreover, new advanced features like remotely disconnecting meters create new vulnerabilities and make smart grids an attractive target for cyber attackers. We claim that, due to the nature of smart grids, unforeseen attacks and failures cannot be effectively countered relying solely on proactive security techniques. We believe that a reactive and corrective approach can offer a long-term solution and is able to both minimize the impact of attacks and to deal with unforeseen failures. In this paper we present a novel approach combining a Models@run.time-based simulation and reasoning engine with reactive security techniques to intelligently monitor and continuously adapt the smart grid to varying conditions in near real-time.

Keywords: Models@run.time · Reactive security · Reasoning engine · Smart grid · Model-driven engineering · Meta-modeling

1 Introduction

The vision of the smart grid promises to significantly increase the efficiency and reliability of the electricity grid and to seamlessly integrate micro generations and renewable energies. New services for electricity consumers, producers, and distributors will be created. One big step to turn this vision into reality is to use modern ICT to enable a two-way communication between customer devices and smart grid providers. On the one hand this facilitates advanced new features like remotely reading usage information from a meter or controlling devices through remote commands. On the other hand these new abilities make the smart grid more complex, making it inevitably more prone to failures, and more vulnerable

© Springer International Publishing Switzerland 2014
J. Cuellar (Ed.): SmartGridSec 2014, LNCS 8448, pp. 139–153, 2014.
DOI: 10.1007/978-3-319-10329-7_9

to attacks. This introduces new challenges. Moreover, advanced features like remotely disconnecting smart meters, makes the smart grid a valuable target for cyber attackers. Exploited vulnerabilities can result in the takeover of devices by an attacker, which can subsequently lead to serious crises as city blackouts. In particular, with a view to the rising cybercrime and given the importance of the electricity grid, it is essential to effectively protect it against attacks and failures.

Considering the complexity of smart grids and the fact that security techniques must dynamically evolve and improve over time to face future attacks and failures, we claim that proactive security techniques (like encryption, network-, and protocol security), although very useful, are not sufficient as a stand-alone approach. Instead, it must be anticipated that not all attacks and failures can be successfully prevented using proactive measures. We believe that, besides proactive security measures, a reactive and corrective security approach for smart grids is essential for at least two main reasons. First, it allows to deal with attacks and failures by monitoring and continuously adapting the smart grid to varying conditions like attacks, failures, and potential dangers—which together we refer to as *events*—in near real-time. Second, reactive security techniques allow to minimize the global impact of successful local attacks and failures. In this paper we present a novel approach combining a Models@run.time-based reasoning engine with reactive security techniques for smart grids. We mainly want to address security issues related to the stability and availability of the smart grid. By using an abstract model of state and behaviour of physical smart grid elements, a reasoning engine can simulate and explore potential actions on how to react to an event. For example, when an intrusion into a smart meter is detected, the reasoning engine could react by remotely deactivating the communication module of this smart meter to isolate it in order to avoid cascading failures (like reading potentially corrupted data from it). The models are used at runtime to monitor the smart grid with the intention of filling the gap between software models and the physical grid. Based on the Models@run.time paradigm the reasoning engine can simulate, explore, and evaluate different protection actions and their impacts in near real-time before the most appropriate ones (to secure and stabilize the grid) can be selected and applied to the real system.

The rest of this paper is organized as follows. Section 2 briefly introduces the background of this work: smart grids, Models@run.time, and reactive security. Section 3 details our Models@run.time-based simulation and reasoning engine and Sect. 4 presents numbers from a real implementation of this approach. The related work is discussed in Sect. 5. Finally, Sect. 6 gives an outlook on future work before this paper concludes in Sect. 7.

2   Background

2.1   Smart Grid

Today's electricity grid was designed for the demand of the 20th century where power generation was centralized and electricity was delivered from utilities to customers in a strictly one-way direction. This changes with the integration of micro generations and renewable energies where electricity can be exchanged in both directions. Energy produced from private windmills, for example, can be sold to providers in times of high demand. Furthermore, electric vehicles could help to balance load by delaying their charge cycles or even transferring electricity back to the grid in peak times, as proposed in [10,21]. Modern ICT is applied to automate and control the electricity grid by enabling a two-way communication between customer devices and grid providers. This makes it possible to remotely read (consumption) data from meters and, what is more important, send commands to devices. This modernization of the electricity grid to meet the demands of the 21th century and especially it's distributed control ability is referred to as the *smart grid future* by Farhangi [15]. Bruno *et al.* [7] propose that a distributed control of smart grids can significantly improve its stability by locally smoothing the energy consumption. Among smart grid devices, smart meters are the cornerstones of the new infrastructure. While their initial task was mainly *automated meter reading* (AMR) [15], in future scenarios they tend to become highly interconnected and control other devices—like gas meters and micro generation devices—to build a so called *advanced metering infrastructure* (AMI) [15]. Electricity grids are typically controlled by SCADA (Supervisory Control and Data Acquisition) systems which control electricity production and delivery in real-time. These systems ensure the global stability of the grid by performing dynamic load balancing of electricity production, depending on customer consumption. SCADA systems have strong constraints concerning latency to ensure resilience of the grid in case of over-usage, as described by Aim and Wollenberg [1]. A challenge when designing smart grid infrastructures [7] is the coordination of SCADA systems and new communication networks across smart meters. SCADA systems typically focus on electricity production and delivery management, while smart meters and the smart grid network focuses on local consumption optimization and management.

2.2   Models@run.time

The smart grid aims to become a self-adaptive and self-healing system. Such systems usually need to analyze their surrounding environment and internal state in order to continuously adapt themselves to varying conditions. Therefore, building an appropriate abstraction model, which reflects the current context of the system is of key importance. Over the past few years, an emerging paradigm called *Models@run.time* [6,27] proposes to use models both at design and runtime in order to support self-adaptive and intelligent systems. At design-time, following the Model-Driven Engineering (MDE) paradigm [22], models support the design and implementation of the system. The same (or similar) models are then embedded at runtime in order to support the reasoning processes of self-adaptive and intelligent systems. The idea behind this is that models offer a *simpler, safer and cheaper* [30] means to reason. In addition to the static structure of a system it is also possible to include the dynamic behavior in the model [29] to create a so-called executable model. The dynamic behavior of a system can be expressed using several paradigms such as stochastic queuing theory [36] or finite state automata [9]. State machines [32] are a well known semantic to express behavior in terms of states and transitions, which are triggered in reaction to events.

2.3   Reactive Security

Reactive security follows the idea that it is nearly impossible to proactively prevent all kind of possible attacks and failures. Instead, it must be taken into account that techniques used for cybercrime will continuously evolve and—in some cases—outperform previously installed proactive security techniques. Whereas proactive security has to predict future attacks, which is very hard, reactive security has to minimize the effect of attacks, *e.g.* by learning from the past, which is in many cases easier [2]. Reactive security approaches aim to prevent attacks by intelligently monitoring and early reacting to changes [31], or to minimize the global effect of successful attacks. For example, a denial of service (DoS) or distributed denial of service (DDoS) attack on a smart grid concentrator can be countered reactively by dynamically putting the attackers on blacklists.

3   Models@run.time-Based Simulation and Reasoning

3.1   General Approach

We propose a reactive security approach for smart grids. As smart grids are becoming more and more complex and techniques used for cybercrime will continuously evolve, we believe that effective protection mechanisms for smart grids must be able to react dynamically to successfully counter attacks and failures. Thus smart grids need the ability to continuously adapt themselves in order to react to various events. Therefore, they need to analyze their surrounding environment and internal state. We suggest using an abstract model of state and behaviour of physical smart grid components. Based on the Models@run.time paradigm this model reflects the internal state of the smart grid and is continuously updated with state information of the physical smart grid components. It is a common approach for self-adaptive systems to regularly sample and store the context of the system in order to back the reasoning algorithms up with historical data. That the Models@run.time approach is suitable for large distributed and self-adaptive systems has, for example, been shown in [27,28]. The model is used at runtime to simulate and explore different actions to react to events in real-time. The model, which represents the state of the smart grid at the time of an event, can be cloned to simulate several reactions on independent models. This happens in near real-time. Based on results of different simulations, appropriate corrective actions can be derived and either suggested for manual application or automatically applied to the real system. The basic concept of our Models@run.time-based reasoning engine is illustrated in Fig. 1.

The goal is twofold: first to prevent attacks and failures by intelligently monitoring and continuously adjusting the smart grid and second to minimize the

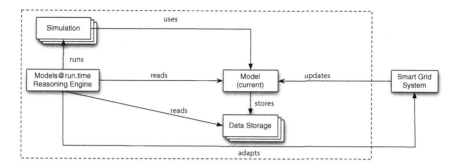

Fig. 1. Models@run.time-based reasoning engine

global impact of (successful) attacks and failures. The key thing to note is that our reasoning engine works reactive. It always searches for appropriate counter-measures to dynamically react to an event. Typical events, which we target to counter with our approach, are:

– **Intrusion detection**: It doesn't matter whether the attack is detected by our reasoning engine or by another tool (specific attacks might be best detected in specific layers by specific tools). The proposed reasoning engine is particularly suitable to detect attacks by identifying deviations from normal behaviour, usually called *anomaly-based detection* [4]. For instance, by continuously monitoring state information, state flapping (state oscillating between two configurations) of devices can be detected. By continuously monitoring network traffic and checking against the expected traffic, attacks like flooding an entity (smart meter, concentrator) with messages can be detected. Also, by monitoring sender and receiver of messages, suspicious messages can be identified. For example, a meter request to send consumption data to a device to which the corresponding meter is not logically registered to, is suspicious. Another example for a potentially suspicious behaviour would be if a large number of smart meters in one area receive the command to shut the electricity down (even if the command is send by a trusted entity). In addition to anomaly-based intrusion detection the proposed reasoning engine can be feed with data from other tools, *e.g. specification-based intrusion detection* systems [4,5] or *signature-based intrusion detection* systems [4]. All this data can be aggregated and analyzed by the reasoning engine and used to derive appropriate counter-measures. For example, the communication module of affected smart grid devices, like smart meters, can be remotely deactivated to isolate it in order to avoid cascading failures. Another strategy would be to blacklist the device so that other devices no longer exchange messages with potentially corrupted devices.
– **Electrical load**: Based on the current load, combined with historical data (*e.g.* last 20 Monday evenings) the reasoning engine can predict how the load will likely develop and if a critical limit could be exceed. Besides creating

alarm messages, this information can be used to delay/encourage electric cars to charge. Similarly, the voltage level can be monitored and predicted to decide if local production units must be connected/disconnected.

- **Communication network traffic**: Based on the knowledge of the used protocols, the network technologies, and historical data the reasoning engine can simulate and evaluate the number of messages required for an action and thus predict the network load. This information can be used to delay actions (like sending consumption data) to keep the overall network load below a critical value.
- **DoS/DDoS**: DoS and DDoS attacks can be detected by the reasoning engine, *e.g.* by monitoring the network traffic and state information of attacked components. Potential attackers could be automatically added to a blacklist. Or, in case of an affected concentrator the reasoning engine could deactivate it and initiate that connected smart meters reconnect to other concentrators.
- **Frequency of disturbances**: In complex and distributed systems, like smart grids, it is normal that from time to time minor disturbances (like meters are temporarily not reachable) occur. By monitoring disturbances over time the reasoning engine can detect an unusual high frequency, which can indicate security problems.
- **State changes**: A frequent change of state (like repeated unsuccessful register intents) often indicates security issues of smart meters. Such problems can be detected by the reasoning engine and can for instance cause to deactivate the communication module of the concerning meters.

The counter-measures found by the reasoning engine can be either automatically applied to the real system or only proposed for a manual validation. It is conceivable that counter-measures first must be manually validated and then, based on this validation, the reasoning engine can automatically improve itself by learning from these decisions. For example, if a counter-measure for a certain event has been manually validated and confirmed for automatic execution, the reasoning engine can apply this solution in the future automatically. If a manual validation indicates that the proposed counter-measure is not appropriate, the reasoning engine can learn which counter-measure should be used instead (i.e. the counter-measure which is manually selected instead the one automatically proposed). Also, for reasons of safety, counter-measures with a very big impact on the grid may be only applied after a manual validation and confirmation.

One risk of our Models@run.time-based simulation and reasoning engine is that the model could not correctly reflect the state of the real system. This could for example be due to the fact that the model has not been updated since the last important state change of the smart grid system. This is known as *eventually consistent* [35]. In general, a model can always only reflect a partial view of a real system. This is a general problem that self-adaptive and intelligent systems face and has to be taken into account by the reasoning engine.

3.2   Smart Grid and Behaviour Model

Topology Model. Our model for smart grids consists of different components: smart meters, repeaters, concentrators, SCADA systems, and a central control system and reflects how these components are connected. The basic structure of our model is inspired by the smart grid configuration currently deployed in Luxembourg [20], as we work in close collaboration with Creos Luxembourg S.A[1] on cyber security for smart grids. Figure 2 shows a simplified topology of the smart grid components described with our model. Each smart meter is connected to a concentrator, either directly or via one or several repeaters, and each concentrator in turn is connected to the central system. One or several SCADA systems are used to monitor and control the physical smart grid processes. The proposed reasoning engine operates on top of a model representation of this structure.

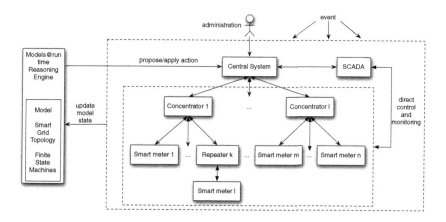

Fig. 2. Topology model

FSM Model for Behaviour. In order to model the behaviour of our structural smart grid components (smart meter, repeater, concentrator, central system, SCADA) we use Finite State Machines (FSM). The suitability of FSMs to model and simulate behaviour has been shown in [17,32]. Each message sent to a component can be interpreted as an event for the corresponding FSM and can trigger a state change. Figure 3 shows a simplified representation how a typical smart grid process can be simulated using FSMs. For the sake of simplicity, all states which are not necessary for the example are omitted. It shows how a smart meter registers to a concentrator after starting up.

The initial state of each smart meter and concentrator is *inactive*. Lets now assume *concentrator 1* and *concentrator 2* are in state *active* and *smart meter 1*

---

[1] Creos Luxembourg S.A is the main grid operator in Luxembourg.

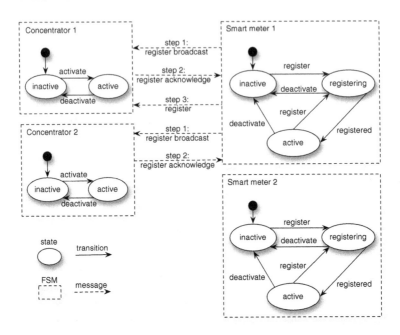

Fig. 3. FSM scenario for registering smart meters

and *smart meter 2* are in state *inactive*. When switching a smart meter on, it tries
to register itself to a concentrator and enters the state *registering*. As illustrated
in the figure, *smart meter 1* broadcasts its registering intent to all reachable
concentrators (step 1). Upon receiving this message the reached concentrators
send acknowledge or deny messages back to *smart meter 1* (step 2). Based on
criteria such as signal strength and number of hops to the central system, *smart
meter 1* decides to register to *concentrator 1*. It then sends a corresponding
register confirmation back to *concentrator 1* (step 3). Depending on the real
smart gird implementation (*e.g.* used protocols) this behaviour may vary. Again,
the described protocol is inspired by the smart grid deployment in Luxembourg.
By additionally taking the average size and payload of messages into account,
even the impact of the network load can be simulated and evaluated.

   This simple example illustrates how we simulate typical smart grid processes
using FSMs to model the behavior of smart grid components. Another example
is to simulate the effects of a deactivated communication link (or electricity link)
of a concentrator; thus how many smart meters are affected, how long it will take
until all of them are registered again, and so on.

3.3   Reasoning Engine Scope

Through observing and dynamically reacting our Models@run.time-based reasoning engine aims to support the smart grid to become self-adaptive and thus
self-healing. Intelligent and self-adaptive software systems need to analyze both

their surrounding environments and their internal state in order to continuously adapt themselves to changing conditions. Therefore, building an appropriate model, to reflect the current context of such systems is of key importance. The model of our reasoning engine focuses on the basic state, structure, and behavior of physical smart grid components. This means that our model reflects if a smart meter is active or not, that a smart meter can receive commands, and that this may change the current state. It also covers knowledge of how these components are interconnected and thereby how certain actions cascade. For example the model contains the necessary information about which smart meters are affected if a concentrator fails. We do not intend to duplicate the complete runtime system, but intend to build an appropriate abstraction containing the relevant parts of the system. It aggregates and combines information collected from different layers. This means our model is not limited only to application oriented layers but can also take information of lower layers (*e.g.* data bases, network traffic) into account. However, it is not the goal of our model to reflect detailed physical processes like the control of electricity production and delivery management. Our smart grid model contains only knowledge which will be used by our reasoning engine to simulate and explore potential actions on how to react to attacks, failures, and potential problems (like local electrical overload). Moreover, we do not intend to replace any existing control systems, like SCADA systems, or security systems. Instead, our proposed reasoning engine complements such systems by aggregating their information to build an appropriate context model.

3.4   Searching Appropriate Counter-Measures

In order to derive appropriate counter-measures to face an event, our reasoning engine must be able to evaluate and compare different actions. Each action can potentially change the state of the model. The goal of the reasoning engine is to propose actions which lead to an *improvement* of the overall model state. First of all, this requires knowledge about what actions are applicable to face an event. This is domain knowledge and is in form of rules integrated in the knowledge base of our reasoning engine. Second, it requires evaluation functions for our model to compare different states.

Counter-Actions are the reactions of our reasoning engine in order to counter events. Examples for events and appropriate counter-actions are:

- Smart meter intrusion detection: deactivate communication module of the smart meter to isolate it and avoid additional damage.
- Disconnected smart meter (customers' electricity is off): send command to restart the electricity link.
- High/low local electric load level: delay/encourage charging of electric cars.
- High/low local voltage level: disconnect/connect local production units (where possible).

Evaluation Functions to evaluate a model we use a set of rules, which are part of the domain knowledge and added to the knowledge base of our reasoning engine. For instance, such a rule is that disconnected (electricity for a customer is down) smart meters are worse than connected ones or that the local electrical load should not exceed (or fall below) a certain value for a longer period of time. Further examples are: Smart meters which are regularly not reachable or have weak connections to their data concentrators lead to a worse state. This applies also for smart meters in error states and especially for smart meters where intrusions are detected. The combination of all rules allows to calculate an overall score for the model. This score in turn is used to compare model states. For example, a failure of a data concentrator leads to a decreasing model state. This failure affects all smart meters connected to this data concentrator since they can no longer communicate with the failed data concentrator, further decreasing the model state. One conceivable reaction could be to connect the smart meters to an alternative data concentrator. Each smart meter which is connected again to a data concentrator increases the model state. By comparing scores of models it can be evaluated if actions improve or downgrad a model state.

Selection the goal of the reasoning engine is to find (and select) appropriate counter-reactions to face an event. The procedure is as follows: from a set of possible counter-reactions (knowledge base), the reasoning engine simulates the (independent) application of different actions using the model and evaluates which actions are the most appropriate ones (leads to the best model state). It is important to notice that the simulation and selection of the counter-reactions happen in near real-time. As a first approach we implemented a greedy [33] algorithm. But other algorithms which are not limited to search local optimums but also consider steps before and after the current, might be far more useful and are subject to study in future work.

3.5   Scalability

Since smart grids can consist of a huge number of components the scalability of our approach is very important. Operations to navigate or manipulate our model at runtime must be very efficient in terms of time and space. Therefore, we are working on a Models@run.time framework, called Kevoree Modeling Framework [16], which is specifically designed for this purpose. It is also conceivable to split the smart grid model into sub-models and distribute the reasoning over multiple nodes. An appropriate strategy is to split the model accordingly to the topology of the grid, such as deploying one instance of the reasoning engine on each data concentrator. Each of these local reasoning engines can then monitor one part or region of the smart grid. The information of the local reasoning engines can be combined on a global level.

4   Case Study Luxembourg

4.1   Scenario

We have implemented a concrete smart gird model based on the approach discussed in Sect. 3. The smart grid test deployment in Luxembourg, which is currently deployed by our industrial partner Creos S.A., is the template for our abstract model. The topology of our model primarily consists of: Smart meters, data concentrators, physical cables, consumption and production data, GPS location data of devices, logical communication connections, and routing tables. Overall, the concrete model of our case study includes around 250 nodes (smart meters, data concentrators), 30 physical cables, and 25.000 consumption data sets per day. We currently cross compile our model as well as our simulation and reasoning engine for the Java Virtual Machine [19] and for JavaScript [11]. For our scenario the model, simulation, and reasoning engine are small and efficient enough to be executed entirely in a web browser running on a standard laptop (MacBook Pro i5 2.4 Ghz, 16 GB RAM).

4.2   Example: Malicious Shutdown Commands

In this example we implemented a detection and protection reaction for potentially malicious shutdown commands. The reasoning engine monitors the state of entities (smart meters, repeaters, concentrators, central system) and detects if a striking number of entities (more than 10 % in a region) are remotely shutdown within a certain time range. The sender of the malicious shutdown commands is added to a blacklist by the reasoning engine to avoid that additional entities in this region will be affected. We implemented a greedy algorithm to detect entities, which are shutdown, and to automatically start them again. A corresponding model evaluation function rates an entity, which is shutdown worse than an entity which is started and the counter-measure is to restart and connect the concerned entity again. If an entity cannot be connected again (e.g. a smart meter can only be connected if a repeater or concentrator is available) the algorithm proceeds and tries the next entity and so forth. The algorithm stops if either all entities are started and connected again, or if none of the remaining entities, which are shutdown can be started and connected. The algorithm is executed in the range of milliseconds to a few seconds (in the worst case that all meters and concentrators are shutdown). This is what we consider near real-time. Since it is conceivable that a large number of entities are intentionally shutdown, e.g. for maintenance, it is possible to deactivate this detection (or only the reaction) for shutdown commands in the reasoning engine. This concrete example demonstrates the feasibility of near real-time reactive security at the range of a city.

4.3   Example: Electric Load Prediction

Based on our discussed approach and model we have implemented an electric load prediction. The idea is to predict if the electric load value in a region—in our case study around 50 smart meters—will likely exceed a critical value. If that is the case, the maximum allowed consumption for the corresponding meters can temporally be reduced by our reasoning engine to avoid an electric overload. Since an electrical grid usually can maintain an overload for a few seconds or minutes [8] the reasoning engine has to react within this time range. The reasoning process consists of an electrical load prediction for a specific point of the grid (one smart meter). Both the current electric load and past values (the consumption history of one month) at this meter as well as from the surrounding meters are taken into consideration. This prediction is continuously performed on a few dozen grid points and a linear regression of the average electric load values of the meters (over a certain period of time) is computed. The complete reasoning process for our case study is computed within a time range of a few seconds. Again, the example demonstrates the feasibility of near real-time reactions of our reasoning engine.

5   Related Work

Cyber security is a major concern of smart grids. Therefore, a lot of work is paying attention to this topic. An analysis of security threats and challenges in smart grids can be found in [13,23,26]. This work indicates the importance of smart grid security and privacy and shows significant weaknesses and attack points of smart grids. Many other authors like [4,12,34] focus their studies on smart meter security: intrusion detection systems, redundant meter reading, and privacy. Others, like Zhao et al. [37] focus their work on cryptography and a secure authenticated key exchange for smart grids. The above-mentioned work discusses important proactive security measures to improve security and privacy in smart grids. Unlike this work, our approach focuses on reactive security techniques, which we believe can complement proactive security measures to improve security in smart grids. In particular we intend to improve the self-healing aspect of smart grids. An interesting approach based on game-theoretic models for reactive security in general (not connected to smart grids in specific) is presented in [2]. Learning based game-theoretic techniques could be interesting for our reasoning engine to find appropriate counter-measures to face events and can be explored in future work. Godfrey et al. [18] suggest to use simulation techniques for an analysis of complex smart grid control schemes. This work focuses mainly on the exact simulation (incl. latency) of control messages. Kundur et al. [24] also use simulation techniques to study the potential severity of physical impacts of cyber attacks. A combination of hardware and software for a detailed simulation of a smart grid is presented in [25]. Their so-called *SmartGridLab* aims to provide researchers with a platform to conveniently and efficiently compare different smart grid designs. Just as the above-mentioned work, our approach suggests to use simulation techniques. In contrary to this work, we do not intend to simulate a complete smart grid one-to-one. Instead, we aim to dynamically counter attacks, failures, and potential dangers by simulating and evaluating different protection reactions in near real-time. Therefore, we use a model abstraction of a smart grid at runtime to be able to perform different simulations in real-time and finally to decide how to react. Baumeister [3] presents an exhaustive litera- ture review specifically on smart grid cyber security. A more general survey on smart grid technologies, which also includes a review of smart grid cyber secu- rity literature, can be found in [14]. To the best of our knowledge there is no related work combining Models@run.time techniques and a reasoning engine to a reactive security approach for smart grids.

6   Future Work

In future work we will explore more complex algorithms, like genetic [33] or game- theoretic [2] ones, to find appropriate counter-measures to face events. Especially algorithms, which are not limited to search local optimums but also consider steps before and after the current, will be subject to study. Another approach we would like to explore is to use techniques and methods from artificial intelligence in order to learn from previous situations and thus automatically improve our reasoning engine. Furthermore, several functions to evaluate the state of our model will be investigated. We will implement and simulate more complex and realistic use cases to continuously evaluate and improve our approach.

7   Conclusion

Ensuring a satisfactory level of security for smart grids is critical and challenging. We introduced a reactive security approach to face this challenge by both (1) rea- soning at high level to take the right decision and (2) reacting in near real-time. Unlike many other works, which mainly focus on proactive security techniques, our approach is completely reactive. Given the complexity of smart grids, we believe that a reactive security approach is essential to either entirely prevent, or at least to minimize the global impact of (successful) attacks and failures. The novelty of our approach is the combination of a Models@run.time-based reasoning engine with reactive security techniques to react in near real-time. Using a lightweight model representation of the physical smart grid elements, our approach allows to simulate and evaluate different counter-measures in real- time in order to dynamically protect the smart grid with the most appropriate ones. We presented an abstract model of the physical smart grid elements and used FSMs to model the behaviour of the elements. We believe that using Mod- els@run.time together with a reasoning engine can introduce a new approach of reactive security for smart grids and can help to develop the electricity grid of today into a more secure and adaptive smart grid of tomorrow that can verify and supervise itself.

Acknowledgments. The research leading to this publication is supported by the National Research Fund Luxembourg (grant 6816126) and Creos Luxembourg S.A. under the SnT-Creos partnership program.

References

1. Amin, S.M., Wollenberg, B.F.: Toward a smart grid: power delivery for the 21st century. IEEE Power Energ. Mag. **3**(5), 34–41 (2005)
2. Barth, A., Rubinstein, B.I.P., Sundararajan, M., Mitchell, J.C., Song, D.X., Bartlett, P.L.: A learning-based approach to reactive security. In: CoRR, abs/0912.1155 (2009)
3. Baumeister, T.: Literature review on smart grid cyber security. Technical report CSDL-10-10, Department of Information and Computer Sciences, University of Hawaii, Honolulu, Hawaii 96822, December 2010
4. Berthier, R., Sanders, W.H., Khurana, H.: Intrusion detection for advanced metering infrastructures: requirements and architectural directions. In: SmartGridComm, pp. 350–355 (2010)
5. Berthier, R., Sanders, W.H.: Specification-based intrusion detection for advanced metering infrastructures. In: Alkalai, L., Tsai, T., Yoneda, T. (eds.) PRDC, pp. 184–193. IEEE Computer Society (2011)
6. Blair, G., Bencomo, N., France, R.B.: Models@run.time. Computer **42**(10), 22–27 (2009)
7. Bruno, S., Lamonaca, S., Scala, M.L., Rotondo, G., Stecchi, U.: Load control through smart-metering on distribution networks. In: 2009 IEEE Bucharest PowerTech, pp. 1–8 (2009)
8. Cepeda, J.C., Ramirez, D.O., Colome, D.G.: Probabilistic-based overload estimation for real-time smart grid vulnerability assessment. In: 2012 6th IEEE/PES Transmission and Distribution: Latin America Conference and Exposition (TD-LA), pp. 1–8, September 2012
9. Cleeremans, A., Servan-Schreiber, D., McClelland, J.L.: Finite state automata and simple recurrent networks. Neural Comput. **1**(3), 372–381 (1989)
10. Deilami, S., Masoum, A.S., Moses, P.S., Masoum, M.A.S.: Real-time coordination of plug-in electric vehicle charging in smart grids to minimize power losses and improve voltage profile. IEEE Trans. Smart Grid **2**(3), 456–467 (2011)
11. ECMA International. Standard ECMA-262 - ECMAScript Language Specification. 5.1 edition, June 2011
12. Efthymiou, C., Kalogridis, G.: Smart grid privacy via anonymization of smart metering data. In: SmartGridComm, pp. 238–243 (2010)
13. Ericsson, G.N.: Cyber security and power system communication-essential parts of a smart grid infrastructure. IEEE Trans. Power Delivery **25**(3), 1501–1507 (2010)
14. Fang, X., Misra, S., Xue, G., Yang, D.: Smart grid–the new and improved power grid: a survey. IEEE Commun. Surv. Tut. **14**(4), 944–980 (2012)
15. Farhangi, H.: The path of the smart grid. IEEE Power Energ. Mag. **8**(1), 18–28 (2010)
16. Fouquet, F., Nain, G., Morin, B., Daubert, E., Barais, O., Plouzeau, N., Jézéquel, J.-M.: An eclipse modelling framework alternative to meet the models@runtime requirements. In: France, R.B., Kazmeier, J., Breu, R., Atkinson, C. (eds.) MODELS 2012. LNCS, vol. 7590, pp. 87–101. Springer, Heidelberg (2012)
17. Fowler, M.: Domain Specific Languages, 1st edn. Addison-Wesley Professional, Boston (2010)
18. Godfrey, T., Mullen, S., Dugan, R.C., Rodine, C., Griffith, D.W., Golmie, N.: Modeling smart grid applications with co-simulation. In: SmartGridComm, pp. 291–296 (2010)

19. Gosling, J., Joy, B., Steele, G., Bracha, G., Buckley, A.: The Java Language Specification, Java SE 7 edn. Addison-Wesley, Bosto (2012)
20. Graglia, R.: Smart grid Luxembourg, September 2013
21. Guille, C., Gross, G.: A conceptual framework for the vehicle-to-grid (V2G) implementation. Energ. Policy **37**(11), 4379–4390 (2009)
22. Caskurlu, B.: Model driven engineering. In: Butler, M., Petre, L., Sere, K. (eds.) IFM 2002. LNCS, vol. 2335, p. 286. Springer, Heidelberg (2002)
23. Khurana, H., Hadley, M., Frincke, D.A.: Smart-grid security issues. IEEE Secur. Priv. **8**(1), 81–85 (2010)
24. Kundur, D., Feng, X., Liu, S., Zourntos, T., Butler-Purry, K.L.: Towards a framework for cyber attack impact analysis of the electric smart grid. In: SmartGridComm, pp. 244–249 (2010)
25. Lu, G., De, D., Song, W.-Z.: Smartgridlab: a laboratory-based smart grid testbed. In: SmartGridComm, pp. 143–148 (2010)
26. McDaniel, P., McLaughlin, S.: Security and privacy challenges in the smart grid. IEEE Secur. Priv. **7**(3), 75–77 (2009)
27. Morin, B., Barais, O., Jezequel, J., Fleurey, F., Solberg, A.: Models@run.time to support dynamic adaptation. Computer **42**(10), 44–51 (2009)
28. Morin, B., Barais, O., Nain, G., Jezequel, J.-M.: Taming dynamically adaptive systems using models and aspects. In: Proceedings of the 31st International Conference on Software Engineering, ICSE '09, Washington, DC, USA, pp. 122–132. IEEE Computer Society (2009)
29. Muller, P.-A., Fleurey, F., Jézéquel, J.-M.: Weaving executability into object-oriented meta-languages. In: Briand, L.C., Williams, C. (eds.) MoDELS 2005. LNCS, vol. 3713, pp. 264–278. Springer, Heidelberg (2005)
30. Rothenberg, J., Widman, L.E., Loparo, K.A., Nielsen, N.R.: The nature of modeling. In: Artificial Intelligence, Simulation and Modeling (1989)
31. Rowe, B.R., Gallaher, M.P.: Private sector cyber security investment: an empirical analysis. In: WEIS (2006)
32. Schneider, F.B.: Implementing fault-tolerant services using the state machine approach: a tutorial. ACM Comput. Surv. (CSUR) **22**(4), 299–319 (1990)
33. Vafaie, H., Imam, I.F.: I.: feature selection methods: genetic algorithms vs greedy-like search. In: Proceedings of the International Conference on Fuzzy and Intelligent Control Systems (1994)
34. Varodayan, D.P., Gao, G.X.: Redundant metering for integrity with information-theoretic confidentiality. In: SmartGridComm, pp. 345–349 (2010)
35. Vogels, W.: Eventually consistent. Queue **6**(6), 14–19 (2008)
36. Wolf, R.W.: Stochastic Modeling and the Theory of Queues. Prentice Hall, Upper Saddle River (1989)
37. Zhao, F., Hanatani, Y., Komano, Y., Smyth, B., Ito, S., Kambayashi, T.: Secure authenticated key exchange with revocation for smart grid. In: IEEE PES Innovative Smart Grid Technologies, pp. 1–8 (2012)

A Survey on Privacy in Residential Demand Side Management Applications

Markus Karwe[1]([✉]) and Jens Strüker[2]

[1] Institut für Informatik ud Gesellschaft, Universität Freiburg, Freiburg, Germany
karwe@iig.uni-freiburg.de
[2] Institute of Energy Economics (INEWI) at the Fresenius
University of Applied Sciences, Idstein, Germany
jens.strueker@hs-fresenius.de

Abstract. Demand Side Management (DSM) is an auspicious concept for managing electricity grids with a high share of renewable energy sources. We provide a survey on privacy energy issues and potential solutions in Demand Response systems. For this we give an overview of privacy issues raised by energy consumption values. We introduce the Smart Metering Gateway concept of the BSI and indicate three technical types of Demand Response (DR). Furthermore we show how the three types can be integrated in the Smart Meter Gateway (SMGW) BSI setting. We present the privacy concerns about three technical DR types and provide an overview of current Privacy Enhancing Technologies that are applicable to mitigate these problems.

Keywords: Smart grid · Privacy · Demand response

1 Motivation

By 2020 the European Union wants to generate 20 % of its total energy consumption by renewable energies. This increased generation of renewable energy calls for an improved energy management as weather dependent photovoltaics and wind turbines will provide most of the renewable energy. In order to keep the Grid stable, the demand and the fluctuating supply must match. Managing the demand side is a promising alternative to costly grid expansion or battery installations. However, today's standard load profiles are made for forecasting energy demand on average. These standard load profiles are not able to address volatile single customer specific demand. In order to match efficiently the volatile demand and production, fine grained consumption data is required. The Smart Grid which can be regarded as an information overlay network for the current Grid, allows to collect such fine grained data for single customers. Yet, this fine grained data creates privacy issues. In the Netherlands privacy issues prohibited the roll out of digital electricity meters [5].

The research leading to these results has received funding from the European Union's Seventh Framework Programme (FP7-SMARTCITIES-2013) under grant agreement n° 608712.

© Springer International Publishing Switzerland 2014
J. Cuellar (Ed.): SmartGridSec 2014, LNCS 8448, pp. 154–165, 2014.
DOI: 10.1007/978-3-319-10329-7_10

2   Energy Privacy

A Smart Meter sends energy consumption values to a Smart Grid stakeholder. Privacy research in the Smart Grid focuses on sent energy values. Those values allow to infer information about the customers. The more frequent the consumption values are read, the more precise the inferences are [13]. A possible inference is the detection of electrical devices. It allows to recognize which devices are running on the customer side and when they are running.

Use mode detection is an even more privacy invasive analysis. Use mode detection tries to determine activities performed by appliances. In [8] consumption values of a TV sent by a smart meter are analyzed with a frequency of 2 Hz. In this setting they are able to detect three movies with a Pearson Coefficient of 0.98, 0.94 and 0.93. In [3] a measurement frequency of 1 kHz is applied to identify which website, out of a set of 8 sites, is currently visited via a personal computer. There the authors reach an accuracy of 60 % without any false positives.

Behavior deduction is based upon appliance analysis as well as use mode detection and tries to infer inhabitant behaviors. In [14] a behavior deduction experiment within a student apartment was performed. The result of the experiment is a precision rate of 90 % for detecting presence events and sleep cycles.

Compared to other privacy research fields like privacy in Social Networks, energy data bears a different threat potential. A smart meter sends energy consumption values regularly and independently from customer actions. Thus smart meters can be regarded as a judas hole into a household.

3   Smart Metering Gateway

The German 'Bundesamt für Sicherheit in der Informationstechnik' (BSI) proposed a Protection Profile for a Smart Meter Gateway as well as an according technical guideline [7]. The standard is criticized on the one hand for the very strong security assumptions and requirements and on the other hand for the poor privacy protection [21]. Concerning data privacy, the standard offers to send energy consumption data, which is not used for billing purposes, with a pseudonym instead of an identity. Smart Grid privacy research shows that this kind of data can be depseudonymised if another database is used. This database should include the identity as well as information which correlates with pseudonymised data [10]. Such information are billing data, even if privacy preservation protocols like [9] are used. A company with access to both databases is able to bypass the privacy protection mechanisms. This lack of privacy protection in this BSI concept depict the need for future privacy protection mechanisms, which match the BSI Smart Meter Gateway Architecture. We will illustrates the privacy challenges in DSM-DR under consideration of the BSI Protection Profile as well as the technical guideline.

According to the guideline, a Smart Meter system consists of a Smart Meter Gateway, an associated Security Module, a Home Area Network (HAN), a Local Metrological Network (LMN) as well as a Wide Area Network (WAN) as shown in Fig. 1.

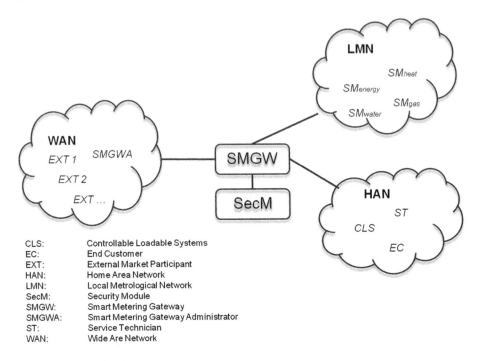

CLS: Controllable Loadable Systems
EC: End Customer
EXT: External Market Participant
HAN: Home Area Network
LMN: Local Metrological Network
SecM: Security Module
SMGW: Smart Metering Gateway
SMGWA: Smart Metering Gateway Administrator
ST: Service Technician
WAN: Wide Are Network

Fig. 1. Smart Metering Gateway environment

The Smart Metering Gateway (SMGW) acts as a security proxy for all three networks. It operates as a firewall and separates those networks. The SMGW further stores measured data and grants access rights only to authorized market participants. Another function of the SMGW is to provide a HAN interface to look into consumption data as well as system information. The LMN consists of Smart Meters (electricity, gas, water, heat) from one or more customers. There are two roles within WAN which are external market participants and the SMGW Administrator. An external market participant can be amongst others a Demand Side Manager or a Distribution System Operator. SMGW Administrator is a special role which acts as a trusted entity. Beside SMGW configuration, this role takes part in the pseudonymization process by replacing the SMGW signature for measurement readings with its own signature. SMGW takes also care for putting rule types for prices as well as specifying who is allowed to gain data from it. Note that the SMGW Administrator is not allowed to gain access to measurement values. The HAN knows three different roles. The first one is a Technician who performs on-site configuration of the SMGW. The End Customer is the second one, who is able to take a look into his consumption data via the HAN interface. The third role is the Controllable Local System (CLS) which might be intelligent household devices or energy interrupters.

4   Demand Response

DSM aims to change the customer's use of electricity. This widespread notion includes the concepts of DR and Energy Efficiency (EE). EE programs try to help customers to understand their own energy use and therefore to show energy saving opportunities. The Federal Energy Regulatory Commission defines DR as 'Changes in electric usage by end-use customers from their normal consumption patterns in response to changes in the price of electricity over time, or to incentive payments designed to induce lower electricity use at times of high wholesale market prices or when system reliability is jeopardized' [4]. There are three types of load changes, which shall be reached with DR. The first one is Peak Clipping, where the electricity consumption is reduced during peak times. The second type Valley Filling, aims to increase the energy consumption during times of low energy usage. The third one is Load Shifting where the electricity usage is shifted from peak times to times with low energy consumption. Several DR-Concepts like DLC or Demand Bidding, where customers accept and execute an offer made by the Demand Side Manager, exist to reach those load shifts. Those programs primarily discern in the economic or contractual level. From a privacy perspective it is important to recognize which parties are involved in the program and which data those parties hold. It is important for DSM from a technical and privacy viewpoint to regard whether a DSM event is dispatched or not and if the control of the load shift is hold by the customer or the Demand Side Manager. Therefore those programs are categorized into non-dispatchable and dispatchable. Dispatchable programs can be further subdivided into direct and indirect. An example for a non-dispatchable program is Time-of-Use (TOU) which is a price structure where the price per unit differs per block of time. In TOU a high price depicts an incentive to reduce load and a low price depicts an incentive to consume more energy.

A direct dispatchable program is DLC where a Demand Side Manager controls customer devices directly. To achieve a peak clipping a Demand Side Manager can turn off electrical devices on the customer side. In a dispatchable indirect program like Demand Bidding, a Demand Side Manager submits a quote to customers to reduce or to increase electricity consumption during a certain period of time. To accomplish an energy goal, a Demand Side Manager needs to get enough positive acknowledgements from customers which will fulfill the load shift.

4.1   Non-dispatchable DR - Tariff Structures

With different prices for different times, incentives are given to customers to change their usage behavior and therefore to create load shifts. According to the BSI guideline, those tariff structures are deposited in the SMGW by the SMGW Administrator. For each tariff time slot, the SMGW stores cumulated energy consumption values. A Demand Side Manager is allowed to gain those values from SMGW for a fiscal period.

Thus a Demand Side Manager knows a_i, tr_i where a_i is the energy consumption amount, tr_i is the tariff structure and $i \in (1, \ldots, |tariffslots|)$. In a uniform tariff the Demand Side Manager would know only a, where a is cumulated energy consumption for a fiscal period.

Privacy invasion in this kind of DSM is similar to privacy invasion regarded in the uniform tariff. Non-dispatchable DR allows us additionally to deduce reactions on price incentives of customers.

4.2 Indirect Dispatchable DR

In indirect dispatchable DR as shown in Fig. 2, a Demand Side Manager sends DR quotes to a customer. Such a quote could be to reduce or to increase load on customers side within a certain time frame by a certain amount. Customers can either accept or deny these quotes [1].

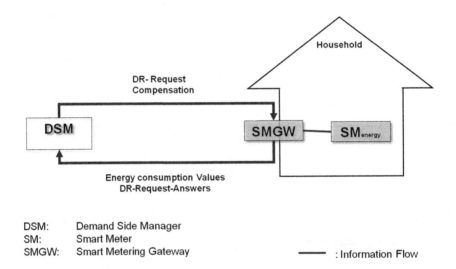

Fig. 2. Indirect dispatchable Load Control

A participating customer bears the responsibility to create such a load shift. This responsibility situation creates the problem for the Demand Side Manager that an accepted load shift quote is not fulfilled by a customer. Thus a Demand Side Manager must be able to measure whether a customer executed the load shift or not. To measure the effectiveness of DSM quotes is regarded as a tricky task due to many possible errors which either happen by incident or willful action like in the Enernoc double accounting case [20]. One way to do it, is to compare actual consumption of a household with comparison data. Such comparison data could be an average baseline consumption of the customer in the recent past. This DR approach, where the customer reacts manually to the DR quotes and fulfills them also manually, is not directly affected by the BSI Guideline.

The Demand Side Manager needs only to request actual consumption data as well as historical data from SMGW. The Demand Side Manager is able to collect a transaction history, which includes whether a customer accepted a quote or not and comparison data as well as the actual consumption within the time frame of the DR quote.

This kind of DSM is much more privacy invasive than non-dispatchable DR. A Demand Side Manager can not only infer information about price sensitivity, she also needs to have historic comparison data as well as actual consumption data. It is also important that customers can be identified individually, in order to give them incentives like a monetary incentive if they reach a certain energy reduction within a certain time frame.

Additionally a Demand Side Manager can infer a reliability value of a single customer by regarding acknowledgements of those quotes and actual performed load shifts. To sum it up, a Demand Side Manager needs historical consumption data, current consumption data as well as payment information and she is able to create a transaction history for individual customers.

4.3   Direct Dispatchable DR-DLC

In Direct Load Control (DLC), as shown in Fig. 3, a Demand Side Manager is able to control customer devices by herself. For customer convenience, she has to respect the preferences of the customer while performing DLC [2, 6]. By applying DLC a Demand Side Manager can be more certain about performed load shifts compared to indirect dispatchable DR and it is considered to be more effective than non-dispatchable DR.

When it comes to privacy issues, DLC is the most privacy invasive variant of the regarded three categories. A Demand Side Manager needs to know all controllable customer appliances, which shall participate in the program. Appliance detection is one of the three major threats regarded in current Smart Grid privacy research. Participants of DLC programs need to show the information, which can be revealed by appliance detection. Additionally comparison as well as actual consumption data is needed. A customer might still try manually to bypass DLC-DR actions like starting or shutting down a device.

The BSI Guideline supports also DLC. It specifies that external market participants are able to send commands to CLS within HAN. They can also get comparison data, as well as actual consumption data from the SMGW, in the context of a DLC program.

The Demand Side Manager is able to collect a DLC command history, she knows all devices which are registered for the DLC program, customer preferences as well as actual consumption data for the DLC quote timeframe and comparison data.

5   Current Technology and Privacy Challenges

Non-dispatchable programs are the least privacy invasive type and similar to privacy challenges for plain energy consumption values. Due to this similarity,

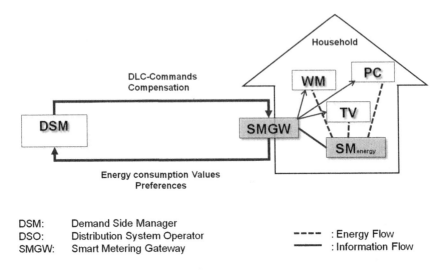

Fig. 3. Direct Load Control

privacy enhancing technologies like group signatures [12] or privacy preserving billing protocols [9] can be applied to this type of DR program. The matter is more complicated for DLC. The problem is the direct control of customer devices by the Demand Side Manager. This problem can be reduced to the problem in indirect dispatchable programs, by introducing a customer owned privacy preserving component. This privacy preserving component would act as a trusted third party (TTP).

5.1 Privacy Preserving for DLC

The privacy preserving component behaves like an intelligent proxy. It hides details about customer devices from a Demand Side Manager. A Demand Side Manager would send instead of direct commands to customer devices a direct load shift command to the privacy component. This command includes the load shift amount as well as the program time frame. The privacy component then takes care for activating or shutting down devices according to load shift request as well as customer preferences. The component would also report to the Demand Side Manager, if a request is not grantable. This concept shifts the responsibility of activating and deactivating devices from the DSM to the privacy component. This TTP acts on household level which reduces the impact factor as a single point of failure (Fig. 4).

For indirect dispatchable demand response such a household TTP approach is possible but not appropriate. This household level TTP means for a DR company that all required data is kept within each single household. An important benefit of the Smart Grid is to use collected data to manage the grid.

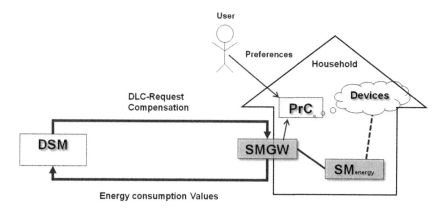

DSM: Demand Side Manager
PrC: Privacy Component
SM: Smart Meter
SMGW: Smart Metering Gateway

- - - - : Energy Flow
——— : Information Flow

Fig. 4. Direct Load Control with privacy component

5.2   Privacy Preserving Options for Indirect Dispatchable DR

Current PET (Privacy Enhancing Technologies) applied in Smart Grid can be categorized in the groups of anonymization techniques, pseudonymization, data perturbation, cryptographic computation, distributed usage control as well as trusted computation.

Anonymization techniques allow to perform operations on data while the original data producer is not identifiable. Group signatures are means to reach anonymity of participants. Where anonymity is in [12] defined as 'The privacy of every customer is preserved. It is impossible for the energy provider or anybody else to get information about the customer's living habits'. The proposed technique is divided in two protocol steps. In the first step, a Smart Meter provides invoicing data to a data consumer. This invoicing data is a time aggregated value which still allows to identify the data producer. Data must be aggregated in such a way that living habits can not be determined. The second step provides anonymous consumption data by using a group signature. With this group signature the data consumer can not determine which Smart Meter sent a signed value [12]. Linkage attacks can be applied to this kind of technique. Consider a group of Smart Meters, where it is known that energy consumption of only one Smart Meter household is lower than all other energy consumption values. A reason for the difference might be that all other households are currently occupied while the single one is not. This information can be used to link one of the anonymized consumption values to the not occupied household. It is unclear to which extend such linkage attacks can be applied for smaller groups of Smart

Meters. It is hard to find an unique identifier in a large group of Smart Meters, therefore linkage attacks are hard to apply if the group is big enough.

In the BSI setting, the SMGW can apply group signatures instead of the Smart Meter. The applicability of this kind of technique is limited for indirect dispatchable DR programs. The anonymized data of this protocol can be used to measure whether a total wished amount for all participating households has been reached. The invoicing data can be used to get household individual data for the program time frame. Comparison data is needed to verify if a household reached the load shift goal. Currently standard load profiles are used. To use these profiles in DR programs means to throw away some energy management advantages the Smart Grid offers. As an example consider a household which uses always less energy than indicated in a standard load profile. With this knowledge a household can always participate successfully in peak clipping but never in a valley filling program. Historic household individual consumption data is wanted for comparison. This data allows to measure the effectiveness of each program but the question arises how to obtain and use this data in a privacy friendly way. Invoice data of old programs is not suitable because for an effective comparison, the time frame of the old and actual program must be identical. While for several households effectiveness of the program can be measured, an individual effectiveness measurement seems not feasible.

In pseudonymization the ID of a data producer is removed and a pseudonym is inserted. In [10] it is shown for smart metering data that linkage attacks can successfully be applied. For this attack access to pseudonymized consumption values as well as additional identity revealing is needed. Frequent re-pseudonymization mitigates the problem, but produces additional overhead. Due to disclosure risk, pseudonymization is not an effective privacy preserving concept.

Data perturbation follows a different approach. A data error is introduced on purpose in order to protect privacy. The differential privacy guarantee can be reached, if the error is introduced in a specific way [11,15]. Differential privacy is a worst case guarantee and can be defined as:

D_1 and D_2 are two Databases which differ in at most one element, ϵ a privacy parameter which can be chosen, K is a sanitizing algorithm, and $S \subseteq Range(K)$.

$$\frac{Pr(K(D_1) \in S)}{Pr(K(D_2) \in S)} \leq e^\epsilon$$

Thus differential privacy provides the guarantee that a single record can join a dataset and the worst resulting information leakage is e^ϵ. In the BSI setting SMGW can be seen as a database. A data requester can ask SMGW for consumption values. SMGW retrieves the information and adds noise to answers. This noise is taken out of a Laplace distribution where the distribution depends on e^ϵ and global sensitivity of the request function. This technique hinders linkage attacks but has also an impact on data utility. Differential privacy can be applied for groups of households. By applying differential privacy for groups again the problem arises how individual household consumptions can be gathered for comparison purposes.

Cryptographic computation is based upon homomorphic encryption. Computational feasibility of homomorphic encryption is limited to simple operators like sum. DR programs need to compare actual with historic consumption data to measure program effectiveness. Relational operators are needed for this and therefore usage of cryptographic computation would lead to additional computational overhead.

Distributed usage control tries to check constant the use of data according to a policy [17,18]. This approach is promising from privacy perspective. Usage of data for a certain computation would be denied if a specified privacy policy, which could be defined by a user, is not stating that the computation is allowed. The downside are scaling problems of usage and distributed usage control [16]. In order to apply an effective mechanism, the control must happen on every system layer on all systems involved.

In trusted computing a TTP performs computations on data and the data consumer receives only aggregated values. Instead of an external TTP, a TTP on the data producer side such as SMGW can perform computations. A TTP itself is a privacy risk. An advantage of a household based TTP is that a successful privacy breach impacts only the associated household. A disadvantage is that it uses only data from one household to perform computations. In UK, DCC implements a national wide central data hub which can be regarded as a TTP [19]. A privacy breach in such a centralized system could impact all participating households. A centralized TTP can perform computations with data from several households on behalf of a Smart Grid stakeholder like a DSO which is one of the main advantages of this approach.

Privacy technologies for DR Applications must allow to address a customer individually while still allowing computation on fine grained energy consumption data in order to create custom offers as well as calculating customer compensation and to determine program effectiveness. Thus PET based on anonymity techniques are not adequate. The need to address customers individually can be fulfilled by data perturbation. It also allows to operate on fine grained consumption values. The key challenge for this technique is whether the remaining data utility is high enough to perform the application, after noise is introduced. Also customer compensation is in question. In general billing do not use noisy data. As a privacy protection mechanism, this noise and henceforth the change in the bill can be seen as cost for protecting privacy. The SMGW can be seen as a trusted database on household level. As a trusted entity, the SMGW can be considered to add noise to consumption values to reach the differential privacy guarantee. Whether privacy can be protected by introducing noise and still be able to perform the operation or not is an open research question. Adaptability of cryptographic computation is limited to its computational overhead. For huge amounts of data a big computational overhead is not suitable for DR programs operating near real-time. Distributed usage control mechanisms allow to address customers individually as well as to perform computation on fine grained data. Scalability of this approach is an open problem. As long as those open research questions are not solved a centralized TTP based solution should be considered.

While the single point of failure introduced with the centralized TTP seems risky from privacy perspective, practical considerations lead already to an implementation for the United Kingdom [19]. There a TTP acts as a central data hub.

6   Conclusion

DR introduces new privacy challenges. Non-dispatchable indirect DR is with existing technology mitigateable. As depicted, DLC privacy problems can be reduced to Indirect Load Control privacy problems, if a trusted privacy component on household level is admissible. Privacy problems of Indirect Load Control on the other hand still propose new research questions. For Indirect Load Control, it is required to address a residential household individually. Homomorphic encryption and distributed usage control allow for that but are both not scaling in terms of time necessary for computing. The computational overhead for data perturbation is significantly smaller than the computational overhead for homomorphic encryption or distributed usage control and it can be integrated into a SMGW. Data perturbation is an option which allows to reach the differential privacy guarantee. The downside of this approach is a reduced data utility. An open problem is to create techniques which enable differential privacy via data perturbation while keeping data utility at an acceptable level. The usage of a TTP helps to mitigate privacy problems but it is itself a source of risk. From application view, a centralized TTP solution is the most feasible as long as the open research questions for the other applications are not solved.

References

1. Earle, R., Newell, S.: Fostering econcomic demand response in the midwest ISO. http://www.energycollection.us/Energy-Demand-Response/Fostering-Economic-DR.pdfl
2. Bhattacharyya, K., Crow, M.L.: A fuzzy logic based approach to direct load control. IEEE Trans. Power Syst. **11**(2), 708–714 (1996)
3. Clark, K., Sorber, J., Learned-Miller, E.: Current events: compromising web privacy by tapping the electrical outlet (2011)
4. Federal Energy Regulatory Commission: Reports on demand responses and advanced metering. http://www.ferc.gov
5. Koops, B., Cuijpers, C.: Smart metering and privacy in Europe: lessons from the Dutch case. In: Gutwirth, S., Leenes, R., de Hert, P., Poullet, Y. (eds.) European Data Protection: Coming of Age. Springer, Dordrecht (2013)
6. Ericson, T.: Direct load control of residential water heaters. Energy Policy **37**(9), 3502–3512 (2009)
7. Bundesamt für Sicherheit in der Informationstechnik. Bsi tr-03109. https://www.bsi.bund.de
8. Greveler, U., Justus, B., Löhr, D.: Identifikation von videoinhalten ber granulare stromverbrauchsdaten. In: Waidner, M., Suri, N. (eds.) Sicherheit. LNI, vol. 195. GI (2012)

9. Jawurek, M., Johns, M., Kerschbaum, F.: Plug-in privacy for smart metering billing. In: Fischer-Hübner, S., Hopper, N. (eds.) PETS 2011. LNCS, vol. 6794, pp. 192–210. Springer, Heidelberg (2011)
10. Jawurek, M., Johns, M., Rieck, K.: Smart metering de-pseudonymization. In: ACSAC (2011)
11. Jawurek, M., Kerschbaum, F., Danezis, G.: Sok: privacy technologies for smart grids a survey of options. http://research.microsoft.com/pubs/178055/paper.pdf
12. Jeske, T.: Privacy-preserving smart metering without a trusted-third-party. In: SECRYPT (2011)
13. Molina-Markham, A., Shenoy, P., Fu, K., Cecchet, E., Irwin, D.: Private memoirs of a smart meter. In: Proceedings of the 2nd ACM Workshop on Embedded Sensing Systems for Energy-Efficiency in Building, BuildSys '10, New York, USA. ACM (2010)
14. Lisovich, M.A., Mulligan, D.K., Wicker, S.B.: Inferring personal information from demand-response systems. IEEE Secur. Priv. **8**(1), 11–20 (2010)
15. Rastogi, V., Nath, S.: Differentially private aggregation of distributed time-series with transformation and encryption. In: Proceedings of the 2010 ACM SIGMOD International Conference on Management of Data, SIGMOD '10, New York, USA. ACM (2010)
16. Biswas, D., Nefedov, N., Niemi, V.: Distributed usage control. In: ANT/MobiWIS (2011)
17. Fromm, A., Kelbert, F., Pretschner, A.: Data protection in a cloud-enabled smart grid. In: Cuellar, J. (ed.) SmartGridSec 2012. LNCS, vol. 7823, pp. 96–107. Springer, Heidelberg (2013)
18. Kumari, P., Pretschner, A.: Deriving implementation-level policies for usage control enforcement. In: CODASPY (2012)
19. Kerschbaum, F. Strüker, J.: From a barrier to a bridge: data-privacy in deregulated smart grids. In: ICIS (2012)
20. Strüker, J., Brening, C., Reichert, S.: Inter-organizational demand response applications: how to address moral hazard in smart grids (2013)
21. von Oheimb, D.: IT security architecture approaches for smart metering and smart grid. In: Cuellar, J. (ed.) SmartGridSec 2012. LNCS, vol. 7823, pp. 1–25. Springer, Heidelberg (2013)

Enhancing Problem Frames with Trust and Reputation for Analyzing Smart Grid Security Requirements

Francisco Moyano[1]($\boxtimes$), Carmen Fernández-Gago[1],
Kristian Beckers[2], and Maritta Heisel[2]

[1] Network, Information and Computer Security Lab,
University of Malaga, 29071 Malaga, Spain
{moyano,mcgago}@lcc.uma.es
[2] Paluno - The Ruhr Institute for Software Technology,
University of Duisburg-Essen, Essen, Germany
{Kristian.Beckers,Maritta.Heisel}@paluno.uni-due.de

Abstract. Smart grids are expected to scale over millions of users and provide numerous services over geographically distributed entities. Moreover, smart grids are expected to contain controllable local systems (CLS) such as fridges or heaters that can be controlled using the network communication technology of the grid. Security solutions that prevent harm to the grid and to its stakeholders from CLS are essential. Moreover, traditional security approaches such as static access control systems cause a lot of administrative workload and are difficult to maintain in fast growing and changing systems. In contrast, trust management is a soft security mechanism that can reduce this workload significantly. Even though there is not any accepted definition of trust, it is agreed that it can improve decision-making processes under risk and uncertainty, improving in turn systems' security. We use the problem frames notation to discuss requirements for a trust-based security solution concerning CLS.

Keywords: Problem frames · Model-driven engineering · Security requirements engineering · Trust · Reputation · UML4PF

1 Introduction

The concept of trust has been in discussion for a long time and researchers in software engineering still work on clarifying its terminology [1]. In addition, several well known applications rely on trust and reputation mechanisms such as Amazon's product ratings and ebay's seller feedback [2].

This research was partially supported by the EU project Network of Excellence on Engineering Secure Future Internet Software Services and Systems (NESSoS, ICT-2009.1.4 Trustworthy ICT, Grant No. 256980). The first author is funded by the Spanish Ministry of Education through the national F.P.U. program.

© Springer International Publishing Switzerland 2014
J. Cuellar (Ed.): SmartGridSec 2014, LNCS 8448, pp. 166–180, 2014.
DOI: 10.1007/978-3-319-10329-7_11

In security engineering, current practice is to mitigate potential threats with hard trust mechanisms, which differ from soft trust ones [3]. Hard trust mechanisms aim to define strict rules in order to prevent access to resources without proper authorization. These rules are often in the form of permissions associated to roles. Using such a set of static rules implies a high administrative burden, they are hard to maintain in dynamic environments [4], and they only provide limited control prior to the access of users; once users are in the system, hard trust mechanisms cannot detect misbehaviours by themselves. Moreover, any misbehaviour may lead to multiple rules updates, which can lead to missing rules due to small IT staff or to wrong rules due to human errors.

Another example of hard trust mechanism is cryptography-supported trust by means of Public Key Infrastructures (PKIs). However, many challenges must be overcome to accomplish its integration into highly distributed and heterogeneous Future Internet scenarios such as the smartgrid. On the one hand, the tight resource constraints of some devices precludes the use of public-key cryptography [4]. On the other hand, in an open market where different vendors manufacture different devices, it is not realistic (at least in the beginning) to assume that they will agree on the format of certificates or on the Trusted-Third Parties that can play the role of certification authorities.

In contrast to hard trust mechanisms, soft trust mechanisms rely on the characterization of trust relationships based on certain factors that influence these relationships. Examples of these factors are previous experience, membership to a group, reputation or detected strange behaviours. Trust values can be used by the trustor itself (i.e. the entity placing trust) to evaluate if it should engage in an interaction with other entities.

The main difference with the previous schemes is that we are empowering entities to make decisions based on personal judgement of its context and knowledge. Trust is no longer based on a set of strict rules or on statement by a certification authority that is trusted by definition. Trust is based on a subjective evaluation that takes into account a set of factors that may lead entities to trust or distrust other entities, and some of these factors can be monitored autonomously. Trust and reputation are attached to entities and people, providing a better decoupling from the underlying organizational structure compared to the previous mechanisms. This is relevant as according to the European Commission [5]: "Over the period from 2002 to 2010, more than 11000 cases of restructuring were recorded by the European Restructuring Monitor". Note that we may still need roles to be an important factor of the trust model, and in that case the decoupling would be lower. The drawback of trust-based security solutions is that they entail certain level of subjectivity and uncertainty and do not provide strong guarantees that security concerns will be correctly solved.

Two main challenges arise when we plan to incorporate soft trust mechanisms in the requirements stage of the Software Development Life Cycle (SDLC). First, how to identify the security requirements for which a soft trust approach is a feasible solution; second, how to represent the problem, that is, the security concern, and the elements of trust and reputation that surround this problem.

In this paper, we address this second challenge by integrating concepts from trust and reputation in the problem frames approach [6]. We choose this approach because it focuses on describing the system-to-be in its environment. The description of the environment is essential for trust and reputation, because they rely on knowledge about external stakeholders or software entities in order to determine adequate trust or reputation values.

Our contribution is a notation that allows specifying the requirements of a system that includes a trust or reputation model. This notation is an extension over problem frames that supports the definition of trust and reputation elements and their integration with the rest of elements (i.e. the environment) of the system. Analysts can benefit from our contribution by grasping a better understanding of the system and its interactions with the trust model, whereas designers can obtain a good starting point for planning the architecture and building trust into the architecture.

In this work, we focus on an analysis of trust and reputation relations in the system-to-be. We propose considering trust and reputation in the early phase of software engineering, because the effort for including it in later phases increases. The challenge of such an analysis is to achieve a coverage of all possible trust and reputation relations.

Goal-based methods, e.g., SI* [7] and KAOS [8], investigate the goals and views of all stakeholders of a system. These approaches model stakeholder relations based upon structured goal models. Hence, they consider all goals and relevant software artifacts to these goals. However, they do not consider a complete view of the system-to-be. Other security requirements engineering methods have a similar approach, e.g., the asset-driven risk management method CORAS [9] identifies assets and determines threats to these assets. CORAS models the system-to-be in artifacts that have a relation to an asset and also do not represent the complete system-to-be. Thus, we do not use any of these methods for our trust and reputation analysis.

The Problem Frames [6] method uses an abstraction of the system-to-be and models the environment of the system around it. Thus, this method is our choice to analyze trust relationships in the software and its environment. The method models the *Machine* and its environment in domains with certain characteristics, and we propose a trust and reputation analysis that uses these characteristic to determine trustors, trustees, claims, and other trust-related concepts. We show a structured method that elicits trust and reputation relations for each domain. In the future, we will also provide computer-aided support for consistency, and security reasoning for this method by using OCL [10] queries on the problem frame models. Hence, we use the benefit of having a complete model of the system-to-be and its environment in domains to conduct a threat analysis.

We use the UML representation of the problem frames method called *UML4PF* [11], because this allows us to write OCL expressions to validate the models that will be included in the UML4PF support tool. Moreover, we aim to integrate this analysis into a structured software development process, e.g., an extension of the ADIT [12] process that relies on UML4PF. We choose the

UML notation, because software engineers are familiar with it to express software design choices. Moreover, if we express the software analysis and design in UML, we do not need to map the analysis results to a different notation for the software design. This reduces one source of mistakes during software development. Hence, expressing trust and reputation analysis in UML allows for a seamless refinement step to software design, by re-using the UML models created during the analysis phase in the software design phase.

The remainder of our paper is structured as follows. Section 2 explains background on trust and problem frames, as well as some related work. Section 3 shows our UML profile, which illustrates elements of trust, problem frames and their relations. We apply our profile to a smart grid example in Sect. 4, whereas in Sect. 5 we draw some conclusions and give lines of future research.

2   Background and Related Work

We explain trust concepts in Sect. 2.1, problem frames in Sect. 2.2, and related work in software engineering in Sect. 2.3.

2.1   Trust Background and Terminology

There has been a huge amount of definitions of trust over the years. We propose the following definition: *trust is the personal, unique and temporal expectation that a trustor places on a trustee regarding the outcome of an interaction between them.* This interaction usually comes in terms of a task that the trustee must perform and that can (negatively) influence the trustor. The expectation is personal and unique because it is subjective, and is temporal because it may change over time. Tasks belong to a context, in such a way that a trustor may place different trust values on the same trustee depending on the context where trust is applied. The concept and implications of trust are embodied in so-called *trust models*, which manage trust relationships between trustors (entities that place trust) and trustees (entities onto which trust is placed). Many trust models have been proposed in the literature, but we are particularly interested in evaluation models, as proposed by Marsh in his seminal work [13]. In these models, factors that have an influence on trust are identified, quantified and then aggregated into a final trust score by the trust engine of the trust model. Uncertainty and evaluation play an important role in these models, as the trustor has only limited confidence on a positive output after the interaction with the trustee, and a quantification process is required to evaluate the extent to which one entity trusts another one.

Regarding reputation, the Concise Oxford dictionary[1] defines it as "what is generally said or believed about a person or the character or standing of a thing". The word *generally* implies that reputation is formed by an accumulation of opinions, which makes reputation a more objective concept than trust. A good

---

[1] http://www.oxforddictionaries.com

approximation to the relationship between trust and reputation was suggested by Jøsang [14], who made the following two statements: 'I trust you because of your good reputation' and 'I trust you despite your bad reputation'. Reputation can be considered as a building block of trust but, as stated by the second statement, reputation has not the final say. One could either trust someone with low reputation or distrust someone with high reputation, because there are other factors that may have a bigger influence over the trust decision, such as the trustor's disposition to believe in the trustee, the trustor's feelings, or above all, the trustor's personal experiences with the trustee.

A core concept behind reputation as seen in web reputation models is a *reputation statement*, which can be defined as a claim stated by a source regarding a target. As an example, if Alice says: 'The film Titanic has a good photography', the source is *Alice*, the target is *film Titanic*, and the claim is *to have a good photography*. A source can be human or non-human. Non-human sources include anti-spam filters, input from other reputation models, log crawlers or recommendation engines. A target can be human, non-human or reputation statements themselves. For instance, a user Alice might claim that the review performed by Bob regarding the film Titanic was useful. In this case, the target is *Bob's review about Titanic*, that is, a reputation statement where the source Bob expressed its opinion (claim) about the target Titanic. Reputation engines take reputation statements about a given target as inputs, and produce a reputation score for the target.

2.2 Problem Frames

Problem frames are a means to describe software development problems. They were proposed by Jackson [6], who describes them as follows: *"A problem frame is a kind of pattern. It defines an intuitively identifiable problem class in terms of its context and the characteristics of its domains, interfaces and requirement."*. It is described by a *frame diagram*, which consists of domains, interfaces between them, and a requirement. We describe problem frames using class diagrams extended by stereotypes as proposed in [11,15]. All elements of a problem frame diagram act as placeholders, which must be instantiated to represent concrete problems. Doing so, one obtains a problem description that belongs to a specific kind of problem. The class with the stereotype *machine* represents the thing to be developed (e.g., the software). The classes with some domain stereotypes, e.g., *CausalDomain* or *BiddableDomain* represent *problem domains* that already exist in the application environment. Domains are connected by interfaces consisting of shared phenomena. Shared phenomena may be events, operation calls, messages, and the like. They are observable by at least two domains, but controlled by only one domain, as indicated by an exclamation mark. These interfaces are represented as associations, and the name of the associations contains the phenomena and the domains controlling the phenomena. Jackson distinguishes the domain types *CausalDomains* that comply with some physical laws, *LexicalDomains* that are data representations, and *BiddableDomains* that are usually people. The stereotype <<causalDomain>> indicates that the corresponding domain is a *CausalDomain*, and the stereotype <<biddableDomain>> indicates that it is a *BiddableDomain*. In our formal meta-model of problem frames [16], *domains* have *names* and *abbreviations*, which are used to define interfaces. Hence, the class *Domain* has the attributes *name* and *abbreviation* of type string.

Software development with problem frames proceeds as follows: first, the environment in which the machine will operate is represented by a *context diagram*. Like a frame diagram, a context diagram consists of domains and interfaces, but the diagram does not contain requirements. *Domain knowledge diagrams* focus on some domains of the context diagram and document further domain knowledge about them in terms of facts and assumptions. Then, the problem is decomposed into subproblems. Each subproblem is represented by a *problem diagram* containing its domains, phenomena, interfaces, and their relations to at least one requirement that expresses the subproblem. Since the requirements refer to the *environment* in which the machine must operate, the next step consists in deriving a *specification* for the machine (see [17] for details). The specification describes the machine and is the starting point for its construction.

2.3   Related Work

To the best of our knowledge no problem frame extension exists that considers trust and reputation concepts with the purpose of describing requirements concerning trust and reputation concepts.

The software engineering community has focused on specifying traditional security requirements, such as confidentiality or authorization, during the early phases of the Software Development Life Cycle (SDLC). Haley et al. [18,19] represent security requirements in problem frames. The authors represent security requirements also as trust assumptions, which describe that the security requirement is fulfilled for a particular context, because it is trusted to satisfy the security requirement explicitly. Further examples for modeling notation that consider security are UMLsec [20] and SecureUML [21]. Other notations take relationships between actors and agents into account during the system specification. Mouratidis and Giorgini [22] present Secure Tropos, a notation that extends the Tropos methodology in order to enable the design of secure systems. Actors in Tropos may depend on other actors in order to achieve a goal. Tropos captures the social relationships in the system by specifying the dependencies between actors using the notions of depender, dependum and dependee, and by modeling the actors and agents in the organization. In a similar direction, Lamsweerde and Letier present KAOS [23], a comprehensive goal-oriented method to elicit the requirements of socio-technical systems. Moyano et al. [24] propose a trust model for Si* [7] in order to detect insider threats in an organizational setting during the initial steps of the SDLC. This work proposes setting users permissions on resources or assets, and a level of trust in these permissions. Then, threats, which are implicit wrong permissions, are discovered by examining and navigating through social relationships among actors. All these contributions put forward the idea of capturing social aspects, but the notion of trust and its influence on the information systems are barely explored. This is partially covered by Pavlidis, Mouratidis and Islam [25], who extend the Secure Tropos modeling language in order to include some trust-related concepts. The main difference is that our extension is over problem frames instead of over Secure Tropos. Problem frames are more focused on modelling the system in its environment, which we consider to be useful for trust modelling, and it represents information at a higher level of abstraction.

3   UML Profile for Problem-Based Trust Analysis

Our profile considers Jackson's domain types (as discussed in Sect. 2.2): *Causal-Domains*, *LexicalDomains*, *BiddableDomains*,

Domain Knowledge consist of *Statements* about domains, in particular *Facts* that we can prove and *Assumptions* that we consider during software development. A *Requirement* is a specific kind of *Statement* about domains that shall hold after the *Machine* has been built. Requirements ≪constrain≫ at least one domain and can ≪referTo≫ further domains. A *securityRequirement* is a statement about the confidentiality, integrity, or availability concerns of domains and ≪complement≫ at least one functional requirement in this regard.

We extend our UML profile for Jackson's problem frame notation called *UML4PF* [12] and its dependability extension [15] with required elements to describe trust relationships and trust requirements. We use the profile to create context diagrams, domain knowledge diagrams, and problem diagrams using the elements described in Sect. 2.2. Our trust extension for the UML4PF profile is shown in Fig. 1[2], where all the contributions of this paper are marked in grey. We define relations between Jackson's domains and the elements of Moyano et al.'s trust framework [1]. Each of these elements are now a kind of domain. *Entity* is a domain and *Human Entity* is a *Biddable Domain*. *Trust Information* and *Reputation Information* are *Lexical Domains*.

We aim to build s specific set of *Machines* in order to integrate trust and reputation mechanisms into a system-to-be. These are *Computation Engines*, which in turn can be *Trust Engines* or *Reputation Engines*, depending on whether they calculate trust or reputation, respectively. *Trust Engines* are in charge of calculating *Trust Values* for *Trust Relationships* among *Entit*ies. These engines take *Trust Factors*, associated to *Entity* as input, which may be *Objective Factor* or *Subjective Factor*. Factors can be assigned explicitly or can be obtained by some sort of monitoring; in any case, they are responsible for some other *Entity* playing the role *factor producer*. *Computation Engines* can have different mathematical mechanics, including *belief* or *fuzzy* logics. *Uncertainty* estimates the probability of a trust or reputation value being accurate. The *Time* states when a trust relationship or reputation related statement or information was defined.

*Entit*ies playing the role *Source* can make *Claims* about other *Entit*ies with role *Target*. This information is aggregated in the form of *Reputation State-ment*s, which are used by *Reputation Engines* to compute reputation scores.

---

[2] Note that for readability purposes we simplified the profile and several domains are not illustrated in Fig. 1, e.g., display domains and assets.

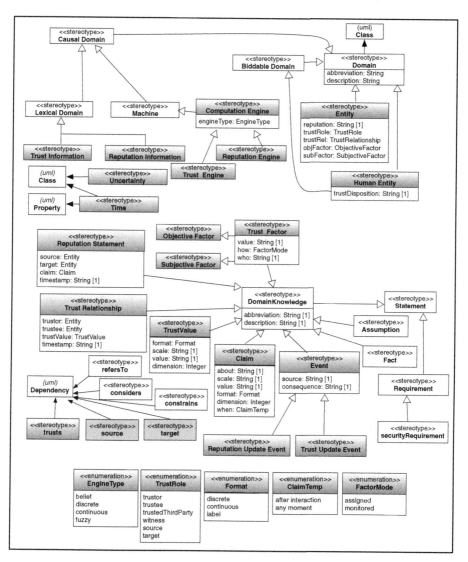

Fig. 1. A trust extension of the UML4PF profile

A *SourceEntity* can make *Claims* *after an interaction* or just at *any moment*. The model considers *Human Entities*, who have an implicit *trust disposition* and who value their *Assets* and wish to minimize *Risk* to these *Assets*. *Countermeasures* reduce the risk to *Assets*. Finally, *Events* are circumstances in the system that trigger a trust or reputation update. These events can be visualized by behavioral diagrams, such as sequence diagrams, as depicted and further discussed in Fig. 6.

4   Applying the Trust-Extension of the UML4PF Profile to a Smart Grid Example

We use the protection profile for the smart metering gateway [26] as an example for our approach. The gateway is a part of the smart grid. This is a commodity network that intelligently manages the behavior and actions of its participants. The commodity consists of electricity, gas, water or heat that is distributed via a grid (or network). The benefit of this network is envisioned to be a more economic, sustainable and secure supply of commodities. Smart metering systems meter the production or consumption of energy and forward the data to external entities. This data can be used for billing and steering the energy production. The protection profile defines security requirements for a smart metering gateway [26] and we use the UML profile as the source for the following example.

The context diagram shown in Fig. 2 describes the machine to be built in its environment. It is part of the overview description of the security target. The ≪Machine≫ is the *SmartMeteringGateway*, which serves as a bridge between the Wide Area Network ≪wan≫ and the Local Network ≪physical≫ of the *Consumer*. The *Meter* is connected to the machine via a Local Metrological Network ≪lmn≫. The Meter is an in-house equipment that can be used for energy management. The Controllable Local System *CLS* can be, for example, an air conditioning unit or an intelligent refrigerator. The *Consumer* can also access the *Machine* [26] via a *ConsumerBrowser*. We extended the description with the following phenomena. The *Meter* sends meter data to the *SmartMeteringGateway*. The *SmartMeteringGateway* stores this data. The *Meter* can also receive updates from the *AuthorizedExternalEntity* forwarded via the *SmartMeteringGateway*. The *AuthorizedExternalEntity* retrieves sent meter data in fixed intervals from the *SmartMeteringGateway*. The *SecurityModule* provides cryptographic functionalities for the *SmartMeteringGateway* such as key generation and random number generation. The *Consumer* can retrieve meter data via the *SmartMeteringGateway* and the *ConsumerBrowser*. The *Consumer* can also configure the *SmartMeteringGateway*, send commands to the *CLS*, receive status messages from the *SmartMeteringGateway* and store *UserData* in it.

We iterated over the domains in Fig. 2 and identified the *MeterData* as an ≪ asset ≫. Figure 3 presents a domain knowledge diagram that contains the description of this asset. The meter data has value for the *Consumer*, because his/her billing depends upon it and a behavior profile about the *Customer* can be created from it. Integrity, authenticity, and confidentiality of this data need to be protected. Another asset of the *SmartMeteringGateway* is the *GatewayTime*. The asset is revealed via investigating assumptions about the *SmartMeteringGateway*, namely that the meter data is recorded with a correct time stamp. The time is used in *MeterData* records that are sent to *AuthorizedExternalEntity* for, e.g., billing. Its integrity and authenticity have to be protected and especially the time adjustment using an externally referenced time is critical.

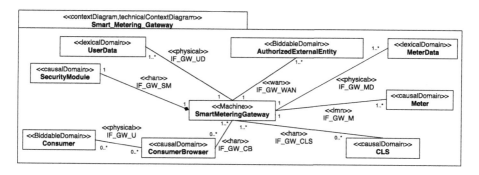

Fig. 2. The Context Diagram of the Smart Metering Gateway

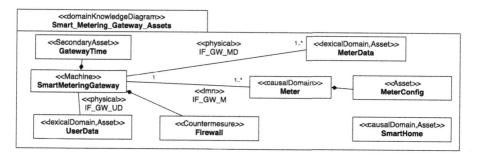

Fig. 3. Domain Knowledge Diagram Concerning Assets and Existing Countermeasures

Some functional requirements of the smart metering gateway are:

R 1 The *CLS* can receive energy consumption data from the *Meter*
R 2 The *CLS* can communicate with an *External Entity* using the WAN
R 3 The *Consumer* can communicate with the *CLS*

We model the trust relationships relevant for the aforementioned considerations in a domain knowledge diagram (see Fig. 4). We focus on the trust relationship *Consumer_CLS_Trust* between the trustor *Consumer* and the trustee *CLS*. This relationship expresses the trust that the trustor has in the trustee concerning the integrity of its configuration and the preservation of confidentiality of private billing information.

We also illustrate in the figure that *OtherConsumer, AuthorizedExternalEntity*, and *SmartMeteringGateway* are trust entities (i.e. ≪Entity≫) in the sense that they are sources of reputation for the *CLS*. Concretely, *OtherConsumers* can report their experience with the *CLS* after interacting with it by using a continuous number between 0 and 1. For example, *OtherConsumer* could be another home user (not the main user), who after asking the fridge for a list of food that is running out, could physically check whether the information was accurate and evaluate with a value between 0 and 1 accordingly. *AuthorizedExternalEntity*, who may represent administrators or technicians, can report the

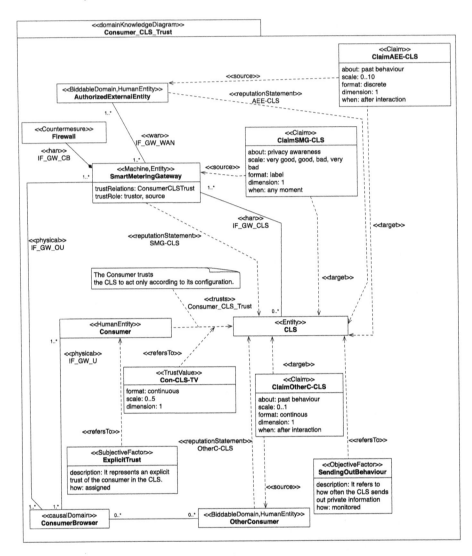

Fig. 4. Domain knowledge diagram concerning trust relations and reputation

same information after a check-up of the *CLS*, but this time by using a discrete value between 0 and 10. Finally, the *SmartMeteringGateway* can report a claim about the behavior of the *CLS* in terms of privacy awareness. Each time the *CLS* sends some information outside the home environment, the gateway analyses the information and issues a claim in a labeled scale between *very good* and *very bad*, according to the sensitivity and quantity of the information sent.

We draw a problem diagram for each requirement in order to refine it. We present a problem diagram for **R1** in Fig. 5. **R1** ≪constraints≫ the *CLS* in such a way that it can receive ≪MeterData≫. Moreover, we use the information in

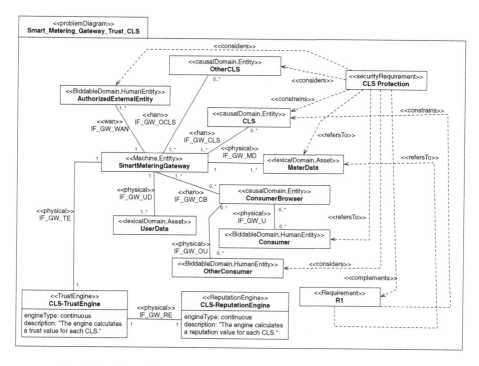

Fig. 5. Problem diagram considering a trust and a reputation engine

Fig. 4 to devise a trust-based security treatment. The ≪securityRequirement≫ *CLS Protection* describes that we must preserve both the integrity of the configuration data of *CLS* and the confidentiality of the *MeterData* of the *Consumer* when it is used by a *CLS*. *CLS Protection* ≪complements≫ **R1**. We require a ≪TrustEngine≫ called *CLS-TrustEngine* to calculate the trust values, which in turn relies on a ≪ReputationEngine≫ called *CLS-ReputationEngine*. The *CLS-TrustEngine* considers both the reputation score and the explicit trust of the consumer when calculating trust values, whereas the *CLS-ReputationEngine* uses the claims made by *AuthorizedExternalEntity*, *SmartMeterGateway*, and *OtherConsumer*. *CLS-TrustEngine* considers the trust factors and the *CLS-ReputationEngine* the claims illustrated in Fig. 4. For simplicity's sake, we do not show these again in Fig. 5, but they have to be considered during the refinement of the problem diagram into an implementable software specification of the trust and reputation engines.

Figure 6 illustrates the use of trust in the system, and concretely, an event that causes the update of a trust relationship between the *Consumer* and the *CLS*. We consider that the *SMG* has a built-in firewall that allows controlling the information flowing to and from the *CLS* as well as preventing changes to the *CLS* configuration. The Common Criteria protection profile [26] states that the gateway has already a firewall to protect the *Meter* functionality. We propose to extend this firewall to protect the *CLS* functionality, as well.

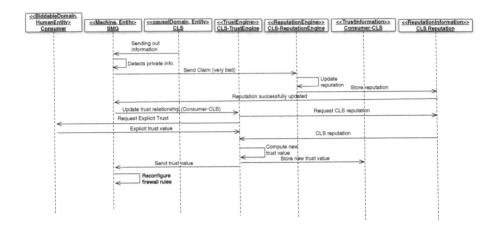

Fig. 6. Sequence Diagram for Trust Update Event

The *SMG* detects that the *CLS* is leaking private information that (in its understanding and according to some policy) should not be passed through. In addition to blocking the information, the *SMG* sends a claim, which triggers a reputation update. Once reputation is updated, *SMG* requests an update of the trust relationship between the *Consumer* and the *CLS*. In order to compute the new trust value, the *CLS-TrustEngine* needs the explicit trust value defined by the *Consumer* for that particular *CLS* as well as the reputation of the *CLS*[3]. Upon receiving the new trust value, the *SMG* updates the firewall rules. For example, in case the *Consumer* does not trust the *CLS* above a given, configurable threshold, all requests from the *Consumer* to the *CLS* are blocked by the *SMG*, and all the messages flowing out from the *CLS* are also blocked, isolating this device from the rest of the system.

5 Conclusion

We have extended UML4PF, which is a UML-profile based on Jackson's Problem Frame notation, with concepts of trust and reputation. In particular, we related these concepts to Jackson's domains and gave some hints on how to describe security requirements that consider trust and reputation. We applied the extended UML4PF profile with trust and reputation concepts to a smart grid example and illustrated the following:

---

[3] We are assuming a trust model consisting of two factors: an explicit trust assigned by the user and the reputation of the trustee, which is computed by aggregating different claims of *OtherConsumers*, *AuthorizedExternalEntity* and *SmartMetering-Gateway*. However, any other kind of trust model that considers other factors can be specified.

- How to elicit trust and reputation information for a specific context.
- Explicit documentation of domain knowledge in terms of trust relations, reputation relations, claims, trust values, etc.
- Describing security requirements that consider trust and reputation domain knowledge with the purpose of building trust and reputation engines to protect assets.
- Refine the static descriptions of trust and reputation engines in problem diagrams with descriptions of their dynamic behavior in UML sequence diagrams.

In the future, we will create a structured method with tool support for creating trust and reputation engines. In particular, we will focus on supporting the modeling and we will provide OCL-based consistency checks of the models. In addition, we will analyze the relations of security controls of the ISO 27001 [27] standard to trust and reputation concepts. We assume the results will provide insights into which ISO 27001 controls can benefit from trust and reputation engines.

References

1. Moyano, F., Fernandez-Gago, C., Lopez, J.: A conceptual framework for trust models. In: Fischer-Hübner, S., Katsikas, S., Quirchmayr, G. (eds.) TrustBus 2012. LNCS, vol. 7449, pp. 93–104. Springer, Heidelberg (2012)
2. Kirtland, A., Schiff, A.: On a scale of 1 to 5: understanding risk improves rating and reputation systems (2008). http://boxesandarrows.com/on-a-scale-of-1-to-5/
3. Rasmusson, L., Jansson, S.: Simulated social control for secure internet commerce. In: Proceedings of the 1996 Workshop on New Security Paradigms, NSPW '96, pp. 18–25. ACM, New York (1996)
4. Roman, R., Zhou, J., Lopez, J.: On the features and challenges of security and privacy in distributed internet of things. Comput. Netw. **57**, 2266–2279 (2013)
5. European Commission: Restructuring in Europe 2011: restructuring and anticipation of change, what lessons from recent experience? (2012). http://eur-lex.europa.eu/LexUriServ/LexUriServ.do?uri=SEC:2012:0059:FIN:EN:PDF
6. Jackson, M.: Problem Frames: Analyzing and Structuring Software Development Problems. Addison-Wesley, Boston (2001)
7. Massacci, F., Mylopoulos, J., Zannone, N.: Security requirements engineering: the SI* modeling language and the secure tropos methodology. In: Ras, Z.W., Tsay, L.-S. (eds.) Advances in Intelligent Information Systems. SCI, vol. 265, pp. 147–174. Springer, Heidelberg (2010)
8. van Lamsweerde, A.: Requirements Engineering: From System Goals to UML Models to Software Specifications, 1st edn. Wiley, Hoboken (2009)
9. Lund, M.S., Solhaug, B., Stølen, K.: Model-Driven Risk Analysis: The CORAS Approach, 1st edn. Springer, Heidelberg (2010)
10. UML Revision Task Force: OMG Object Constraint Language: Reference, February (2010)
11. Côté, I., Hatebur, D., Heisel, M., Schmidt, H.: UML4PF - a tool for problem-oriented requirements analysis. In: Proceedings of the International Conference on Requirements Engineering (RE), pp. 349–350. IEEE Computer Society (2011)
12. Côté, I.: A Systematic Approach to Software Evolution. Deutscher Wissenschafts-Verlag (DWV), Baden-Baden (2012)

13. Marsh, S.: Formalising Trust as a Computational Concept. Ph.D. thesis, University of Stirling (1994)
14. Jøsang, A., Ismail, R., Boyd, C.: A survey of trust and reputation systems for online service provision. Decis. Support Syst. **43**(2), 618–644 (2007)
15. Hatebur, D., Heisel, M.: A UML profile for requirements analysis of dependable software. In: Schoitsch, E. (ed.) SAFECOMP 2010. LNCS, vol. 6351, pp. 317–331. Springer, Heidelberg (2010)
16. Hatebur, D., Heisel, M., Schmidt, H.: A formal metamodel for problem frames. In: Czarnecki, K., Ober, I., Bruel, J.-M., Uhl, A., Völter, M. (eds.) MODELS 2008. LNCS, vol. 5301, pp. 68–82. Springer, Heidelberg (2008)
17. Jackson, M., Zave, P.: Deriving specifications from requirements: an example. In: Proceedings of the 17th International Conference on Software Engineering, Seattle, USA, pp. 15–24. ACM Press (1995)
18. Haley, C.B., Laney, R.C., Nuseibeh, B.: Deriving security requirements from cross-cutting threat descriptions. In: Proceedings of the 3rd International Conference on Aspect-Oriented Software Development, AOSD '04, pp. 112–121. ACM (2004)
19. Salifu, M., Yu, Y., Nuseibeh, B.: Specifying monitoring and switching problems in context. In: 15th IEEE International Requirements Engineering Conference, 2007, RE '07, pp. 211–220 (2007)
20. Jürjens, J.: UMLsec: extending UML for secure systems development. In: Jézéquel, J.-M., Hussmann, H., Cook, S. (eds.) UML 2002. LNCS, vol. 2460, p. 412. Springer, Heidelberg (2002)
21. Lodderstedt, T., Basin, D., Doser, J.: SecureUML: a UML-based modeling language for model-driven security. In: Jézéquel, J.-M., Hussmann, H., Cook, S. (eds.) UML 2002. LNCS, vol. 2460, p. 426. Springer, Heidelberg (2002)
22. Mouratidis, H., Giorgini, P.: Secure tropos: a security-oriented extension of the tropos methodology. Int. J. Softw. Eng. Knowl. Eng. **17**(2), 285–309 (2007)
23. van Lamsweerde, A., Letier, E.: Handling obstacles in goal-oriented requirements engineering. IEEE Trans. Softw. Eng. **26**(10), 978–1005 (2000)
24. Paci, F., Fernandez-Gago, C., Moyano, F.: Detecting insider threats: a trust-aware framework. In: 8th International Conference on Availability, Reliability and Security, Regensburg, Germany, Nov 2013, pp. 121–130. IEEE (2013)
25. Pavlidis, M., Mouratidis, H., Islam, S.: Modelling security using trust based concepts. IJSSE **3**(2), 36–53 (2012)
26. BSI: Protection Profile for the Gateway of a Smart Metering System (Gateway PP). Version 01.01.01(final draft), Bundesamt für Sicherheit in der Informationstechnik (BSI) - Federal Office for Information Security Germany (2011) https://www.bsi.bund.de/SharedDocs/Downloads/DE/BSI/SmartMeter/PP-Smart.Meter.pdf?_blob=publicationFile
27. ISO/IEC: Information technology - Security techniques - Information security management systems - Requirements. ISO/IEC 27001, International Organization for Standardization (ISO) and International Electrotechnical Commission (IEC) (2005)

CryPLH: Protecting Smart Energy Systems from Targeted Attacks with a PLC Honeypot

Dániel István Buza, Ferenc Juhász, György Miru,
Márk Félegyházi, and Tamás Holczer[⊠]

Laboratory for Cryptography and System Security (CrySyS Lab),
Department of Networked Systems and Services (HIT),
Budapest University of Technology and Economics (BME), Budapest, Hungary
holczer@crysys.hu

Abstract. Smart grids consist of suppliers, consumers, and other parts. The main suppliers are normally supervised by industrial control systems. These systems rely on programmable logic controllers (PLCs) to control industrial processes and communicate with the supervisory system. Until recently, industrial operators relied on the assumption that these PLCs are isolated from the online world and hence cannot be the target of attacks. Recent events, such as the infamous Stuxnet attack [15] directed the attention of the security and control system community to the vulnerabilities of control system elements, such as PLCs. In this paper, we design and implement the Crysys PLC honeypot (CryPLH) system to detect targeted attacks against industrial control systems. This PLC honeypot can be implemented as part of a larger security monitoring system. Our honeypot implementation improves upon existing solutions in several aspects: most importantly in level of interaction and ease of configuration. Results of an evaluation show that our honeypot is largely indistinguishable from a real device from the attacker's perspective. As a collateral of our analysis, we were able to identify some security issues in the real PLC device we tested and implemented specific firewall rules to protect the device from targeted attacks.

1 Introduction

For a long time, the majority of industrial control system operators relied on security by obscurity, this means they assumed that control devices cannot be accessed from the Internet and hence the operators made minimum effort to protect these devices. This behavior was motivated by the special requirements in control systems, namely high availability, time-critical services and the huge costs of a potential blackout. Security improvements were mainly considered as a potential risk that can disrupt the normal operation of the system.

In recent years, the threat model of industrial control systems has changed. The Stuxnet targeted attack [15] demonstrated that sophisticated malware is able to penetrate into the isolated part of the control system that were traditionally separated from the parts connected to the Internet. Stuxnet in particular

© Springer International Publishing Switzerland 2014
J. Cuellar (Ed.): SmartGridSec 2014, LNCS 8448, pp. 181–192, 2014.
DOI: 10.1007/978-3-319-10329-7_12

contained modules that attacked PLCs in the target system and consequently caused physical damage in the physical equipment. Recent work [16] demonstrated that attacking PLCs is relatively easy and this makes them an attractive target when attacking industrial control systems.

There have been some efforts to detect attacks against PLCs and to protect them against these attacks [17]. One of the most promising defense mechanisms is the application of honeypots [20] specifically adapted to PLCs. A honeypot is a system that seems to be a PLC based on network behavior, but does not provide any operational functionality in the system. A honeypot practically serves as a trap for attackers. One of the honeypot's aim is to maintain the attacker's interest and thus observe the attack methods against real PLCs. This way, previously unknown attack methods can be revealed that can be analyzed to improve the security of real PLC devices.

There are three kind of honeypots depending on the level of sophistication [19,20]. Low-interaction honeypots simulate only basic network services (or only a base part of the basic network services). High-interaction honeypots simulate different complex network services. The advantage of the low-interaction ones is that they are easier to design and maintain. They can be more stable but they are easier to discover. The high-interaction honeypots are able to keep the attacker's attention longer. But they are much harder to implement because they have to implement the already known bugs and incorrect activities as well. Hybrid honeypots try to combine low and high interaction parts to get the advantages of both. Hybrid honeypots usually simulate different services on different interaction levels.

There are a few existing PLC honeypot implementations. The Scada HoneyNet Project [21] was started in 2004 by Cisco Critical Infrastructure Assurance Group (CIAG) and was discontinued in 2005. It consists of a set of python scripts, each of them implementing a service of the simulated PLC. The project heavily utilises Honeyd [18,19], which is a small daemon that creates virtual hosts on a network. The hosts can be configured to run arbitrary services, and their personality can be adapted so that they appear to be running certain operating systems. The Honeyd daemon can be set to simulate a computer that has the OS fingerprint of a PLC and runs the given Cisco scripts on the appropriate ports. With the help of these scripts the Honeyd PLC realises a Telnet, FTP, HTTP and Modbus services. In summary, these scripts seem unfinished, the services are only partially implemented and the realised functionality is nor realistic neither interactive. Also, it is worth to mention that bugs and mistakes are present in the code, for example, if the log file does not exist, the script doesn't create it, instead it throws an unhandled exception. Even an inexperienced attacker would notice in seconds that the simulated PLC is not real, and the information provided by the logs can not be used to uncover the identity or the methods of the attacker, therefore the SCADA HoneyNet Project clearly fails to reach its goals.

The SCADA Honeynet [7] is maintained by Digital Bond and is freely available from their website. It utilises two virtual machines one of which is a

Generation III honeywall (by The HoneyNet Project [10]) extended with Digital Bonds Quickdraw IDS signatures [7]. The purpose of this unit is to monitor all network activity to identify and log every malicious attack that may occur against the simulated PLC. The other virtual machine simulates a popular PLC that runs five services (FTP, Telnet, HTTP, SNMP, Modbus TCP), the FTP, HTTP and Modbus services are implemented by different Java applications while the Telnet and SNMP services are realised by python scripts. The core of the VM is Honeyd that routes the created virtual host's network traffic (the data streams and datagrams) from the appropriate ports to these applications and scripts. The Digital Bond's SCADA Honeynet is a huge improvement over the Cisco Honeynet Project. With the returned service banners and OS fingerprint it can make scanning and information gathering tools (such as nmap or nessus) believe that it is a real PLC, thus it can be effective against automated attacks and tools. However, the simulated services provide very little interaction, and they might not be able to keep an attacker attracted for long enough to uncover new targeted PLC attacks.

The Conpot project [1] by The Honeynet Project [3] was released in May 2013, and it is available for everyone from their website. Conpot is an ICS honeypot with the goal to collect intelligence about the motives and methods of adversaries targeting industrial control systems. The honeypot realizes two major ICS protocols: Modbus and SNMP. There is also an HTTP service, and a logging system in the honeypot. These services are implemented with Python scripts. The honeypot emulates a Siemens S7-200 CPU type PLC by default, but it can be easily reconfigured through various profiles. The base concept of Conpot by The Honeynet Project is good, but it still have some defects which really need fixing. The honeypot is easy to install and use, but to reach it's full potential, it needs a lot of customization. The HTTP server is not working yet, but it's an important part of a honeypot, because it is a major attack surface where we can examine the behaviour of an attacker. Because of the little interaction the honeypot provides, it's possible that the attacker moves on before it's methods and behavior can be discovered.

The contributions of the paper are the following:

- We implemented a PLC honeypot, which is superior to existing solutions both in usability and indistinguishability.
- The implementation was tested against a real PLC to find differences. The test highlighted only minor problems.
- The honeypot was installed in a public network to gather real attacks successfully.

The remainder of the paper is organized as follows: In Sect. 2 we introduce our CryPLH implementation. The evaluation and public testing is described in Sects. 3 and 4 respectively, while the summary of the paper is in Sect. 5.

2   PLC Honeypot for Security Monitoring

In this section, we present our honeypot implementation for security monitoring of industrial control systems. For the reference implementation, we selected widely used PLC, namely a Siemens Simatic 300(1) PLC device. This device has a IM151-8 PN/DP CPU and it uses firmware version 3.2.6. The PLC has four network interfaces, the first one is a serial port that uses PROFIBUS protocol to control the devices attached to it in a real production environment, the second interface is a Fast Ethernet port that is used to manage the PLC, it should be connected to the management network. The third and fourth interface can be used to form a ring topology of the PLCs. Our goal in this reference implementation was to develop a high-interaction honeypot which appears identical to the real device from an attacker's point of view. We developed a system which is complex but easy to configure, so it can be extended to simulate different (but similar) PLC types.

We have setup a test environment to assess the properties of our Honeypot implementation as shown in Fig. 1. We used an attacker machine equipped with Backtrack Linux R5 [11] to test and analyze the services offered by the PLC and our PLC honeypot. The PLC and the PLC honeypot were installed in the same subnetwork as the virtual machine that runs the Backtrack R5. The initial nessus [12] and nmap [13] scans showed that the Siemens Simatic 300(1) PLC runs four services these are the http, https, isotsap and snmp. The Siemens PLC's port forwarding guide [14] also confirmed that the PLC is capable of running these services.

After implementing the services mentioned above, we integrated them onto a virtual machine to create the honeypot (as presented in Fig. 2). The VM runs a minimal version of Ubuntu Linux, that only has the necessary services and libraries installed. We also implemented a bash script that can start, restart or stop the honeypot. It is run by *(initd)* on every start up. Every simulator has its own way to fine tune it, however there is a main configuration file of the honeypot. In this file global settings can be set, such as the IP and network interface that the honeypot is being run on. The startup-script reads these values and configures each service simulator before it launches them. The script also sets iptable rules to block all incoming connection that are not destined to one of the simulators. The TCP connections are refused by a TCP reset, just like on the real PLC. The UDP datagrams that are not sent to the SNMP service are simply dropped. The script starts tcpdump to capture the network traffic on the honeypots interface. The final step is to change the behaviour of the TCP/IP stack. The files in /proc/sys/ipv4/ provide an interface for this on Linux. These files contain values, that can be read or written and control the operation of TCP and IP. The IP ttl is set to 30, and the MTU is 1518, also the PLC has a fixed TCP window size, which unfortunately can not be exactly set, because of the limitations of the /proc file system. Some of the TCP related values are compiled into the kernel, so they cannot be changed through these files. Currently this is a minor limitation of the honeypot which we will address in our future work.

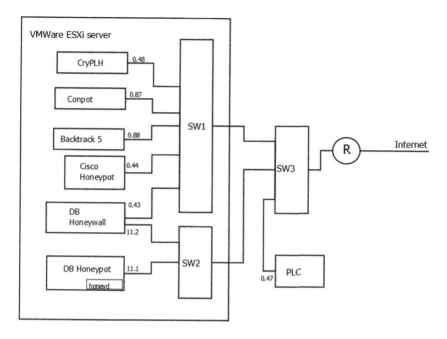

Fig. 1. The laboratory setup of the honeypot testbed

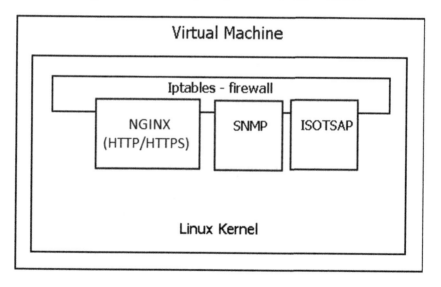

Fig. 2. The abstract model of the integrated honeypot

2.1   Hypertext Transfer Protocol (HTTP) implementation

HTTP is one of the basic protocols on the Internet and it is also implemented on
the Siemens Simatic 300(1) PLC device. Secure HTTP (HTTPS) is an extension

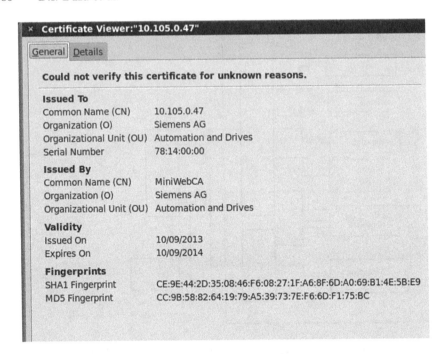

Fig. 3. Details of the PLC's certificate

of HTTP service. It is not an independent protocol it is layering HTTP over SSL/TLS protocol. The device uses a web server from the MiniWeb project [4] that was developed in the C language to provide a small HTTP server with high efficiency and high portability. It also implements a login procedure to access the device.

The device also implements the HTTPS service. There is no difference of the served data and pages. The device uses a self-signed (not trusted) certificate as it is shown on Fig. 3. The certificate is issued to Siemens AG organization issued by the same organization with MiniWebCA common name. The signature algorithm is SHA-1 with RSA Encryption and it uses an 1024 bits long public key. Observing different PLC devices we found that each device use a unique certificate (instead of using the same certificate on every device).

During the test we found that sometimes the PLC is not responding that is probably an indicator for a bug in the firmware. Also, requesting `Portal.mwsl` without parameters causes a complete crash of the system [2]. This can cause security issues when an attacker can send arbitrary URLs to the web server. To improve the safety of a PLC it is strongly suggested to use a firewall to filter HTTP requests and drop the ones which contain `Portal.mwsl` without parameters. We implemented this function by `iptables` as well using `-m string` option.

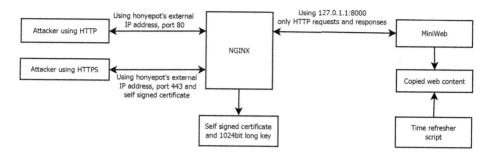

Fig. 4. The HTTP/HTTPS service environment

We simulated the behavior of the MiniWeb server on our PLC honeypot. We had to manage some changes in the copied files to remove all links to the real device. And we rewrote the login mechanism (there is no name and password check) to simulate that there is a password but the attacker failed to guess it. After the changes we were able to simulate the HTTP service with static pages.

We also simulate the HTTPS service. We used OpenSSL [6] and generated an 1024 bit long key and a self signed certificate. We added the same meta-information (e.g. location, common name, organization) to the certificate that the device adds to it's self signed certificate. To simulate HTTPS we used nginx [5]. With suitable configuration it tunnels HTTPS traffic to the miniweb server over HTTP. An another advantage of using nginx is that we can separate the HTTP traffic into two parts: traffic between the honeypot and the outside network and the traffic inside the honeypot (between nginx and miniweb). Thus the system becomes more configurable. Figure 4 illustrates the complete developed structure.

In spite of the substantial implementation effort, the honeypot device has some features that allow an attacker to detect it. Visually there is no difference between the websites on the real device and the honeypot. But on the honeypot's site it is impossible to log in because we pretend that there is a valid username and password combination but the attacker's guess was wrong. On the honeypot's page there is no effect of selecting other languages (it only uses English language). We have to note that on the real device's site it is also impossible to reach any other offered languages because it does not have enough memory to contain the language files. We do not simulate any changes of the visual presentation of the PLC on the site (e.g. the LEDs state never change). We can say that we pretend that the environment of the simulated device never changes. It can be believable that a device's environment does not have changes which change the PLC's running state. We do not simulate the already known bug by requesting `Portal.mwsl` without any parameters however a script can be easily added to stop all communication for a while after visiting the page. If needed, these additional features can be simulated at the cost of making the honeypot implementation more complex.

2.2 Implementing the Simple Network Management Protocol (SNMP)

The SNMP service is commonly installed on intermediary and end network devices such as PLCs, because it provides a simple and easy way to monitor and manage the device. In a typical SNMP conversation there are two participants, a manager, that queries the requests and a managed device, that replies to these. The managed device runs an SNMP software that is called the Agent. The Agent interprets the queries and returns the requested data to the manager. The whole hierarchy and the metadata (variable names, permissions and types) are described in Management Information Databases (MIBs) which use ASN.1 notation.

After the thorough exploration of the Siemens PLC SNMP database and implementation, we created the SNMP service on the honeypot device. After carefully analyzing existing SNMP implementations, we decided to implement a custom SNMP Agent that provides more flexibility. The realised Agent, just like the original, listens on the UDP port 161, and accepts SNMP requests and replies to them. Instead of using real MIBs it parses an XML file that contains the list of records that are present on the real PLC. All these records have an OID and a type attribute. They either contain the static data (e.g. the system descriptor, or interface description) that they represent or they contain a special mark and string that tells the interpreter how the dynamic data (e.g. the system uptime, or the number of received IP packets) should be created or retrieved.

There are variables that an attacker could directly or indirectly alter. Such variables are for example the number of received packets on the connected interface or the number of received ICMP echo requests. The value of these records can not be simply generated because an attacker can try to modify these and check if the returned numbers vary accordingly. To avoid the detection of the honeypot, these values are read from the /proc file system which contains information gathered by the OS on Unix systems. The script receives the name of the interface and this name is used when reading device related information from the /proc/net/dev file. The IP, TCP, UDP and ICMP related data is acquired form the /proc/net/snmp. The purpose of this file is to provide information about these protocols for different SNMP Agents. The TCP current establishments value is read from the /proc/net/sockstat file. As it was mentioned before, the script keeps track of the SNMP related events. It uses the data gathered this way to serve requests for SNMP records.

We tested our SNMP implementation with snmpwalk. The result of the test corresponded to the expectations. Later, the Agent was tested against different Get and GetNext requests, the response format was always identical to the original PLC's responses. It is important to note, that there is a known limitation of the SNMP Agent. If a specific group of records are queried from the local network, the returned data is not valid. However it is not a real limitation, because we assume that the honeypot will be put on a public address, where local network is not defined.

2.3   Step 7 Protocol Implementation

Siemens SIMATIC STEP7 [9] is an engineering software for configuring and programming Siemens type controllers. We can setup and program several automation systems, for example SIMATIC HMI panels, or Siemens PLCs. The communication is going through TCP port 102 of the PLC and uses the ISO-TSAP protocol. We found that the PLC is protected from unauthorized access. This means that we can not download the firmware to the PLC until we entered the correct password. We decided that we are going to simulate this behaviour on the PLC, but without a correct password. So whenever someone tries to access the PLC, the response always will be that the entered password is incorrect. On one hand, this is a fairly simple solution, but it is also believable: a system which has such a great responsibility in controlling facilities or power plants should not be accessible to anyone. On the other hand, if we would like to simulate the programmability, the response to various inputs could be problematic.

We implemented a simulation of the STEP 7 protocol on the PLC honeypot with a python script. STEP 7 queries the PLC for specific parameters and we included these parameters in our response packets to simulate the behavior of the real device.

3   Evaluation

We performed the needed tests for the single services, and presented the results in the related sections. After integrating the services into a PLC honeypot implementation, we successfully tested that the communication with the modules worked properly. Then, we checked the difference between the honeypot and the real PLC. We found that the PLC honeypot is mostly indistinguishable from the real device, yet there are a few characteristics the attacker can use to spot the PLC honeypot. Although we tried to mimic the PLCs networking stack, due to operating system limitations, we were not able to emulate a fully identical TCP/IP stack. Thus, based on the `nmap O` operating system scan, one can distinguish between the two devices with some probability. If the attacker is close to its target (same LAN segment), then in the nmaps operating system guess report there is an entry for Linux when scanning the honeypot (with several other guesses), but Linux is not guessed when the PLC is scanned. If the attacker is a few hops away from its target (which is the more likely scenario), then the honeypot and the real PLC are indistinguishable using the oeprating system fingerprint. Reliably fooling nmap with the proper TCP/IP parameters is difficult if the attacker is on the same LAN segment. One solution can be writing a TCP proxy, which re-frames the outgoing packets, so it would seem it is coming from a real PLC. Another solution is to rewrite an existing TCP/IP stack to be fully identical to the one used in the PLC. We left this effort as a future work.

4   Public Testing

The honeypot was installed on a public network to gather real traffic and possibly attacks. The public IP address of the device was set within an university's IP range. This is not ideal as targeted attacks against industrial control systems do not scan educational IP ranges, however we found some interesting traffic. In the future we want to install our implementation to more appropriate places, where more interesting intelligence information can be collected.

Two tests are described in the followings. The first took eight days and all the logs were analyzed thoroughly. The second test took approximately one month and only the interesting traffic were filtered and analyzed.

4.1   Short Test

In the short (eight days long) test no traffic accessed neither the TSAP nor the SNMP port. Several pings and port scans were carried out on the honeypot, and also several attempts were made to gain access via ssh to the machine (most of the ssh scans are originated from China with 6000 as source port). These attempts were all rejected by the firewall.

The web server was accessed several times, but the attackers were mainly looking for vulnerable PHPMyAdmin pages or vulnerabilities in CCTV camera firmwares. The most interesting attacks against the web server were scans for open proxies, where the attacker tried to download scientific journal papers using the university's subscription. As the PLC honeypot does not offer such services, these attempts were unsuccessful. The whole content of the web server was crawled by robots several times as well.

In general no PLC specific attack accessed our honeypot during this test period.

4.2   Long Test

In the long test (1 month long), we observed similar attack patterns like in the short test. The only real difference was some traffic to the TSAP port. The TCP streams are most likely originated from Shodan [8], which is a search engine for embedded devices. Shodan made some connections to the TSAP port, and sent some queries to the honeypot. Unfortunately Shodan does not reveal the results of these scans publicly.

5   Summary

The aim of this study was to create a high interaction honeypot called CryPLH, that appears to be a Siemens PLC form an attackers point of view. It needs to be able to log all the action an attacker takes, while trying to exploit the PLC. So that later by analysing these log files new targeted attacks can be uncovered, possibly before they reach the real equipments. In order to achieve this all the existing PLC honeypots were examined, and a real PLC was thoroughly audited.

After the exploration of the device, all the discovered services (HTTP, HTTPS, ISO-TSAP and SNMP) were further inspected. Than the simulators of these were implemented and integrated into a Linux based virtual machine. The resulting VM is the honeypot. Although, currently the honeypot has a few limitations which needs to be addressed in the future, still it preforms its task better than any of its predecessors: it is highly configurable, it implements all the services the original PLC implements, and it is interactive.

The most important current issue is to add more functionality to the TSAP implementation, because probably the most interesting traffic would come to that port. Another less urgent issue is the incorrect TCP window size, which cannot be set to the exact required value because of the Linux kernels limitations. In the future a kernel patch or a TCP proxy (that re-frames all the outgoing TCP PDUs and sends them with raw sockets) needs to be written to overcome this problem. The other known issue is related to the SNMP routing records, but this is a less significant problem, because it only exists if the attacker is on the same LAN as the honeypot. The honeypot was tested by independent professionals and no other issue was discovered.

After the initial tests, the honeypot was installed on a public network, to gather information about ongoing attacks. The honeypot collected many general PC targeting attacks, but none of the attacks were PLC specific.

In our future we want to deploy our honeypot within an industrial control system's IP range and gather more intelligence information. By analyzing the collected logs, we will aim at identifying new threats against industrial control systems. We also want to make our honeypot implementation to be publicly available, after correcting the small problems mentioned above.

Acknowledgement. We would like to acknowledge the help and the provided Siemens PLC device to Óbuda University and the company evopro. This work is partially funded by the EIT ICTLabs through activity ASES 13030.

References

1. The conpot project. http://www.conpot.org. Accessed 4 August 2013
2. Crash per webinterface. http://www.sps-forum.de/simatic/52478-s7-1200-crash-per-webinterface.html. Accessed 16 October 2013
3. Introducing conpot. http://honeynet.org/node/1047. Accessed 4 August 2013
4. Miniweb project webpage. http://miniweb.sourceforge.net/. Accessed 7 October 2013
5. Nginx site. http://wiki.nginx.org. Accessed 16 October 2013
6. Openssl: The open source toolkit for ssl/tls. http://www.openssl.org. Accessed 16 October 2013
7. Scada honeynet. http://www.digitalbond.com/tools/scada-honeynet/. Accessed 17 June 2013

8. Shodan - expose online devices. http://www.shodanhq.com/. Accessed 1 March 2014
9. Simatic step 7 engineering software - software for simatic controllers - siemens. http://www.automation.siemens.com/mcms/simatic-controller-software/en/step7/Pages/Default.aspx. Accessed 18 October 2013
10. Honeywall project site. http://www.honeyd.org/honeywall/ (2009). Accessed 17 June 2013
11. Backtrack linux - penetration testing distribution (2013). http://www.backtrack-linux.org/. Accessed 23 October 2013
12. Nessus vulnerability scanner. http://www.tenable.com/products/nessus (2013). Accessed 10 October 2013
13. Nmap - free security scanner for network exploration & security audits. http://nmap.org/ (2013). Accessed 23 October 2013
14. Siemens product support. http://support.automation.siemens.com/WW/llisapi.dll?func=cslib.csinfo&lang=en&objid=8970169&caller=view (2013). Accessed13 October 2013
15. Bencsáth, B., Pék, G., Buttyán, L., Felegyhazi, M.: The cousins of Stuxnet: Duqu, Flame, and Gauss. Future Internet 4(4), 971–1003 (2012)
16. Gorzelak, K., Grudziecki, T., Jacewicz, P., Jaroszewski, P., Juszczyk, Ł., Belasovs, A.: Proactive detection of network security incidents (2012)
17. Koopman, P.: Embedded system security. Computer 37(7), 95–97 (2004)
18. Provos, N.: Developments of the honeyd virtual honeypot. http://www.honeyd.org/ (2007). Accessed 16 June 2013
19. Provos, N.: Honeyd-a virtual honeypot daemon. In: 10th DFN-CERT Workshop, Hamburg, Germany, vol. 2 (2003)
20. Provos, N., Holz, T.: Virtual Honeypots: From Botnet Tracking to Intrusion Detection. Pearson Education, Boston (2007)
21. Pothamsetty, V., Franz, M.: Scada honeynet project: building honeypots for industrial networks (2005)

Author Index